RIDING THIS ROAD

My life – making music and travelling this wide land with Slim Dusty

JOY McKEAN

hachette AUSTRALIA

People of Aboriginal or Torres Strait Islander heritage are advised that this book contains names and photographs of people who are deceased or may be deceased.

Every effort has been made to contact copyright holders of material reproduced in this book. If anyone has further information, please contact the publishers.

Unless otherwise credited, photos are from Joy McKean's personal collection.

hachette AUSTRALIA

Published in Australia and New Zealand in 2014
by Hachette Australia
(an imprint of Hachette Australia Pty Limited)
Level 17, 207 Kent Street, Sydney NSW 2000
www.hachette.com.au

10 9 8 7 6 5 4 3 2 1

National Library of Australia
Cataloguing-in-Publication data

McKean, Joy, author.
Riding this road: my life – making music and travelling this wide land with Slim Dusty / Joy McKean.

978 0 7336 3154 2

McKean, Joy.
Women country musicians – Australia – Biography.
Singers – Australia – Biography.
Women lyricists – Australia – Biography.

782.421642092

Cover design by Luke Causby, Blue Cork
Front cover photographs: (background) Townsville, 1957;
(foreground) Tamworth, 2010, 80th birthday tribute concert (Newspix)
Back cover photograph: Joy McKean and Slim Dusty (John Elliott)
Text design by Luke Causby
Typeset in Bembo by Kirby Jones
Printed in Australia by McPherson's Printing Group

The paper this book is printed on is certified against the Forest Stewardship Council® Standards. McPherson's Printing Group holds FSC® chain of custody certification SA-COC-005379. FSC® promotes environmentally responsible, socially beneficial and economically viable management of the world's forests.

I dedicate this book to my family.

Firstly I thank my parents, Millie and Silas McKean. They gave me a life, then their love, common sense and sacrifices equipped me to live it to the full.

My late husband gave me, and now my children and grandchildren give me love, support and companionship.

I thank them all.

PROLOGUE

Dad saw me fall.

It was just daylight in the Balmain semi where we lived while Dad taught at Birchgrove Primary School in Sydney. He used to take us – my sister, Heather, and me – down to Mort's Dock for a walk because Blondie needed exercise.

Blondie was the Alsatian dog someone couldn't afford to take with the family when they moved away, and who we couldn't really afford to feed either. The Depression was hitting everyone hard then. Hawkers were regular callers; selling bootlaces, tiny recipe books or anything they could think of. Most were genuine, poor devils, but some were out for anything they could get.

One hot day Blondie was lying in the cool at the end of the hall. The hawker was persistent, and my mother was young and pretty. The man put his foot to the door and pushed the door against her, until she flung it wide open, putting him off balance while she called, 'Blondie! Blondie!' As Blondie barrelled down the hall and left the floor in a growling avalanche, the hawker bounded over the low front fence in a tumbling shriek. After that, we were seldom bothered by hawkers.

Balmain wasn't trendy then, in 1934. It was regarded as a slum area of Sydney – perhaps not so 'slummy' as Redfern and

Macdonaldtown were at that time but, still, it wasn't the best of addresses.

School had finished for the year; I know this because it was about a fortnight before my fifth birthday, on 14 January 1935. Dad had taught me to read when I was three, and I was a bookworm well and truly by the time I was four. On this particular evening, Dad had brought home a comic book for me, but I was not allowed to read it because it was bedtime.

'You can have it first thing in the morning,' Mum had promised. So at daylight I awoke and went into my parents' bedroom looking for the book. I was sneaking out the door, book in hand, when Dad woke and – half asleep still – idly noted that I had fallen or, rather, crumpled to the floor. He went back to sleep.

Unperturbed by the fact that my legs didn't seem to work any more, I crawled along the hall to the enclosed verandah that ran across the back of the semi. The kitchen was at one end of the verandah; at the other end sat the piano, my mother's pride and joy. She had taught me to sing 'Girl of My Dreams', singing the tune and words over and over for me to learn while she played the piano.

It was a lovely piece of furniture, with inlaid roses of golden wood close beside the brass candlestick holders. Mum played it often, having taken some lessons as a fourteen year old. I still have that piano, but the years have not been kind to the old strings, and it will never be tuned to concert pitch again. It was packed up and freighted or conveyed some way or other from one small school district to another; to Sydney and back to the country, to finally come to rest in my home. I've written many songs to the vamping bass of that old piano.

I was lying there beside it on the floor, flat on my tummy, fascinated by the comic book, when Mum came down the hall on her way to the kitchen to make breakfast.

'Mummy, I can't walk,' I lifted my head to mention to her.

'Oh yes, darling. Well, never mind,' she replied. 'Come and have some porridge and you'll be fine. Breakfast won't be long.'

'But, Mum, I *can't* walk,' I repeated in a matter-of-fact way.

When my young parents discovered that I meant what I said, they were bewildered. They did not know that a polio epidemic was in full sway throughout Sydney at the time.

They sat me up on the kitchen table, encouraging me to lift my legs, or to try standing on them. I couldn't do it. They stood me up and tried to get me to walk across the room. I stumbled a very few steps and fell again and again. I wasn't worried, but my parents must have been terrified.

These days, they would have headed for the nearest hospital or doctor. But this was 1934, and Dad was a 29-year-old country schoolteacher recently moved to the city. He and his 25-year-old wife knew no one in Sydney except his family, living out at Granville in the western suburbs. Wages were low, doctors' fees in comparison were expensive and a visit to the doctor was usually a last resort.

So Dad piggybacked me, and Mum carried Heather, as they travelled by tram and train out to Granville, and then walked the twenty minutes to Grandfather McKean's family home, where he and Granny lived with their youngest son and three daughters.

Family conference having been held, I was taken to see the chemist, an old family friend. I distinctly remember being placed on my feet and encouraged to walk across the shop floor to the watching pharmacist. I took step after step, slowly and unsteadily, before my legs folded again and I fell down. I heard him say, 'I think your little girl may have infantile paralysis. You need to get her to hospital as soon as you can.'

That marked the beginning of a long separation from my family. I didn't live at home again for nearly three years.

CHAPTER 1

My father, Silas Lyndsay McKean, was the second son of a country schoolteacher, Matthew McKean, who was born in the old goldfields town of Trunkey Creek, New South Wales. Matt's father, Henry McKean, was a hot-tempered Irishman from County Tyrone who was an untrained schoolteacher, a 'highly moral man', to quote from an inspector's report. Nevertheless, he seemed unable to avoid clashing with any local authorities who appeared to him to be unreasonable or lacking in the respect he felt was due to him.

He came from a farming family in Northern Ireland, but regarded himself as something of a scholar. Landing in Australia late in 1864 with his sister Sarah, he took work first on a friend's farm near Mittagong in the Southern Highlands of New South Wales and then on the Zig Zag Railway being built over the Blue Mountains and ending in the town of Lithgow. The big railway camp at Bowenfels, for labourers and fettlers on the line, included numerous families of the workmen, but there was no school and no teacher for the children.

Eventually Henry, as the only educated man available, was asked if he would take on the job of teaching; a local landowner donated the materials to build a slab school on his property, and after four years in his new country, Henry's future seemed rosy enough for him to send for his Scottish sweetheart, Jessie Crawford. He married Jessie when she arrived, in a double ceremony with his sister Sarah and her husband, and embarked on a teaching career.

Henry's temper may have been part of the reason my grandfather Matthew was such a mild, good-tempered gentleman. Just the same, Grandfather had his share of stubbornness when needed. For instance, he did not approve of the proposed husband of Hazel, his middle daughter, and refused to 'give her away' in traditional fashion, so her eldest brother, Bill, had to do the honours. Although it took quite a lot to rile Grandfather, he was a six-foot monument of intimidating, withering scorn when he did lose patience.

My father, Silas – or Sike, as the family mostly called him – left Parramatta High School at around the age of nineteen and took a job on the railway as a station porter-cum-ticket collector-cum-general dogsbody. This didn't suit Grandfather and certainly did not suit Sike's elder sister, Vera, also a teacher. Sike was hauled off the railway station platform, where he was perfectly happy, and into teachers' college to complete the 'short course' of training. Then he was handed his first assignment; two 'half time' schools in the Monaro Ranges near Cooma in southern New South Wales.

In 1926, Silas boarded with a local family, the Scotts, and took up his duties of teaching in the little slab schools of Anembo and Waygrah. One week he taught three days at Anembo and two at Waygrah, and the following week he reversed the order. This meant that all of the children received five full days' schooling in a fortnight. He had two horses, one called Silkband and the other Graygo, and they carried him back and forth every week, rain or shine and, at times, in the snow. To get to Waygrah school from Anembo, where the school was made of slabs with an iron roof, Silas rode horseback nine miles over stony ridges to the Cooma Road and the little wattle-and-daub schoolroom. Then he rode the nine miles back to his lodgings. He later had to add a third horse, as the two found it hard to keep up the continual journeying under the rugged conditions.

Silas liked the life and the chance to go shooting for rabbits, to play cricket for Anembo against Jerangle cricket club and to be part of the local community. He was a fine athlete; a tennis player and footballer as well as a good cricketer.

In 1927, when Silas was moved to the school at Doyles Creek in the Hunter Valley of New South Wales, he boarded with the Killen family and walked about a mile across the creek and up the hill to his post at the little school. The Killens lived in the same slab homestead built by the first William Killen in the 1860s. Mildred (Millie) Agnes was the only daughter in a family of five sons, and no doubt Granny Killen had other aims for her pretty daughter than a life married to dairy farming, which was all that was on offer in that part of the world. I think she might have been well pleased when the new schoolteacher and her daughter were soon inseparable.

Millie was nineteen when she married 23-year-old Silas in December 1928. All Sike's family rallied around and they loved being up at the farm, so there was quite a big wedding with Una, Sike's youngest sister, being one of the two bridesmaids. The young newlyweds were still living at Woodpark, the Killen farm, when I was born in Singleton, the nearest town, in January 1930. Nevertheless, about eighteen months later they were pleased to take up a new position at Lostock, also in the Hunter Valley, in nice time to welcome the arrival of Heather Colleen Lois in February 1932.

They were a happy young couple, fitting easily into the life of the community around the school and district where they settled. The residence was attached to the side of the school building; this made it a simple matter for Dad to take me into the classroom with him to give Mum a break while she was looking after the new baby. I had a slate of my own and a slate pencil, but I graduated to a book to practise my 'pothooks' as I began learning to write. Best of all, though, I began learning to read. Just by sitting in the classroom with the older children, I picked up the idea of words and sentences without too much trouble at all. Dad soon realised that I was learning, so he helped me further. He was a good teacher despite the fact that it was not his first choice as a career.

In those little country schools, the teacher did everything – cleaning the school at weekends, for instance. 'Everything' once involved picking up a howling small daughter who fell off the desk she shouldn't have been climbing on; I was screaming because in the process I'd slashed open my scalp on the iron foot of the desk. There were other jobs too. The teacher's wife taught knitting and sewing to the girls, and hopefully the teacher got the boys working in the schoolyard tidying up and weeding.

I vaguely remember the pothooks, the slate and the beginning of little books and the ABC style of teaching to read. But my first clear memory is of running from the schoolroom around the side of the house and up on to the verandah, where my mother was breastfeeding my sister, Heather, as she sat there in the sun. Heather, being a very alert little miss already, threw her head back and tried to see what the commotion was about. I remember Mum scolding me and telling me we had to be careful the baby didn't roll her eyes too far back as she tried to see over the top of her head! I must have been about two and a half years old at that time.

It was a couple of years later that Dad was moved to Birchgrove School and we settled in the rented semi-detached home in Balmain, an inner-west suburb of Sydney. The house is still there, but renovated and with a top storey that has distant views of the harbour. A local historian told me that two doors down from where we lived, another girl also contracted polio. We had been in Balmain only six months or so before

I contracted polio in 1934, so it was no wonder that Dad and Mum were glad to soon move out of Sydney to a school at Moonan Flat, once again in the Hunter, in order to have Heather out of harm's way.

My parents had to leave me behind in Camperdown Children's Hospital. I had not shown any unusual symptoms to warn them that I was unwell and the paralysis had a good hold on me before I was diagnosed and treatment begun. My left leg was affected badly, and although it was thought that my right leg was affected from hip to knee, it came good after all.

Following the initial hospitalisation, I was moved to Canonbury at Darling Point. Canonbury was built by an early show business entrepreneur; it was a very big and beautiful building overlooking Sydney Harbour. It had begun life as the entrepreneur's private home, then became a rehabilitation nursing home for returned soldiers from World War I. After that, it was used for children's rehabilitation; there were full physiotherapy facilities, and even a schoolroom with a gentle lady teacher who made sure I learned to tell the time while I was there.

The daily routine included learning to walk with a metal leg brace known as a caliper on my left leg. One wall of the physio room was mirrored so that we could see ourselves walking (or trying to) between two long handrails. I remember the frustration of trying and trying to lift my leg in the physiotherapy sessions; trying to move my foot up or down. No matter how much I wanted to send the message to my leg from my brain, it would not get through. These exercises would go on for the next eight years, either at home or in such places as the Sister Kenny Clinic at the Royal North Shore Hospital (RNS) in Sydney.

After being discharged from Canonbury in about June 1935, I stayed with Mum and Heather in the McKean family home in Granville. As Mum was supposed to be teaching the

Moonan girls how to sew and knit instead of taking me to the Outpatients clinic at the hospital or to the Kenny Clinic, Aunty Una stepped into the breach, moving to Moonan Flat and keeping house for her brother, my dad, and teaching the girls their sewing and knitting. This was only a stopgap arrangement, of course, and Mum had to find someone to board me and get me to the Kenny Clinic every day.

The someone my mother found was a Scottish widow, Mrs Graham. She had three daughters – Margaret, Elsa and Barbara (a schoolgirl) – but boarded the elderly Mr Imrie, and another adult polio victim from the country, Amy. Mrs Graham lived in Naremburn, which was walking distance from RNS. In those days, it was quite safe for me to walk to and from the clinic on my own, and I did that five days a week for nearly two years. When I left Canonbury, I could walk quite well with the aid of my caliper, but my leg refused to lift or move much without its help. The caliper was uncomfortable in the summer heat, and it felt heavy and cumbersome at times but I adapted quickly to its constant use. I couldn't walk as fast as some, but I could keep up with a normal child's walking pace most of the time. I could even walk about the house without the caliper for a little while so long as I held my hand on my leg above the knee to make sure my leg didn't bend suddenly and let me down.

Mum and Heather returned to Moonan Flat and I moved into a little bed in Mrs Graham's bedroom with a jar of butterscotch on the mantelpiece. One piece daily was the ration.

On alternate weekends I went to stay with my aunties and grandparents in Granville, or with my mother's brother, George Killen, and his family in Redfern. I spent more weekends in Granville than in Redfern, I believe, but I looked forward to them both.

When I was to go to the aunties, Mrs Graham would take me on the tram to the city centre, where my aunty Hazel worked as a stenographer. If we went in a bit early, Mrs Graham would take me to the Australian Museum on College Street and leave me there for an hour or two while she did some shopping. I loved it; the guides always took an interest in a little girl walking around studying the exhibits and didn't seem to mind explaining things to me. If we went into town late on Friday afternoon, I would spend the last couple of hours of the working day under Hazel's desk in the office, keeping out of the way of the boss, amusing myself drawing or reading, until Hazel took me home with her on the train.

Weekends with the aunties and Granny and Grandfather McKean were a highlight in my quiet life. Uncle Milton, still a young bachelor living at home, always had a big black car in the yard and nearly every weekend the aunties would sandwich Granny and young Joy in between them as Mick (as Milton was called) drove us out for the day. Sometimes we went up to the Hawkesbury River and waited in the queue of cars and motorbikes for the ferry to dock and load up. On the other side of the river we'd picnic at Mooney Mooney, and I would see the Aboriginal hand prints and carvings on the rocks.

More often we'd go to the Blue Mountains, with the boot of the big car loaded with homemade sandwiches, cakes and homemade cordial, plus tea, sugar and even milk packed in wet tea towels for the trip. Sometimes we went past the mountains to visit relatives around Bathurst and Orange in the Central West of the state.

Grandfather seemed to prefer a weekend without his family around him. Maybe then he could get a bit of peace and quiet for a change. At other times, the refuge for this quiet, gentle man was the Mitchell Library in the city, where he would spend the day reading and sometimes copying by hand items from favourite books.

Mrs Graham was very good to me, though she was strict with my upbringing. I learned my table manners, how to clean silver and, if I stayed there for the weekend, how to use a carpet sweeper ('Both hands, Joy, not just one'). I also learned lots of hymns because if I was there on Sunday mornings I went to church with her; I was drilled through 'Onward, Christian Soldiers' and others so I would not disgrace her. Each afternoon, she spent an hour or so sitting in her private porch, sewing or knitting, and perforce I learned too. I also learned embroidery ('fancy work') and how to crochet the edging to small d'oyleys; and late in 1936 I learned how to knit little soft, white baby singlets without realising that I was adding to my brother Robin's baby trousseau. Robin arrived in December 1936 at Scone Hospital.

I went daily to the Sister Kenny Clinic at the RNS Hospital. Sister Elizabeth Kenny was a Queensland bush nurse who had hit upon an innovative treatment for polio patients. She used hot foments – cloths heated in water – to ease the spasms brought on by the disease, so that movement was then possible and further physiotherapy and other treatment could be introduced. I had not suffered these spasms; I seemed to go straight to the paralysis stage. Sister Kenny had achieved remarkable results here in Australia and in America, where she was treated as a heroine.

Part of the treatment included immersion in an ordinary bathtub; the nurse held a short hose attached to the bath tap. The idea was to aim a sharp spray of alternating hot and cold water up and down the spine to stimulate the blood flow. Afterwards, there were the usual physio exercises plus electrical stimulation of the weakened muscles.

I only saw Sister Kenny once. I was walking out to the foyer and saw her coming down a staircase opposite. She wore a plain black dress, and her white hair was quite noticeable in the hospital surroundings. I have since seen her museum in the little village of Nobby, Queensland, and I have seen calipers on view there. But she preferred that patients did not use them … or not in my case, anyway. So she, or her nurses, decreed that my caliper should be removed, and that I use elbow crutches instead. This way, I think she believed, my leg would gain more usage and therefore, hopefully, more strength.

However, although I had a lot of fun on those crutches, my knee gradually stiffened so that I could not straighten it. By the time my parents were told that I was no longer progressing, probably because I was fretting for my family, I had a bent knee but I was about the fastest thing on crutches in the Southern Hemisphere. Dad immediately applied for a transfer back to Sydney and I was reunited with my family after three years away, except for school holidays.

CHAPTER 2

I had school lessons while I was in hospital, but none while boarding that I remember. Possibly Grandfather and Aunty Vera gave me some lessons when I spent weekends with them, but when Dad and Mum came back to Sydney and rented a house at Naremburn, I began correspondence lessons at home. I was still going to RNS each day and it was not till the clinic told my parents they could do nothing more for me that I eventually spent a little time in fourth class at Naremburn Public School. I can only assume that the teaching at Canonbury's little schoolroom on top of Dad's informal teaching at home, and then the correspondence lessons while at Naremburn, brought me up to fourth class standard, as I do not recall any other standardised school lessons.

My return to my family was also marked by music. My mother played piano and I think Dad must have learned a bit too, even though the only piece I ever heard him play was 'In the Sweet Bye and Bye', complete with crossing over of hands with a flourish to finish the last refrain. Mum and Dad joined the Hawaiian Club run by Norm and Arthur Scott, brothers who, as the Singing Stockmen, also recorded some sides for the Regal Zonophone label.

It was at the club where Mum and Dad learned to play the Hawaiian steel guitar in the same style most musicians play the dobro these days. I was totally intrigued by the guitar, especially as my parents showed me how to vamp and strum an accompaniment for the songs I sang around the house. To keep me happy, they also gave me a little cheap ukulele and a book of lessons: an E-Z tutor. Between the piano strumming, ditto on the guitar and then on ukulele, I was having a fine time and singing every song I could learn, including the Aeroplane Jelly song.

At this stage, I don't recall Heather being too interested in the music, but it wasn't much later that she decided to join in. Heather Colleen and I were close friends and teammates; from the time she could say a few words, she was always on my side. Her favourite expression was 'I no know'; when Dad looked for me when I'd been naughty so he could tan my hide, her reply to his enquiry was always 'I no know'. It probably saved me a few deserved smacks, and I would return the favour when she was in bother, by never knowing where she was or who was responsible for whatever our parents were irate about.

We were living at Naremburn when my brother Stuart was born in December 1938. He was a tiny baby when we spent Christmas at the Doyles Creek farm that year. There was a heatwave over the summer period, and the baby suffered badly from the high temperatures. As he lay in his cosy-bye under the shade of the grapevines, Heather and I took turns to fan him. We would also soak old blankets in water that Mum and Dad, Heather and I would bring up in kerosene tins from the dam at the bottom of the hill. Then we'd hang the wet blankets in the doorways of the bedroom building where any slight breeze might cool the air with evaporation. We put the baby in the cosy-bye between the two doorways and kept fanning. Stuart survived the summer, but it was not an easy victory.

The next move for the family was to the little school at Yanderra in the Southern Highlands of New South Wales. As usual, arrangements were made by letter to rent a house and have the furniture (*and* Mum's piano) sent by rail or removalist van to be installed by the willing hands of our future neighbours and school parents. I've often wondered how Mum felt that night, as we arrived in the dark, in freezing weather to no transport, no welcome, and a long walk carrying a baby, comforting a toddler and shushing two cold, tired little girls. In her gentleness, I doubt that she would have let her frustration or tiredness show when she and Dad finally shepherded their little tribe into the first lamp-lit house they came to on that long gravel road. Luckily, it turned out to be across the road from the house we were to live in, and where our beds awaited us. Our neighbours were mortified that we had arrived to such a non-welcome but were certain that we were not expected till the next day.

Heather and I were up at the crack of dawn the following morning, going outside to walk barefoot in the hard frost and take a good look at where we had landed this time. It was a weatherboard house, with some sheds nearby where apparently there had been some poultry farming carried on. Further down from the house, wire netting enclosed a large patch of bush and a small chook house. There were even some hens still there, including two Cochin China bantams that Heather and I fought over. We each wanted the prettiest one, but I think Heather won this time. We envisaged our own chickens and our own fresh eggs.

The water supply was the usual tank on a high stand with a tin dish under the tap to catch any drips. We were fascinated to see that the water in the dish was frozen solid. We found that would be the case in the laundry shed too; if Mum put any tea towels or such into a tub to soak overnight in winter, they had to be thawed the next day before they could be boiled up in the copper or washed in the tubs.

There were sliprails in the front fence in place of a gate, and the bush surrounded the house on three sides with the road in front. We found a sapling down in the back bit of bush, and a handy V on an old log, and there we were with a good seesaw made to order.

The furniture our neighbours had unpacked was probably all in the wrong places at first, but Millie and Sike made short work of turning it into a homey setting. The floors were bare boards, but my parents always carried linoleum squares on their moves. These squares were patterned around the edges, and when Mum and Dad varnished the floorboards around them in brown lacquer, each room looked quite neat and tidy.

In the cold winter weather on the Highlands, the kitchen stove was a favourite gathering place in that little house. With the oven door open, and the fire built up, those who could get closest to the stove toasted their toes with one foot leaning on the oven door. My polio leg had really poor circulation; chilblains from knee to ankle were the usual result throughout winter. But Heather and I loved to each put a brick into the oven and then wrap it in an old towel to place in the foot of our bed to make it cosier at bedtime.

The schoolhouse was about a mile up the road towards the railway and the only little shop, the Log Cabin. Over the time we lived in Yanderra we moved twice more, each time closer to the school. It was a small Provisional school; this meant that if attendance dropped any further, it stood the risk of being closed. However, one way or another, it kept up the requisite number of scholars – which included Heather and me – while we were there. At times, children of railway workers came for a while then moved on.

There was a small wood stove in the classroom for heating but we still froze in winter, and fried in summer. Nevertheless, we loved being there. Dad made study trips into the bush a fun episode; we all collected specimens of bushes, the numerous wildflowers and trees, and Dad as teacher sent them to the Sydney Botanic Gardens Curator to be identified and then proudly displayed in little homemade boxes on the school walls.

Yanderra children moved around in groups and made regular sweeps of the railway lines for coal that had fallen from the steam trains. It was a lot of fun to stand by the lines as a train passed by, yelling out to the passengers to throw us their newspapers. We usually collected plenty of reading matter as well as plenty of fuel for our family stoves and open fires. In one exciting event, there were pound notes scattered around in the aftermath of an attempted train robbery. I never did hear the rights of that story, but there was a lot of excitement and scrounging around the railway lines by young and old.

While all this was happening, I was having the time of my life running free in the bush on my elbow crutches. For the first, and probably the last, time in my life I could run as fast as the other kids, though I had some busters when the crutches tangled with vines or stones in the bush while I was moving full pelt. The crutches came in handy, too, when I was tearing along a narrow track through the bush to the school and a bandy-bandy snake lay across the track ahead of me. The bandy-bandy was a small, flattish snake banded in white stripes on a black background. I was too late to stop, but the crutches flew me over the sleepy snake and off at an increased pace as I put distance between Bandy and me.

Unfortunately, the bent knee caused some distress to my parents and they kept taking me back to the Outpatients clinic at Royal North Shore Hospital. These visits entailed a train trip from Yanderra to Sydney and usually took the whole day to complete by the time the steam train puffed to the city, we waited in the Outpatients clinic for my turn to be seen and then the train puffed its way back to the Southern Highlands. The doctors at the clinic suggested that I really did need to wear a caliper and to have the knee bandaged into place so that by tightening the bandage daily the tendons in my knee would eventually straighten out. I don't think Mum and Dad enjoyed the process any more than I did. It was painful and it took some time to work, but my knee did straighten out at last.

It was at Yanderra that I began singing in earnest, and before too long, Heather joined in. On occasional visits to Granville Picture Theatre matinees, I had seen some films starring an American comedienne called Judy Canova, who mostly acted the comedy hillbilly girl. Judy's singing and yodelling were featured in her films and that got me started. I found that I could yodel quite well, and when I heard some records by an Englishman called Harry Torrani, who specialised in Swiss-style yodelling, I was hooked. Before long, I was learning 'hillbilly' songs (as they were called then) and I was singing and yodelling to my strumming on Dad's or Mum's steel guitars. Heather was beginning to sing along with me too, and we would sometimes sing a couple of songs for a school concert or at a church function.

Before making any rash decisions about further music lessons, Mum and Dad decided to take me for an audition with Norm Scott in Sydney at the Hawaiian Club. I played Dad's Stella guitar and sang and yodelled a couple of songs for Norm, who was very kind in his review of my efforts. It was not long before a small guitar had been made for me, and a Michigan ukulele bought for Heather, and we began fortnightly rail trips to Sydney for our guitar and uke lessons at the club. Soon after this, Norm and Arthur had us performing on the club's weekly radio show on 2GB. So we were on radio at the ages of ten and eight years.

As we were often asked to sing at school or church concerts and any little local fundraising concerts, Mum brought out her sewing machine and made us stage outfits. We wore black slacks (slacks covered my caliper and built up shoe), white blouses with red neck scarves, and black and white gauntlets on our wrists. The big investment would have been the two black cowboy hats fashioned with dents in the crown, as we'd seen on Canadian Mounties' hats. Perhaps we were thinking about the Canadian cowboy singer Wilf Carter. Heather and I had learned some of his songs, and his yodels as well.

The outfits stood us in good stead when we appeared on the Harry Yates 2UE Sunday Diggers Concerts at the Tivoli, and the following year on *Australia's Amateur Hour.* The *Amateur Hour* was a nationwide radio talent quest, and we entered in 1941. Heather was nine and I was eleven years old. We did quite well, though the stage appearance was daunting. Heather was such a little girl and as she walked out onto the stage after me, her eyes swept over the huge audience in the theatre and, shocked, she came to a full stop. Neither of us had ever seen so many people in one place in our lives.

I finished fourth class and then spent fifth and sixth classes as my father's student. During the latter part of 1941, all sixth class students had to take an intelligence quotient (IQ) test as part of the year's programme. Shortly afterwards, Dad had to take me to Sydney to the Education Department for further tests; I would guess that because my father was the teacher who administered the tests, the department thought the results might not have been quite correct. Anyway, there was one point's difference in the result their own people obtained, so Dad was in the clear and I was officially noted as having an IQ of 163 points. Also noted was that my mental age was nineteen years ... How they worked that one out, I have no idea. I know I was a precocious child, but I would normally put that down to the fact that I had spent so much time with adults and in hospital surroundings.

Millie and Silas were very good parents. They did everything they could possibly do to assist me to grow up as an independent person; someone who adapted to my disability and did not regard it as an unassailable hurdle to my aims in life. They encouraged me to do anything I wanted to do and they fostered my singing and music as a special gift that helped make up for any physical drawbacks I might encounter. They had been told at some stage that should I break that bad leg, it might not heal properly, and they must have worried as I climbed trees, searched caves, explored the bush and walked miles up and through the surrounding bushy gullies and tracks around Yanderra.

In September 1939, war in Europe was declared and Australia moved onto a war footing. Dad raced home from school at lunchtime to hear the war news; supplies of khaki wool arrived at the school and we were all knitting 'socks for the soldiers' as fast as we could turn them out. By the latter part of 1941, Australia had declared war on Japan as the Japanese war machine turned to the South Pacific.

It was in September 1941 that I was placed in the Margaret Reid Orthopaedic Home, in St Ives in Sydney's north, for in-house hospitalisation and rehabilitation, mainly to improve the strength and movement of my left leg. My parents still held hope that maybe, just maybe, some treatment would make me more mobile and would help keep me strong enough to live a normal life despite the caliper and the drag of the bad leg.

I was intrigued by this new hospital, its wards open on one side to the elements. The only time the wall facing the gardens was closed by its shutters was when rain beat in. It was still cold at times in September, but we wore cotton bib-and-brace shorts over a bare torso, and a shortsleeved cotton blouse if it was very chilly. The only time we wore a woollen sweater was when it was just about freezing. As summer approached we wore cotton headgear shaped like a fisherman's rain hat, with the long piece at the back to shelter the neck. It may have been a very bracing style of acclimatisation, but I did not suffer a head cold for two years after I left there. I was one of the lucky ones who was quite mobile. Many children there were strapped onto frames, or wore heavy plaster casts ankle to hip. There was even one lass aged fourteen who had a severe case of rheumatoid arthritis and had great difficulty in walking around the ward.

The patients were expected to share any treats, such as chocolate, that we might have received from family, and we had small jobs to do sometimes. I loved the music teacher who played the 'Barcarolle' on the piano as we tapped our little triangles in time. I also liked vamping on the piano and singing my country songs, especially when one of the visiting doctors returned with his guitar to lend to me. He joined me in singing 'Hillbilly Valley', to the amusement and entertainment of the nursing staff.

CHAPTER 3

I was still in Margaret Reid when Dad was moved to Cudgera Creek in the Tweed Valley of the Far North Coast of New South Wales. Heather and my two little brothers went, of course, but I was left in Sydney once again. It was not long before my mother rebelled, saying it was too much to be separated once more for what little gain? I think she felt that a strong family life, where she could help with my exercises, and a normal childhood would be better for me and for the family as a whole.

At this time in late 1941, the threat of Japanese invasion of Northern Australia was too real to be ignored. So when Mum, Dad, Robin and Stuart left Doyles Creek after spending Christmas 1941 at the farm, they left Heather and me with Granny Killen in the safety of the dairy farm until they could see how the war developed. This gave us about six weeks of freedom as Granny Killen coped with two girls who had ferocious arguments and differences, but who seemed to entertain themselves without problem.

In the farmhouse, there was no electricity or phone, and no water piped to the kitchen or tubs. Granny had to wash and iron our dresses as well as shirts and trousers for my uncles Bill and Jack. This got a bit much for Granny at her age of seventy-odd, so she bought some brown patterned cotton from the Assyrian hawker's van and fashioned some straight-up-and-down shifts that took much less ironing and fussing. We were not at all happy with these because Jackie – our youngest Killen uncle and a handsome man of Irish good looks with black wavy hair, olive skin and brilliant blue eyes – delighted in telling us that all we needed were some Sam Browne belts to finish off the picture. Although we did not know what a Sam Browne belt was, we could understand it was not something overly attractive and we sulked. He had to bring us bags of boiled lollies from town to get back in our good books.

Now and again we went to Singleton or to Denman with Granny and Jack or Billy. Both towns were about twenty miles from Doyles Creek. We had cousins to visit in Denman, and Granny always took along things such as pumpkins or melons or such to the aunties. I should mention at this point that Heather's name(s) caused some confusion in our extended families. Dad's background was Scottish and Mum's was Irish, so Dad called her 'Heather' and Mum called her 'Colleen' and their families followed the leader. To tell the truth, I called her Colleen until her teens, when she announced to all and sundry that from now on she was to be called Heather. (I know Slim always called her 'Coll' if he wasn't careful.)

The main store in Denman was Campbell's and Granny would sail in, dressed in black and jet beads, to be greeted with respect: 'And what could we do for Mrs Killen?' Heather and I stood around and stared at the counters where the groceries were measured into brown paper bags and stacked up. Granny had an account, I think, but there were certainly plenty of cash payments being made. To do these, the invoice and the customer's money were placed in a screwtop container which was then attached to an overhead pulley. One pull by the shop assistant and the money would fly over our heads to an office above, where the cashier opened the receptacle from its flying fox, placed the required change therein and, with a sharp pull on the dangling handle, sent the money whizzing back to the counter and customer. Fascinated little girls watched in trepidation: What would happen if the flying fox contraption broke? Would everyone's money be stuck up near the roof forever?

If we went to Singleton on market day, Granny would take masses of her famous perfumed stocks. They were beautiful flowers, and how she managed to grow them with her limited supply of water is still a mystery to me. She would take them to the market and leave them for sale as she purchased other things she wanted on the day. At lunchtime she would shepherd us to an upstairs lunchroom run by two spinster ladies whose names I cannot recall. They presided over a long dining table where, from tureens and platters, they served a set menu to people who came for a good home-cooked meal. Going to a cafe was not Granny's idea of the right thing for a widowed lady with two little granddaughters to do; if only she could see how things have changed now.

Back at the farm, Heather and I, to our later shame, took delight in teasing old Aunt Eliza. Aunt Eliza was Grandfather Killen's unmarried sister; after Grandfather's death, Aunt Eliza still lived at Woodpark and wandered in and out of the buildings, the store and saddle room, happy in her memories of the past. She was a tall old lady, and Granny told me that Eliza had been a real 'belle of the ball' when she was young.

There was some mystery regarding Eliza; in her old age her situation would have been classified as senility, but Granny – who was not a particular fan of Eliza, as she had to look after her – was generous in describing her beauty and hinted that a would-be beau had 'put something into her tea at suppertime at the dance' and that Eliza had become terribly ill and remained vague and otherworldly for the rest of her life. Then I heard the story of her being alone at the farm when a hawker called; the resulting encounter had scarred her and her mind for life.

So apparently she had been quite normal until some episode – whatever it might have been – took place in her young life and she was so affected by it that she became this haunted, quiet shadow around the house and the yard.

It was not until I was up at the farm as a teenager that I came upon Aunt Eliza in her little room, and I sat down with her. I brushed her long silver hair and looked properly, for about the first time, at the fine bone structure of her old face. More importantly, I listened to her properly for the first time. She talked quietly of her girlhood, of old faces and old friends, of the parties and balls she had gone to and remembered. Years later, I wrote the song 'Old Aunt Eliza'; my daughter, Anne, recorded it. I still have Eliza's little ivory fan; I like to think of her as a beautiful, tall young woman waving the little fan as she sat in the ballroom amongst the other girls. But the reality was a tall, gaunt old lady in long dresses and cotton sunbonnets sitting in the saddle room where two mischievous little girls amused themselves by pouring cups of water under the door to alarm and disturb her. I still feel guilty when I think of it. But perhaps it didn't worry old Aunt Eliza too badly. I hope not.

By the time the 1942 school year began at Cudgera, it was decided that it was quite safe to bring Heather and me up to the Tweed. We were so excited to travel on the train to Murwillumbah and to be driven out to the little school in the midst of banana plantations and dairy farms. Cudgera was a district of farming families some twenty miles from Murwillumbah, which was the main town in the Tweed Valley. The school was in a grassy lane with the teacher's residence alongside it. There was one neighbouring house, the Quinns', and then the local hall. On the hill behind, and all around, were banana farms. In the backyard of the school residence were pawpaw trees and a Japanese mulberry tree. Out in the lane, near our neighbour's front fence, was a huge mango tree. We had received a case of pineapples from Mum and Dad when we were down at the Creek with Granny, so we knew there would be more to come of all these new and luscious fruits.

Dances and school events were held in the little hall, and the local ladies would decorate the stage with frangipani flowers crowded into vases. I could not work out how the sweet frangipani flowers grew the long stalks that they flaunted en masse in their tall containers. The secret was this: the children went into the paddocks and picked multitudes of paspalum grass stalks and impaled the frangipani blossoms on the top of each stalk. Simple? Labour intensive! The effect was beautiful and the perfume almost overpowering, but lovely.

I began the first year of high school in the classroom there by receiving correspondence lessons from Sydney's Blackfriars Correspondence School. It was not ideal, as Dad was teaching every class, from first through to sixth, in the one room. He had an assistant, Isobel Blanch, who took the kindergarteners (and possibly the firsts) in the hall down the lane. I don't think I learned too much in the way of languages and algebra that year, although I suppose I must have made some progress.

Dad was getting very restless as the war news grew more ominous. He ended up enlisting in the Army early in 1943, despite the fact that he was 36 or 37 and married with a wife and four children to look after.

When Dad left for the Army, we moved into Murwillumbah, to a house on Church Hill, walking distance from high school for me and primary school for Heather. The walk was sometimes enlivened by the discovery of a green tree snake in the small trees growing along the footpath. I was put into a second-year class and had to try to catch up on the bits I'd not learned back in the classroom at Cudgera.

Heather and I were singing a lot in those days, and we were performing in war fundraising concerts around the district. She was eleven and I was thirteen. There were American soldiers stationed near Murwillumbah and the town was lively with dances and concerts. Dad came home on leave before too long but was then sent to Townsville.

Mum wrote to him to consult him about the proposal made to her by two of my aunties in Granville. Hazel was married by this time, but Vera and Una, plus our Uncle Milton, still lived with Granny and Grandfather in the big old two-storey house at Malcolm Street. Aunty Una worked at Granville Baths and had become good friends with swimming and diving coach Tom Penny. Tom had moved on to coaching young swimmers and taking a strong interest in swimming for disabled people. He was keen to coach me and use swimming to improve my general strength and, in particular, to help my polio-affected leg. My parents were very open to anything they thought would be helpful for me and the decision was made for Mum and the family to move to Sydney, to share the house in Malcolm Street.

Accommodation in Sydney was almost impossible to find in those days. Rents were high and 'key money' was the norm – if you did find a house or flat to rent, you had to pay a cash fee on the side before the key was handed over. Authorities brought in what was known as a '5A lease' in an effort to combat this but, as is always the way, there were many methods of getting around it.

In those war years, and for a short time afterwards, clothing, tea, butter and sugar were strictly rationed, and petrol even more strictly rationed. A blackmarket mentality grew up even amongst the more conservative of householders. I remember that because Heather and I did not drink tea until I was at least about eighteen years old, Mum and her mother swapped tea coupons for butter and sugar coupons instead. There was always someone who could get you a dress length (for a price, of course); smokers were keen to become regular customers at one particular tobacco outlet so that when the small stock of coveted Australian brands of cigarettes arrived to be hidden 'under the counter', they would be certain to be given the nod that now was the time to get a packet or two. English and American cigarettes were more readily available but not so much to popular taste.

I fear the aunties might have found that having a family of four youngsters around all the time was a bit trying, especially as the two boys of six and eight years of age had to be constantly 'shushed' and trained to not run in the long hall or past the staircase. In summer, the cooking had to be done on the one gas stove in a little annexe near the bathroom. Mum cooked for herself and us children, and she shared the stove with Aunty Vera, who often cooked on the same stove for the rest of the family. It could be awkward and stressful, but we were much better off than many other families at the time.

Crowding was the usual way of life when accommodation was so expensive and hard to find, and when other cousins came to visit it was a case of 'topping and tailing' in the old double beds. We used to talk half the night because we'd wake each other as our toes would tickle the nose of the cousin occupying the opposite end of the bed. It was sometimes by accident, but more often it was definitely on purpose.

Heather and I began school at Parramatta High, which our father had attended. In third year I studied for my Intermediate Certificate lying flat on the floor in the old front room, under the Tiffany silk-shaded lamp. The walls of the room were painted a soft red – the same colour as the silk in the lampshade. An old black player piano sat in one corner, while a wind-up cabinet record player stood at the opposite end of the room. Peacock feathers sat stiffly in a pair of Mary Gregory vases on the mantelpiece. That front room was the one quiet room in the whole house; I had always gravitated to it since I was old enough to read. Grandfather's bookcases lined part of one wall and one held a set of Children's Encyclopaedias. Although I read a lot of general information, I found that there were stories at the end of each volume and they were a greater attraction than the worthy information in the rest of the pages.

Tom Penny lost no time in beginning my swimming lessons. Over the next three years or so, I trained under his coaching, which was often criticised as being too hard on young swimmers. He was simply ahead of his time, however, and his coaching showed results. Accused of being likely to 'burn out' his young charges, Tom ploughed ahead regardless and kept his youngsters winning club and some state trophies. There was no possibility of my reaching that standard, but Tom aimed for me to be able to compete and have some success. I believe now that he knew how important it could be for my self-confidence to be able to compete with able-bodied swimmers and have some wins. He trained me hard in fresh water at Granville Baths, and joined me up into the Manly Ladies Swimming Club as well. Training in fresh water and then competing in salt water helped me swim an improved time. Because the handicapper couldn't keep up with my rapid improvements, I managed to win a respectable number of the handicap races. In retrospect it was a bit rough on the Manly handicapper, but I worked like a robot to get those results and it did wonders for my self-confidence.

The next goal was to train me as a long-distance swimmer. My leg was gaining some strength but it did not contribute much help to my kick. The right leg kicked so strongly that it drove me off to one side unless I compensated by extra drive from my left arm. These were all problems that Tom tackled one by one. The usual freestyle swimmer breathed once each two strokes; Tom taught me to take a breath every three strokes and that saved me precious seconds in a short race. I had strong arms and back, and good lungs, and although I was slower than most, I had staying power, and I usually had enough left in me at the end of a mile or half-mile to increase my pace for a finish.

In the mid 1940s, the only heated pool in Sydney that we knew of was in Tattersalls in the city. However, Tattersalls was a 'men only' club, so there was nowhere for me to train in winter when the local pool was closed. On weekends Tom took his little team – including me – over to Manly, to train in the outdoor pool. That pool was actually an enclosed area of the harbour, and as I swam lengths I could see great holes in the wire fencing below water level. Being a country girl, I had a terror of sharks and I didn't co-operate very well with my training. Tom promptly put a stop to that by insisting that I dive through the main hole and out onto the rocks nearby and see for myself that no sharks were waiting there to eat me for breakfast. I wasn't convinced, and cried my way up and down the pool when he started me on my lengths again.

The next idea that struck Mr Penny, as we all called him, was when he discovered that the clean water issuing from Bunnerong Power Station in Matraville was a few degrees warmer than swimming water anywhere else. So he took me and a couple of others to an open paddock where the water raced quickly down a channel from the power station outlet. The only change room was the paddock behind a low wall of old corrugated iron, and the wind was very brisk indeed. I took my goose pimples to the edge of the water and reluctantly waded in. The water may have been a few degrees warmer than anywhere else, but it was still very cold, and to top it off Tom had me swimming like mad against a strong current. He probably thought it was a good workout, but I don't remember ever repeating the performance.

I wasn't alone in being at the baths every spare minute in summer; Heather was in and out of the water like a little fish. She was a good breaststroke swimmer, and showed promise as a diver. Mr Penny had his eagle eye on her diving, if I remember rightly. It was a heavy blow to all of us when Heather contracted polio in the summer of 1944–45.

By this time, Dad had been discharged from the Army and was teaching again in Sydney. Our furniture and household goods were still in storage in Murwillumbah, where the storage facility stood near the banks of the Tweed River. When the river flooded our belongings were inundated, too, and most of Mum and Dad's treasured wedding and family portraits were ruined by the floodwaters. The lounge suite smelled of dirty water, but wonderful neighbours still in Murwillumbah went down and got the furniture, hosed it and dried it to the best of their ability.

Heather showed symptoms of polio at nine in the morning and by noon she was in Prince Henry Hospital over near Botany. She spent weary months in hospital, losing a girlfriend who died there one night after existing in an iron lung for weeks. It was while Heather was in hospital that the family was split up for a while. Friction in the double household built up to a point where Dad and Mum thought they should move out. I was boarded with the family of a classmate while my parents rented rooms in a nearby suburb. It was a very disjointed life and I was relieved when things went back to normal.

We were ecstatic when Heather was discharged with what appeared to be nothing more than one shoulder a little higher than the other and flattened arches of her feet. It wasn't long before she was swimming and hurdling again. Small in stature, she could run like a hare and, with no technique at all, could leap hurdles with ease. But she didn't want to return to Parramatta High, where all her peers had moved on to other classes. Instead, she joined some other friends at Auburn Home Science School and did her Intermediate Certificate there.

Heather and I were doing a lot of singing and performing by now, as we entered various talent quests that were very popular then, and we were in demand to appear for charity fundraisers and concert parties as well. It was when Heather was walking from school to Auburn railway station one afternoon that she saw a poster outside the town hall offering auditions for artists to appear on a big talent quest. She went inside, where auditions were in full swing, and when told she could enter the quest, promptly asked, 'Can my sister come too?' I suppose the entrepreneur thought, The more the merrier, and so the next afternoon after school, Heather and I took ourselves off to Auburn with guitar and ukulele to sing some of our songs for Dick Sawyer. Through this, we became regular performers on Dick's many concerts throughout the suburbs, but before too long we had to cut down on our show bookings, because school studies reared their demanding heads.

The next episode in this saga of country concerts in the heart of the city came with the arrival from America of one Willard Ferrier and his young daughter, Dot. Bill Ferrier had problems at home and was determined to keep Dot with him, so he came about as far from his marital worries as he could, landing in Australia, where he told Dot to always keep a pound note tucked into her shoe in case she was 'abducted by her mother'. We were quite entranced by all of this, but most of all, we were fascinated by the shows we appeared on and the artists who starred in them.

In Sydney, the Tivoli Theatre was the centre of live entertainment. Roy Rene ('Mo') ruled as king of the vaudeville stage; when one Bob Dyer arrived as part of a hillbilly act, he not only married Dolly from the chorus line but stayed to become part of Australian radio and television history with his *Pick a Box* show. He still liked his hillbilly or country music too, and bought himself a ticket to a Bill Ferrier show in Sydney Town Hall. Of course, he was soon spotted and coaxed onto the stage to say 'hello' to everyone. He was a good sport about it.

Jack Davey was his pretend opponent for top honours in the radio industry, and Bob and Jack provided the entertainment in a Henry Lawson–Banjo Paterson style of argument. There were quite a few live music shows on radio; community singing shows were very popular. In the 1940s and early 1950s, most radio stations played a mix of musical styles. This consisted of anything from light classical to popular, jazz, country (still called 'hillbilly' then), instrumental or blues. It made for interesting listening, and music was the main component of radio programmes (as opposed to today's prevailing talkback shows).

When I finished high school at the end of 1946, I began collecting character and ability references that I enclosed with my application to enrol at teachers' college, with the aim of following our family tradition of becoming a schoolteacher. Much to my dismay, I received a blunt refusal on the grounds that because of my disability it was decided that I 'could not relate to the children' I would be teaching. That took a bit of swallowing, but I changed my goal and set my sights on a university Arts degree that included psychology. I thought I could possibly do a good job working with disabled people. However, the sticking point to a university degree (teaching, at that time, was a diploma) was having the money to pay for the education. Another hurdle to overcome but, in the meantime, I needed a job.

CHAPTER 4

I was just seventeen at the beginning of 1947. I had a good pass on my Leaving Certificate and I had to find a way of continuing my education or getting a job. First, though, early in February, I had to have an operation on my left ankle. I was admitted to Royal North Shore Hospital, where I stayed for more than five weeks after the procedure. Once back at Malcolm Street I spent three weeks in a wheelchair and another three weeks on crutches. That did not stop my girlfriends visiting, nor did it stop one of my church-group friends rolling up on his motorbike and sitting me and my plaster cast on the pillion to get to meetings. While I was more or less immobilised at home, I managed to earn my pocket money by knitting jumpers for women. I charged 2/6 (two shillings and sixpence) per skein knitted, but they had to do their own sewing up. This filled the slow hours during the days when everyone else was away at work or school, and gave me a bit of money of my own.

Heather and I even did some performances while I still had the plaster cast on my lower leg and foot. I wore black slacks and a black sock over the cast, along with all the rest of my stage outfit. As all hall and theatre stages of the time had full length curtains, my method of getting onstage was to have the curtains drawn while I hobbled or hopped into position onto a chair mid stage and the compere introduced the McKean Sisters out front. When the curtains opened, there we were in front of the microphone.

I sometimes wonder now about the balance of our harmonies, but I think these appearances may have taken place when we mostly sang and yodelled in unison. As we were growing up, Mum opposed my singing and yodelling in harmony with Heather, as our voices were not strong enough separately to be heard properly. (It should be remembered that we used to appear on concerts where there might not have been a microphone, or there was only one and it had to be shared.) The harmony singing was a natural thing for me to do, and gradually, over the next year or so, we perfected our style and, I suppose, our vocal strength, so Mum let us go ahead and do it our way.

Over the years, there has been a fair amount of debate about my harmony yodelling, because the harmony line does not follow the usual style of copying the melody of the lead line a couple of notes above or below. I could not have said how I used to do it – it was something that came naturally to me, so I didn't try to work it out – but a studio musician told me that I was yodelling a counterpoint melody to Heather's main melody. Apparently, that means I yodel a completely different tune that fits and harmonises with the lead melody. That sounds complicated, and perhaps it is because I don't quite understand how I do it or why! This exasperates my daughter, Anne, when she wants to learn the harmony yodel line for a performance. Someone has to perform the lead line and I can then sing or yodel the harmony, but I can't just sing or yodel it without the lead melody to pitch against.

Once my ankle had healed fully, I had to find a job and after a series of unsuccessful interviews that were basic, and very different from what job interviews are today, I came up against the same problem: I was disabled, and apparently a caliper on my leg meant I couldn't keep the books or answer the telephone where I could be seen by clients or customers.

Having heard the remarks made by one prospective employer as I left his premises, and assuring myself that it was his loss, not mine (I had tickets on myself at seventeen), I decided I should undergo a vocational guidance test at the office of the Vocational Guidance Bureau in Martin Place. Surely that would give me some pointers about the sort of career I could aim for, and I would be given advice on how to get started towards it. So I made the appointment, sat for the test and was interviewed by one of the psychologists there, Joy Charlesworth.

Joy was a lovely lady, and very encouraging in her attitude towards the possibilities she laid before me, but her emphasis appeared to be on my pursuing a university degree in the immediate future. That was going to be easier said than done, because tuition fees had to be paid up front. I didn't have the money and neither did my family.

After the morning's testing and the psychologist's interview, I was most surprised to be called in for an interview with the bureau head, who offered me a job at the Vocational Guidance office. I was especially surprised about this because I couldn't use a typewriter, and the job was typing the psychologists' reports each day after the morning's testings. He must have had a lot of faith in me, though, because I was enrolled for a week's solid tuition in typing at the business college in Parramatta, and then I began work at the office in the city. Before too long I was promoted to writing brochures about different careers; the booklet had to set out what qualifications were required, how to attain those, what could be expected in the workplace, and the prospects for advancement. Current rates of pay were also included. I enjoyed this part of the job as I could 'clock in' a little later each morning and then set out from the office to interview key people in different businesses to get the facts and figures about each career.

I was very happy there at the Vocational Guidance Bureau, especially as after all those years that ankle operation meant I was able to wear a surgical shoe on my left foot instead of an ankle boot. For a teenager wanting to wear pretty dresses, it had been a real trial to wear a boot on one foot and a black Oxford lace-up shoe on the other. It was especially hard when everyone else was dancing around in high-heeled ankle strap sandals with their summer dresses. I still had to wear black lace-up shoes, but that was a minor problem compared to some other people's troubles – although a teenager couldn't be expected to see it in that light at times. I was a normal young girl who indulged in some bouts of whingeing, though I usually stamped on it as firmly as possible.

Most of the time, the fact that I wore a caliper and walked very badly was not my problem so far as I was concerned; if it was a worry to anyone else, that was their problem instead. After all, the only things I could not do were run and dance, but even the dancing was alright when old-time ballroom was the norm at the dances I attended. In the days when we all wore long dresses to a dance, one polished ballroom dancer who believed he was Australia's answer to Fred Astaire did not realise that I wore a caliper. He was kind enough to honour me with an invitation to share the floor with him, and nearly dropped in his tracks after he asked me, 'Do you have a stiff leg?' and I answered, 'Yes, I do! Didn't you know?' Obviously, an experienced dancer could tell by the way I moved that my left leg did not work the same way as the other. Naturally enough, that was the last time I danced with him but it gave Heather and me a wonderful laugh. His face was worth a picture.

When rock 'n' roll came in, with jitterbugging and such, Heather and I had some absolutely hysterical sessions as she tried hard to teach me how to do the steps, making allowance for the stiff left leg. I gave that up after a while as I could see there was a limit to my abilities, after all, and Heather was not a magician.

The McKean Sisters were appearing on concerts run by Dick Sawyer, on Bill Ferrier's shows and at local concerts such as visits to nursing homes and to the mental asylums at Peat Island and Milson Island on the Hawkesbury River. It is strange and, indeed, pitiful to think that in the 1940s even people with Down syndrome were placed in such institutions. One young boy called to me from behind a high mesh fence to tell me that he shouldn't be there because his only problem was epilepsy. I was only seventeen and did not know what I should do to help him, if he was genuine. No one took any notice of me when I asked about it while on the island, and after we left I had to let it go. It was little consolation to know that everyone had enjoyed the amateur concert and pressed us to 'come back again soon'.

All through 1947 and into 1948, we were getting so many offers of appearances that we decided we should 'turn professional' and begin to charge a fee. A number of the charity engagements dropped off, naturally enough, even though we still did many of those. One of the engagements we enjoyed and worked fairly often was on board the Showboat that cruised Sydney Harbour every Saturday night. At these shows we used guitar and ukulele and did a straight singing and yodelling act. They were always full of good-humoured crowds who liked to sing along and asked for favourite tunes.

Part of the fun for the Showboat crowds was pushing money into the sound hole of our instruments as we worked close to the audience. One particular night when we arrived home from the show, we made so much noise shaking out coins from the guitar and ukulele that our mother was woken and came downstairs to see what on earth we were doing. She ended up laughing and helping us find and count all the coins that rolled out.

It was a bit later, when the square-dancing rage hit Sydney, that we began calling and teaching at private parties. For the square-dancing part of our act I played piano accordion and called the instructions, while Heather played guitar and taught the beginners how to do the steps. It was the best way we knew of to get a party to loosen up and start having a good time.

It was also one way of just about breaking our backs, hefting that 120 bass piano accordion down to the railway station and back again after the gig. We took it in turns: one carried the accordion and the other the acoustic guitar and we generally swapped a couple of times in the journey.

One of the nicest jobs we did was in a fancy home on the north shore of Sydney, for a house full of executive-type business people who really let their hair down and got into the swing of the square dancing. They booked us again for another evening and said that they would arrange transport for us. Malcolm Street came out in full force to inspect the polished black hire car that glided to a halt outside our house, and the uniformed driver who very formally took charge of our heavy instruments and ushered us into the vehicle. Our neighbours couldn't believe their eyes, and we couldn't believe our good fortune. It was the easiest trip to and from a job that we ever had, and it filled us with ambition to save up for a small car of our own that we would go travelling in, to cross the Nullarbor and see Western Australia. (I don't know why we had this fixation about driving across the Nullarbor but I did get to drive across it eventually.)

All through 1947 I looked at ways to get into Sydney University; I really wanted to have that Arts degree. Eventually, I scored a small scholarship that paid my fees for one year plus 30 pounds towards the cost of textbooks. Then a former student donated his textbooks and I was lucky enough to benefit from this generosity. I was able to begin the degree in 1948 but found that working some days, and performing with Heather every weekend and some nights, plus the lack of any room at home to study, played havoc with my schedule of lectures. I knew I would have to change to evening lectures the following year, and my psychologist friends at the Vocational Guidance Bureau managed to get me a position at the Tutorial Classes Department in the university grounds.

They gave amazing support – I will always be grateful – and I had a good year there in 1948. But in 1949 Heather and I were performing so much that my drive towards an academic career fell way into the background. I became tired of juggling work, lectures at night and our performing jobs. If I didn't take an engagement, then neither could Heather as our bookings were for the McKean Sisters duo. I was writing songs too, and gaining good reception for these when we tried them on stage. All in all, music was giving me far more satisfaction than my studies did and again, it was a battle to find anywhere to study. Every day, I walked twenty minutes to the railway station, travelled over half an hour to Central Station and walked another twenty minutes or so to the university. After working in the office all day, and attending evening lectures I covered the same route home, arriving about ten o'clock at night. I studied on the train and in Fisher Library at lunchtime, and on the floor of the red front room under the Tiffany lampshade at home.

Music took over to such an extent that when we were offered an engagement to appear for two weeks with Sorlie's big tent show, based for a time in Newcastle, I burned my bridges and resigned from my job and my lectures.

I will always be glad we took that engagement, because it gave us another slant on show business. Sorlie's was one of the first of the touring tent shows: there was an orchestra in the pit in front of the stage, a full chorus line and a soubrette leading them out front; there were singers; and variety acts, including one popular act of the time, Will Mahoney. His wife, Evie Hayes, was famous in Australia as the lead in the stage musical of *Annie Get Your Gun*. The couple were Americans who had come to Australia for the Tivoli Circuit – a series of venues where entertainers performed variety and vaudeville shows – but decided to stay permanently. Will used to finish his act by dancing on his xylophone and tapping out the melody with his toes.

Heather and I liked to sneak down the side of the stage and hide in the curtains, where we could watch the other acts, especially Will's. We had no idea we were doing anything out of place, until someone said to us, 'I'm surprised Will Mahoney hasn't gone crook at you two – he doesn't like anyone watching from the side.' We stopped, of course, but not before Will, dancing fantastically in the finale of his act, glanced over at two stagestruck youngsters, and winked and smiled at us.

A highlight of the programme was the comedy sketches, headed by comic Bobby Le Brun. He had a great team to act out the skits – people such as Maurie Fields and Val Jellay, and Bobby himself was a top comic actor. He had good material and his timing was spot on. After George Sorlie's death, Bobby and his wife, Gracie – who usually played straight roles in the skits with Bobby – bought Sorlie's big tent show from George's widow, Grace, and took it back on the road. As a very minor act in the show, we McKeans did not get to know the stars such as Bobby and Gracie (but years later Slim and I would come to know them very well indeed and Bobby would help Slim with material for sketches for our travelling hall show – they were good people).

Appearing with the big tent show was Heather's and my first taste of living in a residential hotel with all the other members of the show, and getting around with the girls from the ballet. If this was show business – sleeping in each morning, setting our hair to look good for the show that night, getting dressed up in our stage outfits in the canvas dressing rooms before opening time, being in the midst of all the glamorous costumes and benches of makeup and hairdos – then this was for us, we thought. But it was back to reality when, our engagement completed, we returned to Sydney and faced the fact that we needed day jobs as well as our night performances if we were going to keep up our shopping.

This time I concentrated on getting an office position, and I ended up as the secretary in the real estate office of

P.L. Ashley & Co. in Parramatta. Having to work Saturday mornings, I was allowed Thursday afternoons free instead and I would head straight into the Tutorial Classes office at the university. There, my previous workmates and I used to catch up on their doings and mine, and at times we'd go out together after work.

Working in the real estate office was interesting for me, and as my boss always gave me a 10 per cent commission out of his own earnings if I actually made the sale, I was a very keen secretary and assistant. This commission usually amounted to five pounds on a house block, for instance, and I did my best to earn myself that extra. In doing that, I learned quite a lot about selling businesses and real estate in the area, and I got to know the values around the western suburbs. It stood me in good stead later on.

An erstwhile school friend named Rosalie was working in Alert Radio and Music Store in The Arcade in Parramatta and I often called in to see her. Rosalie played piano and, with her, I was often invited to visit the home of Alert's co-manager, Gerry Ormsby, and his wife, Kate, to join one of their parties and music evenings. When Rosalie left Alert, I joined the staff. I demonstrated guitar, ukulele and piano accordion as Gerry did the selling, and I installed Alert's first record bar. I loved the job because it meant mingling with the customers, the staff were a happy lot and I was in music, even though it was in a different way.

At this time, Gerry was persuading his co-manager, Jack Sandler, that Alert Radio should keep up with the times and do some radio advertising. What better way than to utilise the talent on hand – namely, one Joy McKean with her sister, Heather – and promote Alert Radio's musical sales via the McKean Sisters on a Saturday night 2KY programme of live and recorded country music? Jack gave in, and Gerry bought fifteen minutes of airtime and installed the McKeans in *The*

Melody Trail Show. It was a runaway popular success, as it turned out, so Gerry – that enthusiastic salesman of radios, musical instruments and anything else that was sitting on the shop floor – canvassed his neighbours in The Arcade and nearby, and was successful in getting them to share the cost of another fifteen minutes on 2KY to bring *Melody Trail* to a full half-hour show every Saturday at 6.30 p.m. It would continue for eleven years.

At the ages of seventeen and nineteen, Heather and I were unusual radio hosts, but we were enthusiastic and gave country music listeners all the latest music news, played new release records and old favourites, sang our songs and requests live in the studio, and encouraged other country artists to visit and sing on the programme. Every year on Granny McKean's birthday, we sang for her the old Carter Family standard 'Happiest Days of All'. The late Jimmy Little made his first radio appearance on *Melody Trail* as a shy seventeen year old with a beautiful voice. Nearly everyone who was performing in country music at that time called in to say hello and sing a song live in the studio. We received mail from all over the east coast, from the Territory, the top of South Australia, from King Island and Oodnadatta, and even from New Zealand. We may not have been the most professional of broadcasters, but we probably made up for it in other ways with the live appearances and the news about concerts and artists' doings.

The 2KY studios were housed in the Dymocks Building in George Street, Sydney, and John Harper was king of the airwaves on that station. The treatment he meted out to any Andrews Sisters record that fell into his wrathful hands made him something of a byword in Sydney radio; there would be a resounding crash through the microphone as another boogie by the famous American group met a sudden death on the studio walls, or floor, or even John's desk. He just couldn't stand their music.

John Harper was a big man, rather formidable to many but always very nice to us. Heather remembers that Mr Harper disliked working in shirt, collar and tie, preferring a singlet at times, but that he said he always put on his shirt when the 'young ladies' were due to arrive. He was a good supporter of ours, though we did not see him regularly. It was John Harper who used his influence to make sure our half-hour spot in such a strong position was never in danger of being taken over by anyone else on the station. He had his own way of doing and saying things, but he was such a valuable asset to the radio station that he was able to go his eccentric way and *get* his eccentric way too. We were most appreciative when we heard he waged war on our behalf when our treasured timeslot was being negotiated for by someone else. John put down his large-size foot and the McKeans stayed right where they were.

Country music was big in Sydney in the 1940s. Hillbilly acts were popular on all the live concerts that were held everywhere, and by 1948 and '49 country was on radio stations 2KY (McKeans), 2SM (Tim McNamara) and 2CH (Bob Moore). Tim McNamara was hugely popular and began promoting live country music talent quest-style concerts in many suburbs. At one stage, I think you could see a country music concert somewhere in Sydney on any night of the week if you wanted. Tim's shows were being packed out, and the McKeans were one of his main acts. We recorded some back-up singing on a couple of Tim's Regal Zonophone recordings and began thinking that we would like to do some recording ourselves. I teed up an audition at the Homebush offices of Columbia Graphophone, the forerunner of the modern EMI company. But on meeting Tim, coming up the steps to the railway station as we headed down, he talked us out of doing the audition and going instead to Rodeo Records, where he was now going to record. He had a lot of influence over us in that he was an older, much more experienced show business person, and as we knew little about the music industry, we relied a lot on such advice. That's how we ended up on the Rodeo label in 1949 rather than on Regal Zonophone.

We recorded eighteen songs for Rodeo during 1949 and 1951. Many of them were my own compositions, and there were also a few songs from abroad, such as 'Between Two Trees' and 'The Bluegrass Waltz'. I had begun writing songs such as 'Gymkhana Yodel' to feature our harmony yodelling. I was influenced by our time in the Tweed Valley and featured the country there in my writing.

Southern Music published an album of the sheet music of our recorded songs and we felt that we were becoming quite successful. Best of all, we were having a good time. When I used to attend lectures at Sydney University, I was around when students were organising the annual Uni Revue and were posting notices asking students with any theatrical or musical talent to roll up and audition for a spot. I did the same as Heather had done before me: I went to the auditions and said, 'I have to bring my sister too.' When I look at the photos taken on the night of the show, I think the makeup artists were a bit heavy handed on the eyebrows, but at least we got a kind word from the reviewer, one Neville Wran (who would later become Premier of New South Wales). He got mixed up with the title of a song we sang – in print it ended up as 'Gymkhaniola' instead of 'Gymkhana Yodel', but that was alright with us: we had a write-up in a paper. It may have been *Honi Soit*, the university student newspaper, but it was print and that was definitely fame from our point of view.

Tim McNamara was running so many regular shows, and as we were appearing on all of them we knew just about everyone on the concert circuit in Sydney. Therefore, we were a bit surprised when Tim said to us, 'Come on over to my place on Saturday afternoon if you're not working. I want you to meet some of the people you're going to be working with on the next lot of shows and then we can all go to the Showboat. I'm working there tonight.' We turned up at Tim's house late in the afternoon and met his new performers. One was Gordon Parsons, who was back in town after touring with a rodeo outfit, and the other two reprobates were Shorty Ranger and Slim Dusty.

CHAPTER 5

I've been asked a few times, in a half-joking manner, whether lightning flashed and thunder rolled as I met for the first time the man who would become my life partner and the love of my life. The answer is always a flat 'No'. My first encounter with Slim Dusty was a cheerful enough meeting of prospective stage colleagues, and a very informal chance to get to know people we would be sharing a stage with for the next few months. Tim was running lots of concerts by then, and he had booked Slim to come down from Kempsey and work only for his shows.

Shorty had been boarding in Sydney for some time and writing enthusiastic letters home to Kempsey, to Slim, who was working on the Shire Council road gang and not enjoying it all that much, especially as his older half-brother, Victor, was his boss at one time and made sure that his young brother was worked to his full capacity. Slim sometimes laughed a bit ruefully at the memory, but agreed that Victor, although somewhat stern, was fair and had stuck up for him many a time during his efforts to make singing his career.

The third member of the new group was Gordon Parsons, who recorded for the Regal Zonophone label and called himself 'The Yodelling Bushman'. Gordon was a very happy-go-lucky person with a rather relaxed outlook on life. While Heather and I were eyeing off this mixed crew, we could not have realised that with Tim McNamara added to the mix, we were looking at just about the most talented but also most boisterous and party-minded group of the time.

We had to revise our previous visions of these three because we had never met them before, but this unknown Slim Dusty had some counts against him so far as I was concerned. Slim was quite innocent of the fact that over time we'd had gentle but firm reminders from our mother that we should 'take notice of Slim Dusty's diction. You can hear every word he sings.' That was Strike Number One. Strike Number Two was the fact that I had seen his song album with a not very clear photo on the front. This gave me the distinct impression that he was a fair, left-handed and possibly middle-aged man in a turned-down hat. Obviously, he turned out to be right-handed, fair and quite young and the turned-down hat suited him well. But Strike Number Three put him out in the cold for a long time. We all went out that evening on the Showboat and Slim and Shorty did not pay a lot of attention to the McKeans but, instead, to a couple of girls down from Queensland. So!

Apparently, Shorty had briefed Slim on the fact that these McKean Sisters had a radio programme of their own and were working everywhere and especially with Tim – and, therefore, it wouldn't be a bad idea to be polite in that direction. But Slim, being actually a rather shy person, and having me ticketed as a stuck-up city piece who wouldn't be interested in a bloke straight from Nulla Creek, had decided he'd better watch his step if he wanted to get onto that radio programme. It would not be until later, after we had worked together onstage and around the traps with Tim and the rest of the artists appearing on concerts in the late '40s and early '50s, that we both began to revise our earlier impressions.

We became a cheerful, happy group of artists working and singing together, and we all had a great time enjoying our music and the life of show business. But Slim was serious about his songwriting and about the songs he wanted to record, and he was fascinated by the fact that I was writing songs that interested him greatly – there were no other women performing at the time who were writing as I was.

I'd been writing songs since I was about ten or eleven years old. Most of them deserved to be forgotten – as they have been – but I kept writing and the songs began to improve, so that by the time we were ready to record commercially they were of a stronger quality. Actually, it was not long into our acquaintance that Slim asked me to allow him to record a song of mine, 'My Hometown'. I replied that I couldn't, because Heather and I had it earmarked for our own use on the next recording session. I was complimented by the request, but noticed that he was none too happy about the refusal. That interested me, too.

When Tim decided to take his main group with him on a tour to some of the country areas of New South Wales, we all piled into his big old black car with our instruments and suitcases. Tim and his wife, Daphne, shared the front bench seat with Gordon, while Heather and I were sandwiched in the back seat between Slim and Shorty. Talk about getting to know one another!

We soon found out that as the weather became colder down south, we were breathing in wafts of rum that Tim and Co. swore were required to keep them from freezing on the spot. They didn't seem to think the three women needed any assistance in keeping our bodies warm and our fingers mobile enough to play guitar and ukulele. I remember singing onstage at Katoomba, and seeing a dark trickle of liquid seeping out of the wings from the direction of one of the dressing rooms. A quick check when we'd finished our spot told us that we had missed finding their bottle of rum and emptying the contents down the hand basin.

By the time we hit Wagga Wagga, in the south-west of the state, it was freezing indeed, and I have a fond memory of an inebriated Slim holding up a lamppost in the main street and wanting someone to take his fiver and buy him a hamburger. I have no idea if anyone did – because I made sure I disowned him as an acquaintance, workmate or anything else. But I began to see that it was never Slim who was the ringleader in all these shenanigans; he was a much quieter, more thoughtful person than he made himself out to be. I had a good example of this one time when the heel of my surgical shoe broke and the caliper was unusable. I couldn't walk without the caliper attached to the shoe, and it was Slim who sat me in the car while he took the shoe down to be mended on the spot. When he brought it back, he very carefully and gently fitted it on my foot and attached the caliper into the socket of the heel.

I began to take a lot more notice of Slim Dusty. I also began to realise that where I was, Slim was sure to turn up. Heather also took notice, and did not approve. I had a very nice boyfriend back in Sydney who had said to Slim, 'Keep an eye on her for me, will you?' as he handed me into the car, and Slim joked in later years that he certainly did what he was asked to do. However, there was no strong commitment between the boyfriend and me (on my side, at least), so I was not concerned when I realised that Slim and I were becoming very close friends indeed. But Heather *was* concerned. She did not approve of all the carry on by the four blokes in the show, and she definitely did not approve of this fly-by-night country upstart hanging around her sister the way Slim was doing. She made her disapproval fairly obvious to Slim, but, as I found out in later years, Slim was used to getting his own way if he set his heart on it.

Back then I had no idea of Slim's persistence in getting to the career stage he was at. I did not know the obstacles he had overcome to achieve his ambition of recording on Regal

Zonophone; if I had been told about the isolation of his early life and home, and his efforts to break away from their bonds, I would probably have been amazed. If Heather and I had known, no doubt my protective little sister would have been a lot more worried than she was. But neither of us knew just what sort of tough fibre went into Slim's makeup, because he kept it well hidden and went on to get into just as much trouble and nonsense as the others. He enjoyed it, too.

When we finished the tour I went back to my job at Alert Radio and Heather was working at another shop in The Arcade as well. Slim came into Alert one day, and out of the blue asked me to go out with him the following Saturday. I was happy about that and, before long, I knew Slim was becoming serious about our relationship. It was obvious when he kept writing to me while he and Shorty were away on a short trip up north, but even more so when he turned down another tour and set about getting himself a day job and working on the shows in Sydney. As he boarded with cousins in another suburb, visiting me took a lot of travel, changing trains and walking to and from railway stations. Next thing I knew, he'd managed to get an advance on his royalties from the publishing company and bought his first car, Betsy.

Slim bought me an engagement ring in September that year, and we planned a wedding in December when his workplace closed down for Christmas holidays.

By the way, it is true that I accepted Slim as my husband-to-be without even knowing what his family name was. My mother was a bit diffident when she asked me what Slim's real name was, because it couldn't really be Slim Dusty … could it? I felt a fool; I had never given it a thought. I fell in love with the man, not his name.

In planning our wedding, I had to face a very feminine problem: I really did not want to wear black Oxford lace-up shoes with my lovely white lace wedding dress and veil. It looked as though I would have to paint those workaday shoes when, by chance, I saw a woman in a Parramatta street with deformed feet who was wearing what were obviously custom-made shoes of a different design. She was very helpful when I confronted her with my problem and pressed her for directions to the maker of her shoes. I went off with the address and so began my long history of finding surgical shoemakers in Sydney. These first makers were Eric Rendall and Keith Messenger, and they made my wedding shoes, bless them. Slim and I were married in St Mark's Church in Granville on 22 December 1951.

Slim and his cousin Colin converted Betsy's interior to a camping body, and our honeymoon was to be spent travelling down the South Coast and just over the Victorian border to Genoa, then back up to Sydney via the Hume Highway through Cooma and the Southern Highlands. We spent our first Christmas together camped in Betsy on the banks of the river in Kangaroo Valley on our way south, eating Christmas cake and Christmas pudding supplied by Mum. On the way back north we drove over the mountains from around Mittagong to get to Oberon and then to Jenolan Caves. It was growing late when we reached the top of the descent down to the Caves area, so we pulled Betsy over to the side of the road and set up our camp.

It was cosy in the car and when we woke, we started cooking breakfast over the fire Slim lit. When I headed back to the car to get some plates, I stopped in disbelief and looked at Betsy's tyres and hubcaps. They were a solid mass of stick insects – long ones – crawling up and over each other, trying to find a way into Betsy's interior now that a door was open. I slammed the door shut and hastily moved out onto the road, away from where the stick insects were massing near the car. In the middle of the dirt road, I paused and looked around. From every point around me, myriads of huge insects began moving towards me, seemingly with the aim of crawling up me, as the tallest thing in the vicinity. I think I screeched loudly enough to waken the dead and bounded over to Slim and the campfire, giving a good imitation of a very hysterical woman.

To his disgust, Slim had to douse the fire, bundle me and the gear into the car and, without his breakfast, get me away from the hordes of stick insects. When one emerged from the glove box on the way down to Caves House, I screeched again. I bet he wondered whether or not he had done the right thing in taking me camping, let alone marrying me.

After our honeymoon and my introduction to my new husband's fluent vocabulary when Betsy had a flat tyre in the summer heat on a white dust road near Bombala, we settled down in Granville as a part of the McKean household of young people, pets, music and laughter. The old double-storey house in Malcolm Street had been sold when Grandfather and the aunties moved to Northmead, and our family moved into a single-storey house nearby.

Slim was working for 'Uncle' George Prentice at the plaster factory in Thornleigh, aiming to get his ticket as a fibrous plaster fixer. Weekends and nights we both worked shows and saved every penny we could towards getting a home of our own. Heather and I regularly broadcast *Melody Trail* every Saturday night, and life settled into a routine for us.

It was during this period that we became friends with people such as Gordon Parsons' wife, Zelda, and her mother, Ruby Ashton. Through them we also saw a lot of Violet Skuthorpe and her husband, John Brady. Vi was a champion buckjump rider who, with her brother, young Lance, had toured America with their Australian buckjump show. John had been riding since he was fifteen years old, and as a duo he and Vi had also developed a great whipcracking and ropespinning act. They travelled overseas a lot, and John actually did some stand-in and trick riding jobs on films such as *Paint Your Wagon* when they were working in the United States. Vi and Johnny were mostly with either Noel George's travelling rodeo or with the Skuthorpe family buckjump show.

All of us used to congregate at Kippax Street, Surry Hills, at Ruby's place, where show people always called when they were in Sydney in between tours. From the old Ashton Circus family, Ruby was show business royalty in that world, and although retired by that time she was still treated with great respect. I, for one, was quite in awe of her majestic manner. You never knew who you would meet at Ruby's house: circus acts and sight acts – acrobats, jugglers, magicians, trapeze artists, balancing acts – Ruby knew them all and they knew they were welcome to drop in any time.

It was Ruby who used to tell me, 'Now anyone can sing seconds, but thirds! That's not so easy.' By 'seconds' Ruby meant the second line of harmony against the lead melody, and she was correct in announcing that to sing the 'thirds' or third line of harmony was more technically difficult, or is supposed to be. As I only sang seconds, I felt reproved, but I was allowed to sing along on 'Lily of Laguna' or whatever Ruby was playing on the tuba she used to haul out from underneath the bed. It was a real eye opener for me to meet and listen to all these international and local acts swapping news and gossip from every facet of circus, cabaret and variety shows all over Australia and, indeed, the world. Vi and Zelda were close friends, and ladies of beauty and elegance, and they welcomed me into their circle when I turned up as part of Gordon's mate Slim's family.

Ruby wasn't the only one with a lively home: most Friday nights it was open house at the McKeans'. Anyone who was not working that night tried to call in for the get-together to swap news of shows coming up and new songs written or heard. There was a real sense of friendship and helpfulness to each other. There was competition, yes, but not jealousy. Later I would see things change and regret it, but that's the way of the world and the country music world fell into it, at least for a while.

It was during this time that talents such as Frank Ifield, Lily Connors and Reg Lindsay came to the fore. Reg had ridden his motorbike from Adelaide to compete in Tim McNamara's big talent quest and no one was surprised when he won it. His voice was big and tuneful, he played good guitar and his yodelling was spot on. So Reg became part of the Friday nights at Granville, coming into the lounge room pulling hot water bottles out of his jacket after a bike ride through the cold winter night. It wasn't too long before the goal of his visits was not just the company of all the country singers, but of one in particular: my sister, Heather. They married in 1954.

Slim's mother came to visit in 1952 or '53 while we were living in Granville, and she quickly realised that there was no chance of Slim's returning to live and work in Nulla Creek. She was then satisfied to sell the farm and move to Kempsey to live in a house Victor built for her. Slim and I had paid the deposit on a block of land in West Epping, in the north-west of Sydney; in 1952 we were able to complete the purchase, get ourselves a mortgage and think about building a house. Our daughter, Anne, was born that year and was the centre of attention in the McKean household, along with her great companions Flossie the dog and Josie the pet sheep that my brother Stuart had foisted onto Mum one day. But it must be admitted that the house was beginning to bulge at the sides with all the added inmates.

Slim and I were running our own shows at various halls in suburbs all over the outskirts of Sydney, and from the proceeds building up our savings. One night we were opening a show at Engadine and just getting into the programme when a police officer brought us the news that our little girl had been taken to Parramatta Hospital with suspected poisoning. We left singer Johnny Ashcroft organising the rest of the show and took off, with Betsy going the fastest of her dignified life.

Anne was a toddler by that time; she had gone into one of the bedrooms, pulled out a drawer and unscrewed a jar of some sort of face cream. She then proceeded to eat it just to see what it was like. A bit later on, Dad noticed the mess of cream on the front of her overalls. He and Mum searched for the cause of it, and when they found the open jar Dad saw that the cream's ingredients included mercury. He went to the public phone around the corner and, on advice, called an ambulance. Anne was raced to hospital for attention. By the time Slim and I arrived, our poor little girl was pale and worn out after having her stomach pumped. All she wanted was Mummy and Daddy and her 'nightie' – her security blanket. But at least she was alive and comparatively well. In no time at all she was her own little self again, being adored by all of the household.

Anne was a traveller from the day she was born. We had a carry basket and Anne slept in that on the train to Lismore, where we appeared on concerts organised and run by 2LM Lismore. Slim's friend from 2KM Kempsey days, Tom Crozier, now led the 2LM team and even had a country music magazine being issued from the *Radio Ranch* programme. These concerts at various towns on the North Coast fired our imagination and ambition to be able to host these shows ourselves, and when we moved out of the Granville house to share one with Rick and Thel Carey at Merrylands, there was a lot of enthusiastic talk about going on tour with our own show one day.

All this planning may have been 'pie in the sky' at the time, but it all took place at night when everyone was at home. During the day, Anne and I were alone in the house from early morning till early evening. It was the first time I had ever been alone day after day and week after week, with no one I knew, apart from my daughter, anywhere near me. There was no phone in the house, and no public phone nearby. I sympathise with young mothers who have to come to terms, as I had, with the fact that a toddler does not hold very bright or stimulating conversations. There seem to be more mothers' groups or such these days, but there was nothing I heard about where I was living. I could not say I was happy, and I was not unhappy, but it wasn't an ideal situation. Actually, when the house at West Epping was finally completed I was even worse off as we had no friends in that suburb and it was a long way by public transport to visit my parents or for them to visit me, but the land was affordable and it was closer to Slim's work at the plaster factory. We still had no phone until some years later.

Nevertheless, we were so excited to finally move into our brand new house early in 1954. It was the first time we'd had the luxury of a hot water system, and though we had only newspapers for curtains until Mum and I made proper ones, none of that mattered to us. We sat on fruit boxes while we waited for our dining table and chairs to materialise, and once my radiogram and records were moved in we were happy. I bought myself a cookbook and budgeted strictly as we saved hard to cover the mortgage and build up a bank account towards our dream; going on the road.

CHAPTER 6

Almost as soon as we settled into our new house, we seemed to begin planning how to leave it. Slim had never lost sight of his ultimate goal; his own travelling show. He had achieved his ambition of recording on Regal Zonophone and his records were popular; he'd had a taste of travelling with the Foster showground family and with Tim McNamara; we were staging our own little concerts at various suburbs and the McKean Sisters were well known on our radio programme and through our Rodeo Record releases. Slim and I felt that we had the necessary background for having a go at realising the rest of the dream; being able to make a living from our music alone. I was keen on the idea of travelling too, especially as I was used to moving to different places through Dad's teaching career. So the next logical step was to do it.

We finally took the plunge, using the money from our savings and what was left of Slim's share of the Nulla Creek farm sale to pay deposits on hall rentals for a three-month tour up the New South Wales coast and as far as Toowoomba in Queensland, and back down the New England Highway in time for Christmas in Sydney. Our funds bought an old caravan, a Ronette microphone and amplifier, a couple of small speakers and the very newest invention; a Ferrograph tape recorder that weighed a ton, by the feel of it.

We had one guitar between us, as Slim's old one was not up to travelling any more, whereas my Maton was reasonably new; my piano accordion playing was a good addition to the onstage music; we were both recorded artists and our records were doing well – plus, most importantly, we could advertise our shows on 2KY's *Melody Trail* programme every Saturday night. Apart from that, we had a sense of adventure as well as a dream, and we had youth and enthusiasm on our side. Looking back now, I would also say that we had blissful ignorance of what lay ahead, and for that I think we should have been grateful.

The two of us could do the main singing spots in the show, but that was not going to fill the bill for the whole programme – far from it. These days, a main act plus a support can do a whole concert with a backing band, but in 1954 audiences preferred a lot more variety and band backing was not usual in live performances. We knew that comedians and variety acts were popular, but we also knew that we could not afford a professional comic the likes of, say, Freddie Meredith, nor a top variety act from Sydney. Talent quests were a great favourite with audiences and we reckoned we could run one of those without any bother. The Ferrograph recorder would be a huge novelty in the country and the winner of a talent quest each night would be recorded on tape, with the overall winner of the week having his or her tape played on air on *Melody Trail*. This proved to be a fantastically popular prize for amateur artists.

The talent quest would fill and entertain for quite a bit of time in the programme – then the problem of finding comedy and variety arose. We had noticed a young fellow called Barry Thornton entering various talent quests, calling himself 'The Southern Swiss Yodeller', and Slim thought Barry might be very interested in a bit of touring as a change. Then we noted a chap called Malcolm Mason, who did a bit of ropespinning and whipcracking, and had been working now and then with some of the small circuses and in some of the suburban shows.

Luckily our budget stretched to the purchase of a small tent and sleeping gear for these two young fellows.

As for the comedy sketches (or 'skits', as they were more commonly called), well ... we needed a comedian. Slim cast a very speculative eye on Barry, who little knew what was in store for him. Slim reckoned that if Baz was dressed up as a comic character, and if good-natured Freddie Meredith would give us some skit material and coach Barry in the delivery of the comedy lines, we might be able to make a comedian out of 'The Southern Swiss Yodeller'. That was the birth of old Mulga Dan, a favourite of kids in the outback.

Freddie was more than good-natured in the help he gave us. He tutored Barry and gave us the scripts for some of his comedy skits, and even said that he would come to some of the shows on our first trip to help us settle in to the routine of touring our show. No professional artist could have been more good hearted and more open handed in helping us get started than Freddie was.

Getting the Slim Dusty Show's tour properly advertised ahead of our arrival was the next big point to work out. We couldn't afford another car; Betsy was the extent of our tour vehicles and a caravan was the extent of our accommodation. So my young brother Robin (now called Bob by the family), who was very interested in all this touring bit, either volunteered or was pushed to volunteer for the job of advance agent. This was a grand title for the person who went ahead and checked the booking of halls, placed advertisements in the newspapers and radio, put up posters (bills) in shops and sometimes pasted a few posters in suitable positions. With our meagre funds we had bought a motorbike, which may or may not have been a major attraction to a young man; a small tent; and a collection of posters, paste and feltex pens; plus we had a full itinerary for him to follow. My mother was a bit perturbed by all this and protested that we were giving Bob one instruction after another until he wasn't quite sure if he was going or coming. Dad reckoned no one listened to him anyway, so he kept his opinion to himself. He was about the only person who did, though.

However, being more experienced in show business than young Bob McKean, it was Malcolm who went out to do the first leg of advertising the show. Freddie was coming to Maitland to work the opening show with us and help Barry into his Mulga Dan character. We rented the West Epping house to a young English couple who were planning their vegie garden the minute they set eyes on our big backyard, and then we began packing away any of our personal belongings that we would not take with us, as we set out with posters proclaiming *At Last!! The Slim Dusty Show!!* Anyone would think the world had been waiting with bated breath and tongues hanging out for the show to arrive, but that headline was a favourite with all the shows in Sydney, and was plastered all over posters and handbills, so we thought the least we could do was to keep up the tradition.

So, eight months after we moved into our West Epping home, I wrote in my first Trip Book: *We have gambled everything but our home, I wonder how it will turn out?*

I also wrote a lot about trying to pack the old caravan with our necessities while Slim worked just as hard at throwing them out, seeing them as being of no use to a travelling family. My electric iron was the first of a lot of things to be heaved out, despite my protests. His response was along the lines of, 'I bought myself one of those new nylon shirts, so you don't need an iron for that.' My wails about Anne's little dresses and my good skirt fell on deaf ears.

I will never understand why I did not go with Slim and his mates to have a look at the caravan for sale at a private address. Lesson Number One: don't ever do anything like that again. The caravan's major good point was its price – we could afford it. Its major bad point was that it had too many of them. It was egg shaped, so there was no head room or cupboard room at either end; the water pump didn't work, the electricity connection to get power to the lights was nonexistent, and the only stove was a kerosene primus. To add to that, the sides were made of Masonite, which was an extremely strong but heavy material, and the wheels were set so far back that the main weight of the van was on the tow bar. And that is just the beginning of the list.

Slim's idea of an early start was to wake up at 3 a.m. and get moving. In order to do this for our day of departure, he decided we should hook up old Betsy and the caravan the night before, and I was deputised to guide him as he backed Betsy into position onto the caravan tow bar – although I didn't really have a clue about how I was supposed to do this properly. Betsy was a black 1938 humpy-backed Ford, and as Slim backed her up I tried to guide him into position. He was almost onto the tow ball but too low to hook onto it when I called out, 'Wait a minute!' as I put my hand on the tow ball to check the height. Slim thought I'd said, 'Back a bit!' and that is what he did. The bottom of Betsy's boot jammed my right hand between the tow ball and her body, and I screamed blue murder: 'Forwards! Forwards!'

When Slim leaped out of the car and ran to see what was wrong, I had released my hand and was nursing it, covered as it was with blood. Slim managed to get me inside the house before I fainted away as gracefully as possible, giving him the fright of his young life. When I came to my senses, we were able to see that the damage was between two knuckles; the metal had sliced between them without doing any permanent damage to my hand. Then Slim was relieved enough to be able to give me a telling off for doing such a silly thing. I certainly had done it and I had paid for it, too. Lesson Number Two: keep your hands away from tow bars, tow balls and cars, shout directions from at least three feet away and, even better, give the job to someone else.

Once we'd finally packed, Slim nearly howled in despair. 'We'll never even get to Hornsby with it!' Betsy's springs were flattened, so we unpacked the boot and threw everything into the caravan.

Bob and Barry rolled up full of jokes and horseplay that they kept up even as we stacked ourselves into Betsy at about four or five o'clock next morning. Anne was between us in the front seat, quite bewildered by all this nighttime activity but willing to enjoy the company and check out the possibilities of milkshakes that were usually part of a trip in the car.

Slim and I were very careful about talking much in case of an explosion from either one of us. We were tired, and stressed out, and not wanting to admit to each other that we were nervous about the outcome of our big venture. So even though our smiles were a bit strained throughout, at least we did not have a full-scale 'domestic' as Betsy slowly picked up momentum and rolled steadily northwards, with our spirits lifting more and more as each mile passed beneath her wheels. We had nineteen pounds left in our pockets.

You would think that after all the planning of the itinerary, and the careful booking of the halls and theatres, we would have at least planned where we were going to camp for our first night away from home. Actually, we had decided that we would take ourselves to stay with my Aunty Eily, who lived at Maitland. So about mid-morning we rolled up to Aunty's house and announced our arrival. Aunty Eily was quite surprised but took it in her stride and gave us a great welcome. It was only then that we realised we hadn't asked her if we could come and stay for a night or two before the show. My relations were used to family landing on them, expecting bed and board, but I think now that we overdid it a bit – not that

Aunty even blinked an eyelid. She was a lovely little lady with thick, long, snow-white wavy hair and Irish blue eyes.

I was glad to see Aunty, as I wanted some sympathy. I had a toothache, and a tired little toddler to look after. Aunty took over Anne and I took myself to the dentist. He was a jovial soul: 'Thou hast been a bad girl, Mrs Kirkpatrick,' he told me. 'That tooth should have been out years ago.' By the time he got it out, he was upset because he 'didn't like hurting his patients'. So when I faced the crowd in Maitland Town Hall on the first night of our tour, I had a bandaged right hand and a swollen side of my face. All I could do was try to keep the worst side away from the audience as much as possible.

It was raining, and there was a tiny crowd in a very big hall; those nice souls who came along to see us were not overwhelmed by our presentation that night. I think the atmosphere of a small crowd in a big hall got to them, as well as us, that time. Since then, over the years we have been to Maitland many, many times and the crowds have always rolled up and been great to work to. Freddie kept telling us 'bad start, good finish', and we wanted to believe him. But it was not an inspiring beginning.

Nevertheless, we went off next day to Bulahdelah in the rain and Fred returned to Sydney, promising to catch up with us again a bit later. Aunty Eily waved us goodbye and promised to come with us some day.

The road was not sealed and on one hill we seemed to go one foot forwards and three backwards. Then the hatch on the roof of the caravan blew off and we didn't find out till we arrived at Bulahdelah, to discover the floor and surrounding seat cushions soaked with rain. Slim scrounged part of an old tea chest or fruit box and made a new hatch as it was still raining and didn't show any signs of stopping. We pulled the caravan alongside the hall, which stood next to a school, and as we all walked in and out of the van, the mud came along with us. Bob and Barry were to have their meals with us, so there were five of us (including Anne) who tramped mud all over the floor and whose raincoats dripped onto the caravan seats. The boys slept backstage in the dressing room as it was much cosier – not to mention drier – than a small tent would be.

The crowd that night was great: they filled the little hall and clapped their hands sore. We played and sang; we acted out the comedy skits, with Mulga Dan played by a nervous Barry behind his greasepaint mo. The talent quest entrants were judged by the audience and winners duly recorded on the wonderful Ferrograph tape recorder. We were inspired! We were a success! We were going to make it!

You can convince yourself of almost anything when you have an audience like that one, and we soaked up the applause like sponges. I think Baz stopped perspiring and allowed himself to feel rather pleased with his new career. We all talked ourselves silly over cups of tea after the show and collapsed into our beds with the damp seat cushions and muddy floor still to be dealt with in the morning.

Further problems to be dealt with in the morning began with having to find Anne, who had suddenly disappeared, egg on her face, hair uncombed and, although dressed, wearing about the only pair of dry shoes she had left. She was next door in the schoolroom alongside the teacher, who was kindly wondering how she was to control her class at the same time as she ejected the newcomer in the direction of her obvious home; the caravan at the hall next door. After profuse apologies, I took my seemingly neglected child back to wash and tidy her, and I hoped she would keep this pair of shoes out of the numerous mud puddles till I could get the other pairs dry.

Anne's ability to place herself into the centre of attention – either in the neighbourhood of our caravan or up and down the aisle of a hall just before our show began – was a real and worrying problem to me. It was quite charming the way the local children filling the front row of the hall would coax her into this seat, or that one, and would give her a lolly to eat. But it was not so charming when, one night, she disappeared from backstage before the show. Barry and Malcolm ran down the street; we searched the caravan and the hall surrounds, and the boys found her strolling downtown in search of the milk bar and a milkshake.

Anne took to show business at an early age. The Bulahdelah concert provided the stage for her first appearance, when she woke up as Slim was giving his best performance of 'When the Harvest Days are Over, Jessie Dear'. This song was a sentimental, old-fashioned song he'd learned from his dad, and usually a great favourite of audiences, but this time it seemed to get a rather strange reaction. The audience was trying to quietly smile and not break into laughter as Anne wandered onto the stage in pyjamas, curls tied in pink ribbon and her old 'nightie' clasped in her hands as she solemnly regarded her daddy singing for her. Slim was rather confused, to say the least, and I had to haul her offstage to her loud objections.

I used to open the ticket box at seven o'clock before a show, and while I was busy (hopefully) selling tickets to the show, Anne was under the supervision of Slim and the boys backstage. I used to take two of the caravan seat mattresses into the dressing room and make up a comfy little bed for her; she was supposed to fall asleep before we began the show, and usually that was the case. Our instruments were all acoustic, we had only one microphone and two small speakers as our sound system, and therefore the dressing room was reasonably quiet. Anne normally slept there peacefully until I picked her up after we had closed the show. Then her routine was to come home, mostly just out the back of the hall to the van, then sit up and have supper with all of us before we three went to bed.

It was a steep learning curve for me to adapt to caravan living, especially as the van was so basic, with few amenities.

Water was carried from the nearest tap in a big enamel jug, so big you'd call it an urn, really. It was the sort of thing that used to be found in the supper rooms of country halls and it took up most of the space on the bench beside the kerosene primus. Keeping food was a problem and meant shopping nearly every day because the ice chest didn't keep food cool for long, and not every small town had ice available to buy. We had a pump-up Tilley lamp that gave very good light when it was working successfully. It was a big problem keeping up the supply of mantles to it, though, because the rough roads we travelled used to shake the fragile mantles to pieces. The mantle was a net-style pouch made of a material that was something like asbestos and we had to tie it around the cylindrical tube coming from the lamp fuel tank up to the shade. Then we'd light the mantle, which gradually flamed and burned till it was a net of ash that gave a bright light in our little van. We had to keep a regular supply of mantles on hand, and that was not always possible in the small towns where we were showing. There were times when I had to apply my makeup by the headlights of old Betsy.

Caravan parks were few and far between, and those that were available often lacked much in the way of amenities. Those that were better equipped were usually full of permanent residents who seemed to rush to the laundry or ironing boards the minute a traveller pulled into the park. It was not always easy to do the washing for a toddler and two adults when we travelled every day to begin with. I had brooded over my long-lost electric iron and eventually – a lot later – plucked up the courage to buy myself a shellite iron, which had a tank to hold shellite fuel for heating it up. That way, I didn't have to depend on getting electricity to keep our clothes looking reasonable. I nearly blew myself up with that one time, but at least it was an improvement on Granny Killen's old flat irons. I think the flat irons were safer, just the same.

We drove through some beautiful coastal country but the rain didn't stop till we neared the Queensland border. Up till then the mud was a constant aggravation and the job of keeping stage clothes looking anything like glamorous was a bugbear for everyone. Also, as Slim thought we should move early every day and reach the next town to have most of the day there for radio appearances, repairs and so on, we began to show the wear and tear to our nerves after a while. After all, dairy farmers might get up very early, but they also go to bed at a reasonable hour. We were getting up very early, living in cramped conditions and not finishing work until 10.30 or 11 p.m. every night. After the show, we often – in fact, mostly – had to sweep out the hall and possibly stack the chairs before we could go home for a cup of tea and bed.

It got so that we grabbed a sleep whenever we could. Both Barry and Malcolm were very good at taking Anne down to the milk bar to give me a rest now and then. I guess they realised they were able to sleep when travelling, whereas Slim was driving and I was tending to Anne. Also, dare I believe that having Anne with them drew a lot more attention from the girls behind the counter?

The tape recorder was a great novelty in the show. The amateur acts were a source of enjoyment to us; there was one lass who said she would like to enter the quest but would she be allowed to because, and I quote, 'I can't sing through my nose.' I crisply informed her that I didn't mind at all and she was most welcome. Despite her misinformation, she had a very pretty voice, sang an old country ballad and won the talent quest in that show. Further up the coast, an instrumental trio won the night with a young Aboriginal man on electric lead guitar. Another time, a quaint little lass, dressed in jeans and checked shirt, entered the talent quest but confided in me that she was going to ride in a buckjump show.

'Why! Are you a good rider?' I asked, quite intrigued that such a young lady was able to get such a job.

'Oh, no, not yet,' she replied. 'But I've been practising on Dad's poddy calves and they can't toss me too easy any more.'

I wished her luck and kept a straight face.

Hall caretakers were a race apart. They ranged in nature and efficiency from happy, proud of their clean hall and helpful, to the opposite position of snarly, bad tempered, neglectful and lazy. Halls could be anything from clean and basic to filthy and untouched by a broom for years.

Caretaker #1: 'I put out chairs for *no one*!' Caretaker #2: When I complained that we'd paid a deposit that would not be returned if we did not sweep up after ourselves, and yet arrived to find the hall so filthy we couldn't use it without cleaning it, the reply was something along the lines of 'Suit yourself. I've got your deposit and I'm not cleaning it for you.' Caretaker #3: After we swept up and put away all the chairs that we'd had to set out, a caretaker refused to refund our cleaning deposit because he could see one half of one peanut shell stuck between two floorboards. I am not exaggerating.

We got used to remarks such as, 'What a life you've got. Just singing a few songs at night and look at the money you must be making.' I had to laugh when a nice caretaker at one good town remarked after the show, 'My word, just look at the big house you had tonight. And yet when the ABC brings something good, they get next to no one.' My diary added, *Who threw that brick??*

All these remarks and events got a thorough going over during our cups of tea after the show. Barry and Malcolm – plus Bob when he was back with the show after scouting ahead – always had supper with us before they retired to their swags either in the tent in a park or in the dressing room at the back of the hall if we were parked there. There were some hilarious horseplay sessions in and out of the tent at times; one of the fellows was half asleep when he thought he heard an intruder at the side of the tent, near his swag. With great courage and muscle power, he made a wild grab and began cursing while, to his bewilderment, a similar amount of grabbing and thrashing around and bad language was happening on the other side of the canvas. When they got themselves sorted out, they discovered Baz asleep inside the tent, and Malcolm playing hero grabbing poor Bob, who had arrived from a long trip back to the show and was trying to be considerate in not waking the other two as he was about to roll out his own bed.

Freddie Meredith arrived back in Taree with his wife, Marge, and young son Barrie to once more give us a helping hand for a couple of weeks. The Merediths stayed in hotels or boarding houses for this short trip and were a real confidence booster for Slim and me. Freddie again coached Barry as Mulga Dan while he performed his own comic mime act and some of the comedy skits that he was teaching Baz. Slim had banked on having Fred with us when we showed Kempsey. He wanted to do an especially good show in his home town but, even more, he wanted to convince his mother that he was doing alright and, indeed, had his own show on the road with his own family.

Granny was going to take some convincing, seeing that she claimed that she was not – repeat, *not* – going to any show down at the showground hall. Not Slim's, not anyone's, even if it *was* in aid of the Ambulance Cot Fund. She loved having Anne there, and had cooked all of Slim's favourite cakes and slices for him, so she couldn't really fool us that she wasn't pleased to see us. But budge she would not … on the surface, that is. In the end, she came and I am sure she was very proud of Slim, who just about sang his voice into the ground that night. There were lots of entrants for the talent quest, and though the audience was not too sure about their reaction in the beginning, they ended up having a great time and behaved as if Slim could do no wrong.

CHAPTER 7

It was a bit of an anti-climax leaving Kempsey and the Macleay Valley, as Freddie and family departed for Sydney and we headed north to Lismore and Tom Crozier's team at Radio Ranch 2LM, then over the border to Toowoomba. The rain kept falling and I began to think Slim should stop singing 'When the Rain Tumbles Down in July' in the show, because the rain was still tumbling down in September, October and hardly slowing in November. By the time we headed south again, along the New England Highway, to spend Christmas in Sydney with the family, we felt we were going to be able to have another go at this travelling showman life. However, the showman's life still had a lot more things to show us. One old maxim is 'You're only as good as the show you did last night.' Another is that you can't beat the weather, the opposition from local events like balls, weddings and funerals, and, most of all, you can't beat the damage inflicted by roads like iron with potholes like quarries and corrugations like mountains that smash springs and wreck tyres.

We found this out before we reached home, and the repairs and run of small houses ate into our reserves to such an extent that we discovered we were short of even enough to buy petrol to keep heading south. We faced the fact that we needed bailing out of a very risky situation. I was desperate when I rang my mother. I doubted that she would have the money, but she might be able to borrow it for me. It was difficult to believe that, the very week before I rang, she had won 100 pounds in the lottery, and by that afternoon had 50 pounds telegraphed up the road to me. She really saved our bacon, and after a quick three-week tour out west, which was a great success, we were able to survive and pay back the 50 pounds to Mum with lashings of love and appreciation.

There were certainly plenty of pitfalls and traps for young players like us – and we fell into quite a few of them, no doubt – but it was a good life and we were willing to give it another go. This time, though, we'd head south to see what Victoria had to offer us before heading north to Queensland once again, later in the year.

We asked Johnny Ashcroft if he would come on tour with us and John committed to a year on the road, but he needed a car. He bought Betsy from Slim because we needed a vehicle that could carry a bit more equipment than Betsy could manage. Hire purchase was the solution, and it enabled us to buy a Fargo wagon that carried a lot more luggage and pulled the old egg-shaped caravan. This new wagon eventually earned itself the name of Bumbling Bertha.

As we headed south to parts unknown, Freddie brought Marge and Barrie with him, in a caravan this time, and he stayed with us for a couple of weeks through the Central West till Johnny – with wife Shirley and baby Mac – could join us. We had a lot of fun on the way south, but both the latter part of 1954 and the first months of 1955 seemed to be very wet. Roads other than highways were mainly gravel and sometimes dirt, so travel by car and caravan was sometimes dicey, to say the least. Moreover, I was learning that when we had the responsibility of actually running our own show and keeping the wheels rolling all the time, Slim's temper was a very uncertain one.

The cars of that era had a bad habit of vapourising the petrol and just stopping, or they might have a petrol blockage. On the bad roads, punctured tyres were frequent and so were broken springs on a caravan. Sometimes we turned up at a small hall to discover that the power was 32 volt or, in larger places, DC (direct current) instead of the AC our equipment needed. Both events meant that emergency amplification had to be set up. The first time it happened we had to connect our little microphone through the Ferrograph tape recorder to get a bit of amplification for our singing. Later, having had a couple of close shaves with DC power that could have blown our Ferrograph and our speakers to smithereens, we had to invest in a battery set amplifier. We fed this through a speaker on the roof of the Fargo, to drive through towns advertising the show, and many a time hooking it up onstage saved us from blowing our voices trying to do a whole concert with no microphone at all.

With such possibilities in the air at all times, Slim became very irritable and prone to turning the air blue when things went wrong. He was short on sleep and knew I was too, and the weight of the responsibility of having to keep everything going was so new to him that he found it difficult to control himself at times. I sympathised, but also found it very hard to excuse his behaviour. We were all in the same position, it wasn't just him, and his temper was a side of him that kept coming to the fore. It was very unpredictable, too, and after months – and, later on, years – of this unpredictability and the efforts of keeping peace in the camp, I found myself getting very nervy at times.

It would not be until some years later, when I found my own strength, that I was able to stand up to Slim and tell him off when he was behaving badly. The first time or two it happened, he was so surprised that he pulled his head in and tried to do better. I think some people believed that I was, or could be, a very tough lady – even hard. I can only say that if

I had not been strong and therefore, as a woman, classified as tough, I would never have survived my life and my marriage. But it took time to get there.

The other side of Slim I found endearing. This was his kindness and his thought for me and for Anne on those first tours. Often, he would insist on cooking a meal or taking Anne so I could have a sleep or rest, even though he needed one himself. All his life and career, he often visited ill or elderly people who could not get to our shows; he did many kind things that were never known or publicised, and even if it meant cutting in to the little spare time he had, he'd just go and do it. I remember things such as a man coming to see Slim after one of our shows. He said his old dad was dreadfully disappointed at missing out on seeing the show, as he was ill and hospitalised. Could Slim possibly visit him tomorrow? His dad would be beside himself if Slim could. Well, we had a long trip ahead of us the next day, but in the morning there we were up at the hospital. Slim spent quite a time yarning with this old bushman and leaving him a couple of new albums to play. Two days later, there was a telephone call to the town we were playing: 'Mate, Dad died the night after you saw him. Slim, you've got a bed and a feed in my home for the rest of your life. I mean it.'

I could never know when Slim would be an absolute monument of patience and put up with things that I was sure were going to make him blow up. At the bottom of all his mercurial behaviour, he was a very decent man and I loved him for it.

However, he was also a normal bloke who loved what he was doing but got fed up with things going wrong, and besides being 'Stage and Recording Star of Regal Zonophone Records' on the show's advertising, he was a general dogsbody who built a couple of cupboards in our old caravan, went out with the boys to bill towns with posters when Bob, our advance man, had to return to Sydney for a while, and made tin exit lights when the Victorian rules said we had to have exit lights in all halls and it was our responsibility to provide them. He loved singing and getting together with his mates, but he did have the attitude that things going wrong or breaking down were doing it on purpose to annoy him. I had to smile sometimes, but I needed to make sure he did not see me doing it.

On the way south, we were nearly killed when the brakes on Bumbling Bertha failed as we began the last, steepest descent from the Talbingo Mountain. We'd come down through Cooma, gazing at all the new accommodation built in a hurry to house the hundreds of workers moving in to work on the Snowy River Hydro-Electric Scheme; we'd showed Adaminaby and wondered at the fact that this village on the side of the hill would soon be claimed by the waters of the huge dam being built. We'd climbed through the Monaro Range and begun our way down the other side towards Tumut.

When the brakes failed on the new wagon, we were on the mountain with a drop on one side of the narrow road at such a height that the dams in the paddocks below looked like two little mirrors in the distance. The caravan pushed the wagon and we began picking up speed, with a hairpin turn just ahead. Slim knew we would never make that turn, so he flung the wheel into the side of the mountain and our old caravan fell onto its side on top of the rocks and boulders of the mountainside. It pulled us up. I think I was crying with fright and so was Anne. Barry was sitting paralysed in the back seat, halfway through rolling a cigarette. Slim was almost shaking with the realisation of what we had escaped. Barry said, 'Isn't that a cow!' and finished rolling his smoke.

Our caravan had wrecked tyres and a hole in the side, and the interior was a shambles but the damage was not as bad as I thought. That Masonite side was certainly strong, if it was heavy. Slim and Barry unhooked Bertha from the caravan and we crept the rest of the way down in low gear to where the

Ashcrofts were waiting for us to catch up. Shirley had caught a glimpse of us beginning the descent and they were worried when we had not arrived as we should. It took the men three hours to get the caravan back on its wheels, and John brought it down the mountain behind Betsy.

I thought Slim would be absolutely rabid, but all he said was, 'I don't care about the caravan or the wagon, darling. We're alive and well when we could have been killed.' I couldn't have agreed more. Of course, he wasn't so pleased when we had to get all the repairs done as and when we could while we headed south. Suffice to say that we had no luck on that trip. Houses were small, Victorians complained about the price we charged, and the vehicles seemed to be forever breaking down or puncturing tyres, or the halls were filthy or had no AC power.

We were steadily going broke until we went to the Gippsland region. Melbourne country clubs and artists had given us a great welcome, but we hadn't made much money with our shows. In the farming areas of the Gippsland, though, we did much better.

At Warragul I heard for the first time that my husband was supposed to be an impostor. I vigorously and indignantly defended Slim when a man told me the name of 'the real Slim Dusty'. He was convinced that he had been hoaxed, along with a lot of other people. I noted this in my diary and then forgot about it for a couple of years, until it came up again at the Royal Melbourne Show.

When we showed the little town of Bruthen in the east Gippsland area north of Bairnsdale and Lakes Entrance, we made some lifelong friends: the Gilsenans and Mack Cormack and his daughter Allison. It was one of those meetings that are fated to happen, and although Mack's wife, Lorna (née Gilsenan), was unable to attend that night, she later became my closest friend and confidante. The old Boss, Gordon Gilsenan, used to be nicknamed 'Cannonball' in the days when he drove the mail car from Bairnsdale up through all the mountain towns to Omeo. There were times when he couldn't get through flooded creeks or roads, so he took off the tyres and rode on the rims across railway lines on the trestle bridges of the time. I can't help wondering what his passengers thought as he took them on a hair-raising trip like that. A photo of the Boss with the old mail car loaded to the hilt with passengers and mail doesn't give any indication of what he was prepared to do in the tradition of 'the mail must go through!'

There was a fireplace in the front room of the hall at Bruthen that served as a ticket box, and whenever a comedy sketch caused noise and loud laughter, Mr Gilsenan came out with his granddaughter, Allison, to wait in the warm room for the noise to subside. She suffered from an intellectual disability, and with her sensitive hearing Allison could not cope with the noise but loved the music and singing. Slim's singing was the reason for bringing Allison to the concert; she tried to sing his songs after hearing them on the radio.

That's how we happened to be invited to the Gilsenans' home at Metung on the Gippsland Lakes the following Sunday night to see a concert of Aboriginal entertainers. Tourists used to come by boats from Lakes Entrance about half an hour away on the lakes, to walk up the hill from the Gilsenan jetty and sit around a huge campfire on the grounds of Bancroft, the Gilsenans' home. Unfortunately, the weather was so rough on the lakes that Sunday night that the boats could not make the trip, and the concert had to be cancelled. Just the same, we had a wonderful night and had our own singsong in the lounge room while Lorna and her sister Cora sang some of the local favourite Aboriginal songs, Cora's husband, Jim Waters, sang old Cockney songs, and Mack talked bush poetry with Slim. Mack ended up suggesting that one of Slim's lyrics could have been a bit better written, and I must say Slim was quite taken with Mack, to the point that he was polite in saying that Mack should take a go at writing something himself. They both dropped the subject, and we visited again before we left the district to see the full Aboriginal performance one night.

The boats docked at the jetty below the homestead and the tourists toiled up the steep slope to be shepherded into positions around a blazing fire in the homestead yard. Lorna and Mrs Gilsenan were taking scones out of the ovens and making huge pots of tea in the big kitchen, while the singers began with some of the old harmonious songs and hymns the Lake Tyers choir sang in their church. Their harmonies were beautiful and when sung by the campfire beneath a sky of white stars, to listeners surrounded by bush and huge gumtrees, they made my ears tingle.

Several people there were expert at playing the gumleaf and tried to teach the art to some of the visitors. Some of the men threw boomerangs and several tried to demonstrate making fire. They were not successful at doing more than working up a thin trickle of smoke, and gave up. It required the skill and knowledge of the 'fire king', as they called him, to start a blaze in moments – and he was not present. There were a few secrets to good fire making, I was told later. Something to do with the suitable piece of wood used as a base being taken from the heart of a certain tree, and therefore unable to be identified.

Before we left the Gippsland, the Boss and Mack had coached Slim, Johnny and Barry in the fine art of boomerang throwing, and given each of them a 'comeback' boomerang. Mack used to make some himself, but one of his was a daisy cutter, as he called it, and Shirley and I spent a fair time dodging when Slim practised with that one.

We kept in touch with our new friends as we travelled away from Bancroft, and Slim was intrigued and excited when a letter arrived from Mack including the lyrics of 'When the Bushland Boogie Came Our Way'. Slim had uncovered the first of the bush poets we found all through our travelling career. Mack would go on to write lyrics such as the wistful 'Camooweal', the funny 'How Will I Go With Him, Mate?' and many others over the years. Slim ended up regarding him as a second father figure who was a mate as well as a stern lecturer, if Mack believed Slim was not behaving as he should.

By this time the weather had turned freezing at night; we had a bit of cash tucked away in the bag under the front seat of Bertha and reckoned we had better head north and not waste any time doing it. We had to work our way home before heading to Queensland as planned, but we had stayed far too long in Victoria and the cold and rain worked against us. Small crowds, complaints about our price that was still lower than most of our predecessors, good and bad camps; and yet we loved the crowds that came and cheered and clapped for the night. They were mostly more reserved audiences than we were used to in New South Wales, and when we finally crossed the border we looked forward to some 'red-blooded New South crowds', we told ourselves.

When we finally reached Sydney, Slim did some more recording. This time, one he recorded was 'Our Wedding Waltz', a song I wrote when we were still living at home with my family. This was our first duet; I had sung harmonies on 'Losin' My Blues Tonight' and other songs Slim had recorded, but this was a straight-out duet.

I was recording half-hour sessions for *Melody Trail* while I was out on the road. Slim and I recorded tapes on the Ferrograph, firstly with talent quest winners, but often with groups of people and singers we met on the way, giving news of our travels and what country artists were doing when we met them out on the road. We came across the Gills with their buckjump show; old Johnny Foster on the showgrounds; Buddy Williams up on the New South Wales north coast; Dusty Rankin visiting in Melbourne; Ron Peters shopping at the R.M. Williams store in Prospect, South Australia, when we dropped in to do the same thing; country artists like Tex Banes and many others also in Melbourne.

As we had finally bought the magazine *Spurs* from its originator, Tom Crozier at 2LM Lismore, for a small amount of goodwill, I was also sending stories to *Spurs*, where my mother, Millie, was acting as editor for us. We distributed the magazine nationally through Gordon and Gotch, and it had a good readership for the three or four years we issued it. I wrote articles and record reviews, sometimes under another name; news of country recording artists was featured, and contributors and fans wrote in regularly. We were sorry to close it when Millie's deteriorating health and our constant touring made it impossible to continue publication. It filled a gap in country music's information network.

One of my favourite stories was about the old Calliope music box we found in a Greek cafe in Taree, on the mid north coast of New South Wales. When I showed an interest in it, the family who ran the cafe was excited and welcoming. They invited us upstairs to the family quarters and offered us retsina, the resinous Greek wine. As I was a non-drinker at that stage, this was a trial, but I understood the compliment being offered me. Then we heard the story of the music box.

It was a family heirloom and stood just inside the doorway of the cafe. In a tall polished wooden case, similar to a wider version of a grandfather clock, the glass front at the top of the case showed a very large flat disc of brass or bronze with small protrusions of the metal at intervals over its surface. These little flanges reminded me of the holes in a pianola roll, and indeed they worked in a similar fashion. A coin inserted in a slot in the lower timber cover of the case began the disc turning, and the most beautiful melody played as the little spikes passed over a metal bar. They believed that their great-great-grandfather had been involved in the invention of the Calliope music box in the late eighteenth or early nineteenth century. They told us they had been offered good money for it from a museum, but did not want to part with it. Over the years since then, I have sometimes wondered where the Calliope is now. It is a long time since I heard it playing in that cafe in Taree.

At this time, I often came up against the 1950s attitude that the man of the house – being the usual breadwinner – was the one to be given the front running in any publicity, any good songs, any support that was available, and definitely top billing everywhere. There was room for only one star in this family, and that was Hubby. The idea of a partnership was not anywhere in the neighbourhood. The Wife – or maybe The Missus – was there to do every job she was fit for or found to be capable of doing. That is, as well as the normal cooking, looking after the children, washing and ironing, and generally looking after her lord and master. To this, in my case, was added: helping or actually doing the booking of a tour and paying the deposits; writing the advertisements; helping design the posters; getting the quotes and picking up the finished job; working in the ticket box; singing several songs each night; playing piano accordion solo and as backing music for my husband, and perhaps writing the odd song. In many cases, I was also fronting up to pay the rental of a filthy hall and do the protesting; not to mention sweeping up and setting up or stacking chairs before and after the concert. I didn't mind doing my share, but I got a bit browned off when my radio show was used to publicise others more favourably than myself. My ego – which was pretty healthy after all my parents' efforts to boost my self-confidence – took a battering. It wasn't till I pointed out quietly and reasonably that while others would come and go, I would always be there for him, that Slim partly understood what he was doing. He was denigrating what I was contributing to our life and finances without realising or meaning to.

Let me point out, though, that my husband was a great talent and had the staying power to become the star that he did. I was not, and I did not. Furthermore, if he'd not had that single-minded drive that pushed his gift to its limit, we would not have had the life and adventure that we did. As our marriage and life developed into a real partnership, it became stronger and stronger as the years went on, and he appreciated the abilities I brought to our life together. But my songwriting was the thing that finally made Slim treat me as an equal in the industry we had chosen as our career.

Do not think that while I was doing all these varied jobs, Slim was sitting down and taking it easy. No way! He did his share of planning tours and sending out telegrams and cards of enquiry, of designing posters and of going up to every country radio station we advertised on and getting himself live to air on their country music programmes. He kept the vehicles rolling with the help of the other men in the show; when Bob the advance man had to return to Sydney to take his medical for National Service, Slim organised himself and the other blokes into going out to do the billing and putting in the ads. He did the driving for us, because I could not yet drive, and occasionally I even got breakfast in bed. That was very occasionally, but still …

CHAPTER 8

After more than four months on the road, we were glad to get home to the family for a break of five weeks, which was when we recorded 'Our Wedding Waltz'. Then in August we set out for the west and north. Queensland, here we come! By this time Bob's bike was past the point of no return and we invested in a car for him. I think Bob mourned the loss of his motorbike, but he eventually admitted that the car was much more comfortable and carried a few more creature comforts. Nevertheless, we were a small troupe that battled over shocking roads, playing to audiences that looked for entertainment wherever it was available.

We had a very small amplifier system that was quite sufficient for our style of show and our acoustic instruments, but it had no hope of carrying our efforts over the top of the noise generated by hordes of little monsters of kids in the front row, if they were in the mood. I didn't like the job of trying to quieten them down, because there was often a truculent parent on the warpath if their child was the ringleader of the riot and was moved further back away from the front. I don't know how many times I missed out on being physically attacked, but I do know that I didn't miss out on the verbals. It was funny at times, I must say.

There were the usual drunks who managed to get in, despite our efforts to persuade them that the pub would welcome them more warmly. There were the hecklers who came to have a bit of fun by drawing attention to themselves, so that the performers would have to use their favourite putdowns if ignoring the nuisances didn't work. Then there were the domestic dramas we were privileged to witness. I was onstage one night, in the middle of my second song, when an irate man stormed down the aisle and began a furious argument with his wife, who was sitting with her sister and brother-in-law about two rows from the front. He got louder and louder as he proclaimed that if she, his wife, did not get herself outside to 'settle this right now' he was going to leave her for good and all. (Diary: *Why didn't she let him?*) Everyone around them was intrigued with the details we were all getting, but I was working up a head of steam because our tiny sound system couldn't help me drown him out. To my relief, his poor wife finally got up and left in obvious distress. I hoped she gave him the rounds of the kitchen when he sobered up.

These sorts of happenings all gave colour to our after-the-show chat sessions, and many a laugh once we got over being irritated or browned off. We loved the kids at Goodooga who thought interval was the end of the show and were ecstatic to find that there was still more to come. We loved the welcome we received from people who were starved for live entertainment of any sort. There were times when we showed such tiny places that the crowd was too small for us to do the whole show, and we would offer a half-hour free show instead. We decided to do this in one little district hall, but a spokesman for the small audience explained that they really would like to see the whole show and that, actually, every single person in the district had turned up to support us. Guess how we felt – and we worked our hardest to make up for our mistake.

We arrived in Moree in the midst of the clamour about a colour ban being imposed by the local council. It was even proposed that Aboriginal people should be banned from coming into the hall because there had been a brawl there one evening. However, locals kept telling us that there were faults on both sides, and that one group was just as good or as bad as the other. We didn't want to know about it, though; we found our audiences reacted the same to our show whether they were black or white, and we appreciated the support we got from both. We were not there when the Freedom ride, organised by Charles Perkins and others, came into town to protest about the colour ban on use of the town's artesian baths, for instance. Local media tried to damp down ill feeling by giving as little airing on the subject as they possibly could; they seemed to think that the national media was giving it more than enough anyway.

We headed to western Queensland at just the wrong time, when the summer rains were likely to begin. They even started a bit early, just to welcome these new chums to the great outback. Roads were of black soil, mostly, and turned to mud if a cloud so much as looked like rain. I always remember a conversation John Ashcroft had with a local policeman – I think it was at Coonamble in western New South Wales, before we even reached Queensland.

John: 'So you think we won't be able to get out tomorrow?'

Policeman: 'You won't get out of town if there is any rain at all tonight.'

John: 'Well, we do have a show to do at Walgett. How about the train?'

Policeman: 'The railway stops here, mate.'

John: 'Well, what about the plane?'

Policeman: 'You saw that plane land a while ago, didn't you? And you saw him take off again in five minutes? He took off again before he got bogged down, and if there's any rain tonight there won't be any plane tomorrow.'

So there we were … But we took off in the morning and finally paddled and plodded our way through mud to Walgett and then north.

Suffice to say that with the two small children, our Anne and Mac Ashcroft, one of the main aims every day was to find some tank water for them to drink. In western Queensland bore water was the usual fluid on offer, and in some places it was warm or hot bore water that played havoc with stomachs unaccustomed to it. Cow's milk was hard to get too, as goat's milk was the usual milk available. So everyday living was a bit more difficult as we went, and we had to adapt to our new conditions.

It was fascinating to move into all these towns and districts that were new to us; little did I realise how familiar they would become over the years. For the first time we saw places like the old Charleville Town Hall; we kept Anne and Mac out from under the hooves of a herd of goats that camped under the Blackall hall and went home at milking time; we gazed in awe at the interior of the old Aramac hall with its front stage drop covered with hand-painted advertisements for local businesses of years ago, and with a dressing-room ceiling covered with posters from old travelling shows.

We cut across country to Hughenden without going out to Mount Isa, and showed at the local pub at a railway stop; we got into Hughenden and showed in the theatre owned by a neurotic who seemed convinced that we were his employees and were to be treated as such. Whenever anything – even a lighting plant and generator – went missing in a town anywhere in a district, we had to become used to police wandering up and casually walking around our vehicles, peering in the windows and then asking where we had come from, and when we had been in such and such a town. How we would have fitted a lighting plant and a council generator into Bumbling Bertha along with all our own equipment, I'm sure I don't know. We used to just open the doors and invite the local constabulary to make themselves at home and 'have a good look'. By this time, too, we were experts in getting ourselves into some sort of camp, despite council officers coming down to tell us to move and us asking, 'Well, where to?'

There was a caravan park, of sorts, at Charters Towers, but our happiness took a jolt when a dog flew out from under the caravan next door and attacked Anne. We had not known that the dog had pups in a bed beneath the van and Mum Blue thought our toddler was a possible menace. We waded our way over, under and around all the possible pitfalls, and when we arrived in Townsville, we coastal people drove straight through the city to gaze at the blue Pacific Ocean stretched out to the horizon before us. Little did we know then that the west had planted a dart in our hearts that would never be removed.

Life changed from thereon. We took a few days off and revelled in a real caravan park near a beach. We had fresh water and fresh milk, and we had bitumen roads to travel on. The Rowes Bay caravan park on Cape Pallarenda was three or four miles from the town centre, and our vans were parked beneath a huge banyan tree. It was quite a walk at night to the toilet block, but the main deterrent to the trip was the constant shuffling and scuffling noises in the fallen leaves around the caravan. I found the torch and flicked the beam out the door that first night. In the torchlight, numerous repulsive cane toads froze in position and gazed coldly up at me. They were everywhere underfoot and I felt as though I were besieged.

Maybe the toads knew I was not a fan of the frog family, after my sister and her little friend once coaxed me out into the night at Cudgera Creek and leading me, blindfolded (for fun), placed my hand on about the biggest, fattest, coldest green frog they had discovered. They got the reaction they wanted of course, but ever since I have steered clear of the innocent creatures. So the sight of these brown, lumpy-skinned, humpy-backed monstrosities had me bailed up in my van until I told myself not to be a fool and found something to heave into the gathering to shift them from my doorstep. Just the same, they were unnerving in their numbers and with the distasteful musty smell they emitted.

We were to show two nights in the Theatre Royal in Townsville, and the first night was a respectable crowd, but we hoped for a better one on the second night. At interval I took a drink straight from a cordial bottle and felt a jab in the side of my throat. Sure enough, there were chips of glass missing from the bottle top. It had probably been opened without a proper opener. I began coughing and spluttering, then trying to dislodge the glass with my finger. It still sat there, so I tried swallowing balls of cottonwool from my makeup case in the hope that if it did dislodge during the second half of the show the cottonwool would stop it from cutting my tummy to pieces. I had heard horror stories of what glass can do to a stomach.

Diary: *Wasn't game to tell Slim as he would have panicked, so I had to finish the show trying not to swallow and not to breathe too heavily through my mouth as I sang. When I did tell Slim, he nearly had 'conniptions'.*

We went to the casualty ward at the hospital, where a weary young doctor poked things down my throat and couldn't find anything, so concluded the glass 'had gone down'.

Diary: *I thought 'this is the end'. I found heartrending scenes flashing through my mind etc. etc. Quite pathetic it was! In the end, he kept me in suspense for half-an-hour then told me to go home. If I wasn't past history in 24 hours everything was OK and I was not to worry. I'm still alive, anyway.*

Next day, I managed to slice a finger with a tomahawk as I was splitting kindling for the copper fire. I wrote in my diary that, *I am beginning to feel as though I need locking up or something if I want to get home in one piece.*

While in Townsville we had gone out to the Barrier Reef on a fishing trip, driven around to some of the beaches and managed to leave town with everyone happy and rested. Bob had come back to the show for the holiday and we were all in good spirits as we headed south for Christmas at Kempsey. People loved the show, and were so friendly, bringing tropical fruit for us and inviting us to come for supper or tea. Radio stations were happy for Slim to appear live on air to advertise our show, and this was a big plus because since 1 December there had been a ban on playing any EMI records on air.

Two years previously the record company and the radio stations had come to an arrangement that might have been satisfactory to EMI but which was very reluctantly agreed to by the radio stations. EMI was the main record company in Australia and considered that it invested a huge amount of money in making and distributing recorded music, which radio played and used to attract sponsors and advertising to their profitable benefit. Therefore, EMI demanded that an annual fee be paid, the initial amount being, I understand, 5000 pounds. The second year's fee was 10 000 and the third proposed at 20 000 pounds annually thereafter. The radio stations' association considered that this was too much and that they did not know where it was going to end, seeing that in South Africa the fee was 35 000 pounds.

When the radio stations refused to pay up, the record company banned the use of its recordings. This had a huge impact on people like us. Slim's thinking was that getting his recordings on radio not only helped his sales but helped to publicise his performances and our touring show. This ban therefore made his live appearances an even more important part of our advertising. Before long it was also what prompted us, when we were able to carry them, to begin to sell records at our show. If a new record made its way into a district, word of mouth would help people find out about it and ask for it at a record store. And it was through this ban that so many other record labels sprang up in the Australian market and got a good foothold while EMI was fighting with the radio stations.

Slim and I could see that if we managed to keep our little show going, we were going to be touring for quite a bit longer, and, as that was the case, I began agitating for a better caravan. On the coast there were more decent caravan parks and we began to see some very nice new caravans every day.

When we got closer to Brisbane, and we had a night off, Slim and I, with Anne in tow, set off to visit a couple of caravan factories that we had seen advertised. We saw two or three vans, but fell in love with one grey and maroon Arrow caravan. It was not new but it was in perfect condition. The biggest advantage of this van was a permanently made-up bed. You would know why this was important to me if you think about what it would be like to come home after working a show, making cups of tea for a group of people who visited for a while after work, and then having to arrange and make up your bed for the night after doing the same for your little girl. It was an irksome point that niggled at me nonstop.

The cupboards and finishes in this Arrow van were of silver ash; there was a pantry cupboard, and even a shower cubicle of a kind. It had power connections for lighting and cooking, and it had a water tank with a pump that worked! It was everything our old Egg was not.

We hadn't come with the idea of actually buying a van on the spot, but we both knew that this one, the 'Silver Cloud', was just what we wanted. So I did some quick calculations, reckoned how much was in the bank and how much the rent from West Epping was amounting to, and with a bit of cash we had on hand we decided we could just make it, as such an opportunity might not come up again. So off we went, towing our beautiful new caravan behind Bertha, and absolutely delirious with delight. That was until three days later, when we received a telegram to say our cheque had bounced due to a shortage of funds in our account. Slim blamed me, as it was all my idea, apparently, and as the bookkeeper in the family I should have known better. A bit of sympathetic support would have been nice as I was most distressed, but probably I didn't really deserve it, as I had depended on a telephone call to the bank to check the balances and also depended on the regularity of the rent payments.

I did a bit of frantic telephoning and sorted it out, and we went on our way very happily settling into our Silver Cloud. I have always noticed that once one thing goes wrong, everything else will go the same way for a certain period of time. Sure enough, that's what happened. Slim parked our new van too close to a building with wide guttering, and the guttering smashed a hole in the van above the door. None of our usual towns on the way home were any good because it was getting too close to Christmas and people weren't coming to shows, and I was beginning to think I was about to be divorced and drummed out of the family as the jinx in the troupe.

However, we made it to Christmas after a quick trip out west to Walgett and Bourke, and we planned a coastal tour for January 1956. We booked Chad Morgan for this three-week tour, and after that began to book the first leg of our year's tour. This took us down through central west New South Wales, and we met up with Gordon Parsons. Gordon used to come along for the odd show, and he stayed in the boys' caravan. What with a bottle of whisky one night and roars of laughter for hours, Gordon finished composing a ditty he'd been working on now and then, and Chad must have been sober enough to write down a couple of the new verses as they poured out of Gordon. Baz probably slept through most of it; he had other things on his mind, having managed to get himself engaged to a lovely girl.

Next morning, Slim was laughing over the new version of the song; he thought it the funniest thing he'd heard in years. Gordon had a knack of writing odd ditties such as 'My Pal Alcohol' and 'Aussie Doghouse Blues'. Sometimes he would see a funny verse on a pub wall and he would enlarge upon it, or be inspired to write some ridiculous poem or song about it. He had a real wit and used it to great effect. When Slim recorded 'My Pal Alcohol' – a tongue-in-cheek song from the point of view of a cheerful alcoholic – he received a letter from a Queensland Temperance Association reproving him for setting such a bad example. Slim began to realise that his and Gordon's sense of humour didn't always sit well with some of his audiences. But he still thought it was a funny song, and that this new one from Gordon, 'A Pub with No Beer', was just another in the same vein.

Gordon had been doing some sleeper cutting with old Joe Cooper's gang up the coast, and Little Joe Cooper was busy training Gordon to enter the woodchopping competitions at the Brisbane Exhibition. Joe was convinced Gordon had the makings of a champion axeman, and Gordon was quite happy to humour him, as he was indeed handy with the axe. Anyway, someone must have given him or quoted him the first couple of verses of a poem written by Dan Sheahan from Ingham in Queensland. It had been published in the *North Queensland Register* in 1947 and, like all odd poems or bits of folklore, it made its way down the coast to around Dorrigo and Bellingen in New South Wales. Gordon had no knowledge or any idea that it was not one of those anonymous bits and pieces that keep popping up.

The idea of a pub with no beer would have been Gordon's idea of purgatory, so it tickled his fancy to imagine how it would affect some of the characters he had known in his various watering holes. He introduced those characters and built the story around them, put a tune to it and enjoyed hearing his mates laugh at the result. As for deliberately trying to take credit for someone else's work – that would never have entered Gordon's head. Besides, how did he – or Slim for that matter – know what a phenomenon they were unloosing between them? It was just another funny ditty, full stop.

When we got to know old Dan, an Irish canefarmer with a strong brogue, he said that all he would like was 'a bit of recognition'. Slim, in particular, always did his best to see that Dan got his recognition.

When we headed north to Queensland again, after helping Mum and Dad move into our West Epping house, we took the coastal highway and made return visits to many of the towns that had welcomed us so warmly on our very first tour. As we moved up into Queensland, with Chad Morgan an additional member of the troupe, we caught up with the showmen's annual north run of agricultural shows. By the time we got to Gin Gin, we discovered Tim McNamara there with a show that included the Bullet Proof Lady – and Gordon Parsons. A great reunion took place, as well as a bit of reorganisation. Tim had not had a good run to date, and it was by mutual agreement that Gordon joined us for the rest of our trip. Chad was terrific onstage and audiences loved his Sheik of Scrubby Creek and his comic songs. Unfortunately, he was not quite so well loved by his workmates on tour, as some of his eccentric outlook and behaviour was not appreciated. Without going into them, the complaints became so numerous that just one more incident became the straw that broke the camel's back, and Chad was asked to leave.

As Chad was a popular act – and still is – this put a hole in our small company and our onstage programme. When we reached Townsville and found ourselves there during Show Week, we knew we needed something extra to bolster the line-up. There was the full showground contingent of sideshows, music shows, rides and joints; there were big variety shows including Sorlie's tent show and Max Reddy's vaudeville variety show, plus our very small Slim Dusty show in the old Theatre Royal.

We made hurried enquiries that resulted in a dance duo being engaged for the Townsville shows. This consisted of a hula performed by two young dancers: a white girl and a young Islander man. They were beautiful dancers and the act was very well received, but we were particularly interested in Keith Enighi, the Islander man. He called himself Keith Reynolds, came from Yarrabah Mission out from Cairns and was the bishop of Townsville's houseboy. He was so talented that he played guitar and a bit of piano, sang country and big ballads, could tap dance and do a good soft-shoe shuffle – but his hula topped everything.

Keith oiled his skin till he shone, put hibiscus flowers in his hair, donned the hula skirt and danced till he had an audience entranced. His hand movements were graceful and studied; they had a story to tell. Keith said he was 'a coloured man'; that his father was part Islander and Aboriginal, and his mother part Chinese. We asked permission from the bishop and offered Keith a job with our travelling show; Keith – always called Duncan by Gordon – came with us for the rest of the year. He travelled each morning with a pot of tea on hand and laughed like a kookaburra at Gordon's crazy antics and stories. He was a non-drinker but a heavy smoker, and we liked to say that he drank tea till it came out his ears. He was also a very happy addition to our little group and we missed him when he went home at Christmas time.

We had to send Keith's salary back to Yarrabah Mission, where I assume it was to be banked for him, and out of it we were allowed to pay him 30 shillings a week as pocket money, plus full board. In the first week or two we advanced him money from his salary to buy a couple of good shirts and a pair of good slacks, plus some stage gear, including a swimming costume to wear under the hula skirt. That got us into trouble with the Mission authorities and we received a very strong letter on the subject. I thought it was unfair, and replied just as strongly that Keith needed decent clothes for his job. I also thought he was entitled to dress as well as his companions if he wished; he was earning the same level of pay.

Before we headed south again, we showed Cairns and several towns on the Atherton Tablelands. Bob, who had been doing the advance work for over two years, seemed to be spending a lot of time in Townsville compared to out on the road putting up posters. As this was his second visit to that city in two years, he had met people and made some friends, including a young lady. The upshot of this was that we lost our advance agent, who got himself a different job in Townsville and began courting his Queensland lady. I was unhappy at leaving him behind when we headed for the south and home, as I knew Mum was going to be worried about young Bob being so far from home; he was only about twenty.

All the way down the Queensland coast, we used to book the halls ahead and then Slim, Gordon and Barry would head off to bill the towns and book the advertising. Keith would stay behind with Anne and me, and catch up on bookwork and camp repairs. It was a chance, too, for me to send out the telegrams checking availabilities on halls in the towns ahead.

While we were in Townsville, Slim had renewed acquaintance with Frank Foster, who was now independent of the Foster family show and was on the grounds with the LeGarde Twins, who both sang and played guitar, as his main attraction. However, the LeGardes planned to finish working with Frank at the end of the year and move to America to advance their show business careers. They have lived in the United States ever since and, besides performing their country music, have done some acting for television and movies.

Frank saw the respectable crowds we drew against all the opposition and asked Slim whether he would like to join up with him and have a go at working on the showgrounds the next year. Slim was noncommittal; after a bit of discussion in the caravan, we left it at that and went on our merry way, feeling that perhaps it was best to go on as we were.

1927. Millie Killen was just eighteen years old when Silas McKean came to Doyles Creek, NSW, as school teacher. Silas took this photo of Millie beside the dam at Woodpark when he was courting her. They married the following year.

1930. Here I am as an adventurous ten months old baby outside the kitchen door at the Doyles Creek farm. Playthings were rather basic – a tin bucket and wash-up dish.

1937. Heather, me and Robin, aged five, seven and eleven months, in the backyard at Naremburn. I think Dad sent this photo to a newspaper photographic competition, and won a prize. It was taken not long after I rejoined my family when they moved back to Sydney.

1935 or 1936. A street photograph of Aunty Hazel with her fiancé Bob Anderson and me. I wore spectacles at that time to correct a slight squint in my left eye.

1935 or 1936. I was about six years old. I had to wear an unbending caliper until I was nearly eighteen, when I was allowed to have one that would bend at the knee.

Around 1954. Mum, Dad and my younger brother Stuart at Granville. Mum had thick, almost black hair, and hazel eyes, whereas Dad had light brown hair and blue eyes.

1938. Heather at Naremburn; six years old and proud possessor of her first school tunic. She wore it at every possible moment.

1941. The McKean family in Yanderra. *From left*: me with guitar, Mum with piano accordion, Heather with ukulele and Dad with Hawaiian steel guitar. Stuart and Robin are in front.

Heather and me – a souvenir photo from *Australia's Amateur Hour* radio talent quest, which we entered in 1941, when I was eleven and Heather was nine.

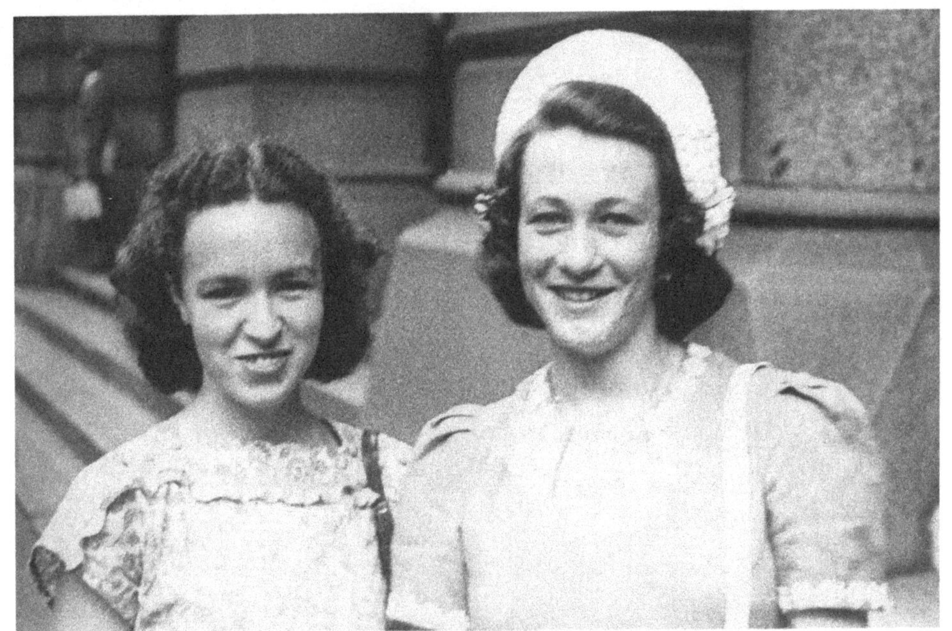

1948. This is me on the right with Bernice, my friend and colleague from the Vocational Guidance Bureau. The photo was taken outside the Sydney GPO, close to our office at the top of Martin Place.

Our wedding day, 22 December 1951. Signing the register with Slim.

One of our 50-foot show fronts. This one featured the Gold Record, which was actually painted with gold leaf. These painted canvas banners were carefully rolled up every time the tent and sidewalls were pulled down, packed and loaded onto the two trucks.

Ready to roll on our first Victorian tour ... Bumbling Bertha and Egg, our first caravan.

Leaving Metung for another year on the road.

On tour in the 1960s. *Left to right*: Barry Thornton, Slim, me and Margaret Mile.

Merlene Foster in her Princess Redwing costume. The headdress was specially made for her in Brisbane.

1956. Taken in Townsville during Show Week. *Left to right*: Barry Thornton as Mulga Dan, Gordon Parsons, Tom and Ted Legarde, Tim McNamara, me, Slim, Glen Davis. This was the year before we joined Frank Foster on the showgrounds.

CHAPTER 9

Frank Foster turned up at Granville over Christmas and finally persuaded us to join him on the showgrounds. He was getting married, the LeGardes were off to America and he wanted to start with a brand new show for the coming year. Having known Slim and Shorty in their busking and showground days, and having seen how our touring show stood up to competition in Townsville, in particular, made Frank sure that with Slim's name headlining on all the banners, we would be good on the show run in 1957.

So Slim agreed, and then spent the next month or so worrying about whether or not he had done the right thing. He took some cheering up, whereas I supported the decision because I knew Slim enjoyed his friendship with Frank and liked old Johnny and Mrs Foster. On top of all this, there was the attraction – for both of us – of having someone else to help with all the work of running a show and keeping it on the road. Slim used to say that Frank was what you might call an Australian version of Colonel Tom Parker, though I didn't fully realise it at the time. Frank had a flair for publicity and the confidence to carry it through.

Another plus for us was the more leisurely lifestyle of the showground. I could look forward to a bit more time to myself and some feminine company, and Slim could look forward to a good fishing and shooting mate in Frank. Barry came too, as by this time he was part of our close team, and for us Baz was part of the deal.

I realised that Frank had put his money where his mouth was when I saw the show front at Nowra in February. We had driven down from Sydney with our caravan, camping opposite Gill's rodeo and beside a trailer of sorts. Slim and Barry had helped put up the big tent, and I gazed in awe. There were two twenty-foot-wide banners gaily painted with Slim's face below a huge boomerang, and at each end a five-foot-wide and 25-foot-high banner with more paintings, including one of me, another of Slim and one of Princess Redwing and her Indian Dance of Death, and promises of entertainment galore. The Dance of Death had me a bit beat till I realised that 'Princess Redwing' was Frank's bride, Merlene.

Then I saw the banners going up across the road, advertising Smoky Dawson's appearance with Gill's, and my confidence took a slight dip as I wondered how we would go against such opposition. Two country music recording artists in tent shows just across the midway from each other was not good business for either one, and we were the 'new kids on the block'.

That would have to wait for tomorrow, though. The owners of the trailer turned up in their old truck, and turned out to be Alan and Alice, who supplied the animal training act in our show. Anne was in seventh heaven playing with their three kittens till one scratched her. Then she discovered three roly-poly pups to play with; she kept clear of the three performing dogs and the three performing ponies, Dixie, Tony and Goldie. The only animals that didn't go in threes were old Dear, a performing cat who was 'in a delicate condition' but still did her act sitting up on Alan's hand to beg, and Artichoke, known as Artie, the goat performer.

In the ring the whole act was smart and polished, and the animals were all loved and well cared for, but that old truck just limped and puffed from one show to another. Alice seemed to spend all her time under it because she was a better mechanic than Alan, and she seemed to get it going long enough each week to make sure they and their menagerie of performers got from place to place.

I was feeling quite lost in this new world. I met Merlene, Frank's new wife, who had her sister Bernice with her, as well as an English girl from Melbourne, Diane. Merle and Bernice were from Tasmania and after Merle's marriage to Frank, this would be her first show with the new outfit.

We did well on this first show, and were the last to pull down the tent and banners that night. Frank was very pleased, as it meant we had done the best of any on the grounds, and we were quietly relieved. We had to drive back to Sydney that night because Slim had more recording to do, and we had to make a quick visit to Kempsey to check on his mother's welfare before we rejoined the show the following week.

I was worried about Anne, who was getting out and around when I was working; on show days I was either in the ticket box or onstage. My mother came down to the next couple of shows to help out, but after finding Anne about to watch a striptease in a show next door, she decided that Anne would be much better off back in Epping with her and Dad. So it was not long before Anne moved in with her beloved Nana and Poppa.

Life on the grounds was a whole new experience for Slim and me. We both did some recording in between shows that were close enough to Sydney, and, to Frank's dismay, I kept the books on each show. He was sure I was getting him hung, but I persevered. 'Frank, I've got to put in a tax return every year,' I told him. 'I have to have these figures and there's nothing wrong with getting them down each week.' Anything that smacked of bureaucracy or officialdom was a bit of a worry for Frank and most 'showies'. Life on the road in those times was often difficult enough given the travelling conditions, without officialdom of any kind demanding the red tape be tied in a bow before deciding all was well and in order, as it usually was … one way or another. Gerry Ormsby had tutored me on keeping the books, and I was trying to live up to expectations as an amateur businesswoman. Caught between the devil and the deep blue sea, I was beginning to earn my reputation as a bit of a nuisance around the place.

Merle and Frank provided the morning entertainment each day. There would be a screech from the caravan next door: 'Fra-a-a-nk!!!' And it would go on from there. The first morning it happened, I sat bolt upright in bed thinking that World War Three had broken out. Nevertheless, I never saw a couple enjoy their fights more than Frank and Merle – especially Merle. But I thought it might be a good idea if we could park our van a bit further away from Mr and Mrs Honeymooners if we wanted a quiet morning. After there was a blue that went on for two hours between midnight and 2 a.m. over Bernice and Diane still being out at a party when they should have been home by twelve, I was sure of it.

Bernice left for home to 'look after the two youngest because Mum's in hospital with pneumonia'. But from the shrieks next door of 'Bernice does more work than Diane, *or* her even if she *is* Mrs Dusty!' I gathered that Frank had fired Bernice and Merle did not approve. I hoped I would not be on the receiving end of any of Merle's shrieks, as I didn't think I had earned the attention, but I guess I was just a handy part of her ammunition. I was still an unknown quantity and needed more sounding out before being dealt with, so Merle reserved judgment and in the meantime she was quite friendly towards me.

We were headed for the show run in Gippsland, Victoria, and Slim and I were looking forward to the Bairnsdale Show, because we could stay at Metung with Cora and Jim, next door to Mack and Lorna and the Gilsenans. Cora was Lorna's sister and had come to Bruthen with Mack and the Boss and Allison.

To get from Bega to Orbost and thence to Bairnsdale, Frank and Slim decided to show at Delegate. It was an unlucky show for Happy Woods and his wife, Frances, (another show couple, friends of ours) as well as for Alice and Alan. The road was mountainous and rough into the bargain; as Happy's truck and caravan headed downhill towards a culvert, a cow wandered out onto the road and parked there. Happy swerved to miss it, and ended up on the very edge of the 'bridge' with a drop of ten or fifteen feet below as the truck rolled into the ditch beyond. Frank and Slim went out to help them get out and then got the news that Alice and Alan's trailer had jazzed across the corrugations on one bad corner and into the ditch. The truck pulled the trailer out but the coupling broke, and the trailer smashed back into the ditch with splintered wood and wheels flying everywhere. However, they began rebuilding it next day, working away as usual.

Mum and Anne were with us when we reached Metung and parked our caravan at Moonah Cullah, Jim and Cora's holiday cabins near the Gilsenans.

Lance McDougall was a one-eyed Aboriginal man who came out in Mack's boat to show us where King Bundawaal's lubra was buried on the shores of Bancroft Bay, beneath a 'honeysuckle tree' by the beach. King Bundawaal was the last of his tribe that was almost wiped out by the whites at an earlier massacre in Boxs Creek. It is known locally as Butchers Creek, and the local Aborigines prefer not to be there at night. Another Aboriginal friend staying was Dave Moore, who sang and played piano and used to entertain Allison, Mack and Lorna's daughter, for hours. He was a good friend who had done so much for Mack during a bad illness that Mack declared, 'Dave's got a licence to bite me for life.' No greater appreciation could be declared, I understood.

As it headed for Queensland the Slim Dusty Show moved north from Gippsland through Orange and Blayney. On the way we took Anne and Mum home to Epping.

That was when Slim made the historic recording of 'A Pub with No Beer'. He realised we were heading for the north run to Cairns and back – far from a recording studio – and he was still one song short for a recording session of four. Gordon had been singing 'A Pub with No Beer' in our show the previous year and though it went well with audiences it had not caused any great stir, but Slim still thought it the funniest ditty ever. So he asked Gordon if he could record it, seeing that Gordon was not recording at that stage and had no plans to do so. That was fine by Gordon; at least he would get something from the mechanical royalties instead of the song just being a fun thing for his own amusement. Little did they know what was going to happen.

Slim recorded the song with only a double bass playing behind him and his guitar, and although he thought his vocal was a bit scratchy on one verse, the producer, Ron Wills, was adamant that it sounded fine and so the 'Pub' went down in one take. Slim thought his song 'Saddle Boy' should be the A-side of the single and the 'Pub' would make a good B-side.

While waiting for the run of shows up to Cairns, we took the show out to a series of agricultural shows in western Queensland. We left the caravans at Roma and stayed in hotels and boarding houses; in one town the men shared a room in what they discovered was the worst bloodhouse in town, where drunks wandered through their room at odd times all night. Merle, Diane and I shared a curtained-off area on the verandah of an old boarding house and froze all night. Still, the men were able to go shooting and bring back ducks to be cooked in the boarding house kitchen, so life was not too bad after all.

We boarded a plane at St George to fly home to see Anne off to her first day at school at the beginning of the May term.

She was to walk to school with my dad, who was teaching there. I brought her a little lunchbox to carry; her hair was in miniature plaits and she wore a little red jumper. It was hard to leave her, though we knew she was very happy with Mum and Dad. So we turned around and headed back to Dirranbandi, where Slim caused a stir singing the 'Pub' – we discovered that during the recent floods the town had been dry for three weeks.

When we reached the coast, the showies were congratulating Slim on his 'hit on the radio'. Our reaction was, 'What hit?' Country music was not being played on radio.

'That pub thing, about no beer,' we were told. 'That one!'

Slim was thrilled at the airplay in Brisbane, and Frank was tickled pink too. I was simply amazed. By some odd chance, a Brisbane announcer, Allan Lappan, heard Slim's recording of the 'Pub' (not on radio), and was so amused at this 'novelty song' that he included it in his daily radio programme. It was a huge success, and then announcer Bob Rogers heard it and was also intrigued. Bob was moving to Sydney and took the 'Pub' recording with him as a popular novelty for his new programme. The rest is history, of course. When the 'Pub' was finally accepted by radio and their hit parades, it stayed on top of the main chart for six months.

I was even more amazed.

We still had the Fargo and our Silver Cloud caravan as we headed on the north run to Cairns. We were travelling one of the worst highways – if it could be called that – in Australia, where the old Redex trials travelled at regular intervals. It was dirt most of the way, with rough corrugations, steep dips and creek crossings in the worst patch between Rockhampton and Mackay. We were held up all day there with a broken petrol pump, till a passing bush mechanic rigged up an oil tin and a gravity feed into the carburettor. Every few miles we had to stop and refill the tin, until we met the garage man from Lotus Creek coming out with the spare part we had asked for ten hours earlier.

Nevertheless, the shows were good on the way up; we attended the Showmen's Ball in Cairns and decided that we would ride the Show Train from Cairns back to Brisbane for the Ekka, as the Brisbane Exhibition is known, held at the end of August. The exodus of show people to Cairns and back to Brisbane every year was the largest of its kind anywhere in the world at that time. As the roads were so bad, the showmen hired a series of carriages and flat-tops behind a railway engine, and the Show Train carried showies and their caravans, tents, banners and eat-up joints; it also carried the entertainers from the big variety tent shows plus the tent workers. It pulled into every show town on the way, and emptied its most unusual cargo into the town for the duration of the annual agricultural show.

We put the caravan onto a flat-top and decided that we'd live in the van while the train travelled, rather than have to sit in a carriage all the way. At each stop, Digger McCarthy, who was quite a character on the show circuit, would come along and take orders for shopping or for blocks of ice. Refrigerators were not the norm in caravans in those days but we all had ice chests for cooling food. Digger bought blocks of the ice for one shilling and sixpence and charged whatever price came into his head at the moment. One big showman complained, Digger withdrew his services, and the showman ended up paying eight shillings for the block. The best way to have Digger help out was to calculate to the closest penny what your shopping list might cost and then just forget about getting any change. Digger had the reputation of being the nicest touch of anyone we knew.

Brisbane was the first capital city show we had ever been to, and I was caught up in everything that needed to be done. While Frank and Slim worked on the publicity and performers for the big show, Merle and I had our own side of the production to handle. Usherettes were interviewed and hired; costumes, hats and boots were made and bought; arrangements were made for daily laundering of show clothes, and, importantly, for meals to be cooked and served to all the staff and performers every day for ten days.

Samson, the strong man, had joined our team and his wife, Kaye, took on the cooking. When she developed an abscessed tooth and did not want to have anaesthetic needles due to her pregnancy, a singer who was moonlighting as a spruiker on the line-up board practised his hypnosis abilities on her; Kaye then went to the dentist and had the tooth pulled with little discomfort. I should mention that the singer was a serious student of hypnotism and later had a career using it in a medical fashion.

It was the last night of the Ekka when a policeman came to me in the ticket box to say that my mother was seriously ill and I should ring Sydney. I did, and discovered that Mum was very sick with nephritis and I should come home immediately. I sat up till two in the morning doing up the cash and getting the wages made up. Then I took the 8 a.m. flight to Sydney, arriving home at about eleven o'clock to find Heather waiting for me. She too had been out on tour, with Reg.

Mum was taken to hospital, where it was touch-and-go for a fortnight with her kidney disease. Once she turned the corner, she still had to stay in hospital for a long, long while. It was a frightening time; she was not quite 48 years old.

We took Anne with us down through Albury on the way to the Royal Melbourne Show. I was the proud possessor of a new caliper that was much lighter than the old one, and I was having a proper pair of stage boots made for the first time. I'd found some surgical bootmakers who were prepared to try to make them: the Perkal Brothers, who knew how to make the European legging-style high boots worn by hunters and hikers, and transferred that knowledge to copying cowboy boots for me. I was excited about the prospect of having good boots to complete my stage outfits.

At our very first Royal Melbourne Show, the question of Slim's identity came up again. I'd been quite indignant when, at Warragul in the Gippsland, I had been informed that my husband was an impostor, and although I was not so indignant this time because the lady speaking to me was so nice and so obviously genuine in her confusion, I was very glad to get to the bottom of this story.

The lady came out of the tent after the performance, and nervously approached me as I sat in the ticket box. 'Is that really Slim Dusty in there?' she asked rather timidly.

'Why, yes, of course. Actually, he is my husband,' I replied.

Then the story came pouring out. This lady was a neighbour of a man living with his parents in the same street, who claimed to be the Slim Dusty of Regal Zonophone records. At intervals he would go away, ostensibly to Sydney to record, and would return brandishing his 'new song album' as well as a new record. He would then organise small concerts in Melbourne suburbs and in outer regions – such as Warragul. His parents and neighbours believed him, and so did at least one other performer who worked on his show a couple of times. This artist told me later that in real life, the impostor looked enough like Slim to pass for his cousin, or to pass for the real thing when only song album covers had photos, and he imitated Slim's singing well enough to get away with it on stage. He disappeared from view as soon as the real Slim Dusty began touring. I still think it was not a very nice trick to play on his parents, though.

By the time we were to work the Sydney Royal Show at Easter time in 1958, we had already taken the show to Hobart for the Regatta, and Merle was expecting her first baby. This meant we had to have a replacement dancer for her Princess Redwing or Firecloud act. We also had to hire two new usherettes for the north run, which was to commence in May or June. The new usherettes were two blondes, and the dancer was a dark-haired lass who could sing well, too. They all seemed to get on well together in the caravan they shared.

Merle's little girl, Robyn Eileen, came home from Dubbo Hospital as we moved up through Moree towards Queensland, just as Slim decided to give up smoking and began carrying bottles of green olives in his coat pockets to stave off the craving. The problem for me was that I was expecting my second child at the time and began eating Slim's olives at every opportunity. By the time I reached Maryborough in Queensland, my hands and feet were swelling badly and I could hardly walk 25 yards without exhaustion. A doctor wanted to put me into hospital immediately but I said I just couldn't do that: my mother and little girl were coming up from Sydney to Bundaberg the following week to be with me. Instead of hospital, I had to go to bed and stay there, and report to a doctor as soon as I arrived in Bundaberg. I would be allowed to travel on to Rockhampton if I rested all the time.

In the meantime, Frank had fallen for one of the blonde usherettes and was shunting Slim onto the other one. I had no idea and I don't think Slim realised what was happening for a while. I did not want to be a spoilsport, and as I couldn't go out I was quite okay with staying home while he and Frank 'took the girls to the pictures for an outing'. During one such episode, I walked past the girls' caravan and, to my surprise, there was the little dancer sitting alone on the van steps having a quiet weep. I spoke and she made some excuse about not feeling well and being a bit homesick or some such thing, and I didn't worry too much about it.

By the time our son, David, was born on main show day at Rockhampton, and I had to get back to the show with the new baby, and with Mum and Anne to accompany me, Slim was getting into the swing of things a bit too much. I didn't know – and it didn't occur to me – that maybe all the new fame and attention was becoming intoxicating for the boy from Nulla Creek.

Mum, Anne, David and I travelled by train from Rockhampton to catch up with the show. The carriage was full of Italian canecutters heading north for the cane season, and they were all very interested in the new young mum as she tried breastfeeding in the corner of the seat with a cloth over the baby. I think Mum was as embarrassed as I was, but there were no unwanted remarks – just genuine interest. I've never forgotten the ordeal, just the same: this was 1958, not 2008.

Back at my caravan home, as we settled back into family routine with the new baby, I began to wonder why Slim spent so much time over at the girls' caravan. Then the blonde lass made the mistake of making a point of (twice) showing me a dress belt: 'Slim made it for me,' she said. I showed no reaction except to admire it and remark on how handy Slim was, but even in my innocence I thought it was time I got back to work and made my presence felt. So I dressed for work and got back onstage.

As I was now just as involved in work as I ever was, it made things a little awkward for any dalliance Slim might have thought he'd have; then I began asking why I wasn't going to the pictures on the nights off, and the excuses were getting lamer by the week. So Slim woke up to himself and called it off with his stand-in girlfriend, who was of the opinion that he wasn't that type anyway. The girl was right: he was not the type, and it is possible that she had been manoeuvred into the situation as well. I, too, woke up to myself then and began to see that if I did not take charge of my family and our life, it could slide downhill before I knew what was happening.

At bottom, Slim knew he was wrong and he had not wanted to hurt me deliberately, but there were influences at play that made me very suspicious. He was nowhere as sophisticated as he thought he was, and I had been absolutely naïve, but when I did wake up, I woke up with a bang. I began to watch out for the pressures on my husband to go along with anyone else's ideas and standards rather than our own, instead of enjoying the partnership we had been slowly building between us; the pressure was always there to leave me in the caravan, making cups of tea and looking after the kids – like the other women in the show – while he was out and about with Frank.

All my life I had been taught to be as independent as possible, and to be a part of everything that was going on. I was not to allow myself to be left sitting in a corner somewhere – and, indeed, that was not what I was planning to do with my life. Others resented me when I refused to be left out of business discussions, and I argued that such work should be shared. When I opened my eyes and looked very carefully around me after this whole upset, I decided that if I could help it, my little family was not going to be hurt or dislocated by any outside forces. So the toughening up began – quietly and casually, but it began.

CHAPTER 10

Once Slim and I sorted out our differences, we got back to our easygoing life together. As I worked on the ticket box in between shows, I heard some funny interactions between the locals and our people. I was listening when two girls went up to Samson and asked him to get Slim to come out the front for them so they could invite him to go with them downtown after the show. With one eye on my flapping ears, Samson (real name: Leon) said, 'Ah, no, he's busy – but I can take you girls out for a good time instead.' As Leon was definitely the glamour boy of the show, in his leopard skin one-piece and his muscles all on display, he was a bit taken aback when they decidedly wiped him in favour of getting hold of Slim. Still, Leon could take it with a grin … and it was just as well they did not accept or his wife, Kaye, might not have been amused.

Local boys who remarked on my 'pretty blue eyes' and 'How about coming down to the dance later on?' were sometimes a bit embarrassed to see me sitting up alongside my husband as we got petrol next morning at the garage they worked at. It was all fuel for Slim and me to have a shot at each other now and then.

All the time we lived and worked on the showgrounds, Slim and I were writing songs, and Slim was recording. The

McKean Sisters act was broken up well and truly when we went on tour with our respective husbands and, of necessity, had to show at opposite ends of the state or country. Country music followers are loyal and keen, but the budget wouldn't stand for buying tickets to the Reg Lindsay Show a few days after the Slim Dusty Show had been in town and vice versa. The only time Heather and I could have got together was when we were showing at the Ekka and old Johnny Foster had Reg and Heather in the family show right next door. That was really funny for us: Slim and Reg swapped stories at the back of the tent while Frank and his brother Pikey traded insults out the front. But, in actual fact, this touring in opposite directions most of the time meant that the McKean Sisters' recording career was over.

My songwriting took a twist away from harmony yodelling and towards bush ballads, and more towards the lifestyle of the people we were meeting all the time in the country and the bush. I wrote 'Saddle Old Darkie' while we were night showing and Slim recorded it in 1953; 'Keep the Lovelight Shining' was the next of my songs to be on Regal Zonophone, with both of us singing it. When the showground began featuring rock 'n' roll artists in the show, Slim began having fun with some rockabilly songs and I obliged with writing some for him: 'I Don't Want No Woman Around' and the 'Ace of Hearts' were a couple of them. We had Johnny Devlin and Lucky Starr showing with us at Brisbane. Lucky had just recorded 'I've Been Everywhere' and it became an immense hit.

'I've Been Everywhere' was written by Geoff Mack, who was better known as 'Tangle Tongue Mack'. He could write great comedy songs and specialised in tongue twisters that not many others could get their mouths around. Along with Lucky Grills, Geoff and his English wife, Tabbi Frances, were co-owners of Carol's Varieties, a tent show that we first enjoyed out at Cunnamulla in western Queensland on the show run there in 1957. My first sight of Tabbi was of a tall blonde lady in top hat and tails, leotard and fishnet stockings, doing her comedy act.

Geoff was working in England and in Europe just after World War II when he met Tabbi, who was one of the famous Bluebell dancers entertaining Allied troops in parts of occupied Europe. All the Bluebell girls were tall, blue-eyed blondes and terrific dancers. Geoff must have been a good talker, because when Tabbi married him and consented to come to Australia with him, she came on the pillion of a motorbike that Geoff rode from England to Perth, freighting the bike when they had to travel by ship. Then he put the bike back on the road, installed Tabbi on the pillion and transported his English Rose across the Nullarbor from Perth to Sydney, in the days when the Nullarbor road consisted of bulldust and potholes and no roadhouses. Believe it or not, she stayed married to Geoff; they're still together. Furthermore, 'I've Been Everywhere' is still a top song after being recorded and translated into languages all over the world.

Over the years we met many entertainers, and very often we would see them again when we were in a capital city for an annual Royal Show. It was great to get into town, whether it be Sydney, or Adelaide or Melbourne, or the Brisbane Exhibition, and go out to theatres, clubs and restaurants and meet up with people in music or show business.

In Sydney, during the first Royal Show we worked at in 1958, an English girl called Sabrina was the rage of the gossip columns and newspapers. Her claim to fame seemed to rest upon her ample bust, which she used to feature well up front whenever a photographer hove into view. At this time Frank had suggested to EMI that with the runaway success and high sales of the 'Pub' they should acknowledge Slim's success with, say, a Gold Record, and the record company had indeed acted on the suggestion with enthusiasm. They manufactured and presented to Slim the first Gold Record ever made in Australia and still the only Gold 78 rpm in existence in this country. The ensuing publicity was a big challenge to Sabrina's campaign, so it was inevitable, I suppose, that Frank and her publicity people would put their heads together.

The PR machine ground into action and next thing Frank had teed up a photo session featuring Slim and Sabrina. I decided I'd stay out of that one, and no doubt I was definitely on the unwanted list anyway. Well, Slim and Sabrina posed with the Gold Record, with Sabrina's famous attributes blocking most of the view of the award; Slim was beaming but wondering what she was going to do next. He reckoned he'd never seen anyone so smart with photos as that girl – she'd catch sight of a camera and it was in with the tummy and out with top. Slim found it a bit nervewracking, apparently, to put his arms around Sabrina to hold a beer glass prop, trying to dodge the famous bust that seemed to be everywhere. He was perspiring, but manfully stuck with it and got the photo session done. I congratulated him on his dedication to our publicity programme, but I had a job to keep a straight face.

We'd had some very good variety acts touring with us on the showgrounds. Vi Skuthorpe and John Brady came with us for one tour. They were polished professional performers at the top of their game, recently returned from overseas engagements. From all their work in the USA, they had authentic cowboy and Spanish costumes to dress their act. Another act, Lloyd Nairn, was a world-class juggler with an open invitation to appear on a top American TV show any time he wanted to visit. Sid Young used to do ropespinning, whipcracking and spinning his silverplated Colt revolvers; big Julie was a lady who juggled firesticks; and the Vilsteys, Bill and Vera, were dental trapeze artists from Europe.

Bill hung by his legs from the top of the trapeze while he held one end of a swivel contraption in his mouth. Vera would swing down from the trapeze, place the other end of the swivel in her mouth and then perform various acrobatics as she pirouetted and swung by her teeth from the swivel held in Bill's teeth. Vera always watched her weight very carefully; it was an important concern in such an act.

One of the most worrying acts for us was young Marlene 'Oakley', who was a sharpshooter and ropespinner. Within the confines of the ring in front of the small stage, Marlene's target box was set up and we had to find one of the lads in the show to act as her assistant. No one volunteered, but in the end Stuart, the new drummer, was coaxed into the job. Truthfully, Marlene was an excellent shot; her father had taught her and trained her in her act. But it still made a drummer extremely nervous when he had to hold chalks between his knuckles for Marlene to shoot them off one by one. Stuart did some calculations and reckoned compensation would be 100 pounds per knuckle.

After his first day on the job, and being still alive and all in one piece, Stuart was quite proud of himself, but he complained about small pieces of lead pinging off the flange of the target box and hitting his hand. So Slim worked on it, to make it wider around the target to protect Stuart (and our audience too, of course) from these tiny pieces. Then Stuart fell over Marlene's ropes; after taking ages to tie on a blindfold for part of the shooting act, he then nearly pulled her hair out as he reefed the blindfold from her eyes, and took a bow to the onlookers who were convulsing with his antics – all unrehearsed, I might add.

Before long, Marlene's dad, Peter, came to see his daughter in action and he was quite disgusted. 'You're shooting too far out,' he told her. 'You should be hitting closer! Here, I'll hold the chalks and you hit them shorter. You're getting lazy, Marlene.'

So Peter took over and Marlene fired closer and closer at each show. Then she hit Peter's little finger at the knuckle and there was great commotion. But Marlene was more interested in the fact that she hadn't aimed for that spot and she was adamant, and so was Peter, that she could not miss or be that far off target shooting from such a short distance. 'I couldn't possibly miss by so much, at that distance,' she kept saying.

When Marlene checked her box of bullets, she found more than one with the top sheared off, and in another she found small chips off the bullets. More than enough to account for the inaccuracy – it was not Marlene's shooting, it was the faulty bullets. Naturally, from then on, every box was checked and every bullet examined before she used it.

We decided to go to the Darwin Show one year, and the men got in some hunting on the way. They rousted out a wild pig one day as the whole convoy was on the road, and the pig was indeed wild at being hunted and shot at. It headed right at the shooters, who banged away with no effect till it looked as if *they* would be the hunted and not the pig. Marlene got out her rifle and stood there while all the shotguns were pounding; as the pig kept coming, she just took aim and dropped it in its tracks with one shot. I suspect that Frank and Slim were in two minds whether to be pleased with Marlene or not.

One of the few friends I had on the showgrounds wasn't even a showie. Joan and her husband had a photographic studio in Brisbane but came on the north run each year. They worked as street photographers, but the street was sideshow alley and all over the showground at each town. On one business trip to Sydney, I bought an electric Beatle bass. Slim had told me to buy an electric bass and amplifier to bring back to the show, and I was silly enough to ask who was going to play it. 'You are,' came the reply. So I was the first bass player in any of the bands on the showground at that time, and as I was practising in the tent the sidewall was lifted and Joan ran in. She stopped in amazement: 'It's you! You're playing a bass!' I said I was trying, anyway. She just began laughing: 'You know what I do back home? I play double bass in a classical quartet!'

Frank was having a ball thinking of new runs to try and new shows to tackle with this very successful show. We went to Tasmania, to the Hobart Regatta, a couple of times and even had Christmas over there one year, filling in the time before the Regatta with some night showing.

Due to my mother's recurring ill health during 1961 and 1962, Anne spent quite a lot of time on the showgrounds with David and us. I organised correspondence lessons for her that were not always successful in catching up with our travels, and when we night showed – as we did that particular year in Tasmania – Anne danced in the opening square-dance sequence. David travelled with us as soon as I could get out of hospital after his birth. He lay in a wicker carry basket when we drove north on the showgrounds and back down the coast to the Ekka. When he was three months old, we realised that I had to have help to look after David when I was working. Mum and Anne were at the Ekka to help me, but after then we were headed to the Royal Adelaide and Royal Melbourne. I had to work all day and late at night for the days of the shows, and my baby needed proper care.

We showed at Mildura on our way through to Adelaide, and I advertised for a girl to travel with me. Bridget Rouse, nineteen years old, arrived at the caravan in answer to the advertisement. She came from Merbein, a nearby town, and was working in a citrus packing shed when her mother spotted the ad. Bridget travelled with us for over three years; we got on well and she loved David as her own.

Next, Frank turned his attention to the Perth Royal Show. This involved crossing the Nullarbor in 1961, with trucks loaded up with the show tent and banners, petrol and spares for the trucks and cars; cars and caravans loaded with show performers and families, and the only fuel and water stops being very few and very far between. There were water tanks at intervals, and – you'd hardly believe it – there actually were idiots who would use them for target practice and let the precious water go to waste.

We had a flash station wagon with a big motor and small cooling system, and more chassis than it needed. Naturally, this was the one that broke down on the way and held up the whole procession. We sent word ahead to the one petrol stop that had a radio phone and camped by the roadside to wait for a part to be sent out from Port Augusta in South Australia.

A group of Aboriginal men and women appeared from the north of the road and began inspecting the colourful convoy. We eventually worked out that these people were some of those who had been moved from their hunting grounds to make room for the Woomera rocket testing grounds. They had been out hunting and were heading back to their new home further south, closer to the coast. This was the first time we had met tribal people who were still using spears for hunting, and we filled in time that first day by asking Lloyd Nairn to entertain them with his juggling. Slim sang some of his songs for them, but I doubt that they had been near radios long enough to recognise him or the songs. Slim sang and entertained in some very different places, but that one must be near the top of the list of the unusual ones. Needless to say, after the isolated trip across the Nullarbor, we decided that we'd return from Perth with the vehicles and caravans on flat-top carriages that unloaded at Port Augusta.

In 1962 Frank and Slim decided to go to the Darwin Show; Anne was with us at that time. It was such a long distance that we teamed up with other show people and did some night shows or 'one night stands' on our way up through New South Wales and Queensland. The Twist was the new dance craze at the time and Merle used to demonstrate it during her dance act in the show. Being keen on her ballet lessons, ten-year-old Anne was an enthusiastic student of the Twist and practised an extra lot at Brewarrina in north-west New South Wales. The next day she complained of a pain in her tummy, and by the time we reached Bourke the pain had become a severe reality.

Anne was booked into Bourke Hospital to have her appendix out and I booked into the Post Office Hotel/Motel to stay in town with her until she recovered from her operation. Bourke is normally a dry place, but that year it rained and it rained until the streets and paths turned to mud. I tried to dry Anne's pyjamas and clothes, but it was a battle. Then the kindness of locals to a stranger in difficulties came to the fore. The wife of the taxi driver who took me to and from the hospital every day offered to dry Anne's clothes in front of her kitchen stove. Regina, the sister of the hotel proprietors, who was acting as a stand-in nanny for their little boy, greeted me on my twice daily return from visiting Anne with a cup of coffee or tea and, if I were late, with a hot water bottle in my bed.

How can you forget such down to earth kindnesses? I always remember Bourke for those, and Anne remembers Bourke for the multiplication tables. Poor Anne! She survived the operation and hospital stay to be greeted with the news that as she was definitely vague on her tables, we would incorporate a daily drilling of them until we were able to take a plane north to Charleville to catch up with the show.

It was on this trip that Slim wrote 'Man from the Never Never'. Some years later, we would see the sign at the turn-off to the pub at Daly Waters; it quoted Slim's words: *We've a pub and general store, what's the use of any more?*

We were quite a big convoy as we headed to Darwin. There were our two trucks loaded with banners, tents and show gear. Next came all the cars and caravans for our show, along with the other showies who travelled and showed their way to Darwin with us. The McDonald Twins had their fairy floss and eat-up van set up out the front of our show, whether we showed in the tent or in a hall; they also performed in the square-dance opening each night. Casey Nelson and his offsider, Joe, had Happy Harry, the double-jointed horse, on display, and the Millers had their sideshow joints plus their old bulldog, Pansy, who found the coolest spot when parked was under the drip tube from the caravan ice chest. But Pansy caused ructions in the Miller household. On one occasion Aub Miller was heard to say, 'The last piece of steak in the place and she gives it to the dog!' His wife protested that while he, Aub, was able to eat something in place of steak, poor Pansy could not, and the convoy was between towns and supplies.

We made it to Katherine in time for the annual show, and Casey nearly had a fit when Happy Harry disappeared from his tent. He blamed Joe; Joe blamed the locals, and Slim and Frank added fuel to Casey's fire by talking about the huge corroboree and barbecue they saw down at the showgrounds after the show closed for the day. The next afternoon Happy Harry was found lazily grazing along the road; he was returned to his family and Joe breathed easily again.

All the time we were showing and travelling on the grounds both Slim and I were writing, and Slim was recording every chance he got. In 1962, Slim's producer Ron Wills suggested that as the American singer Mitch Miller had had a very successful run with singalong records, Slim should do the same with Australian songs. Slim wasn't too sure about this but relied on Ron's advice, which turned out to be correct. The main difficulties were selecting all the songs, abbreviating them in the right places, and fitting the keys and tempos together. Finding the songs in the first place was also a problem. So guess who got the job of that last bit?

I think I haunted every music publisher in Sydney, especially the ones who had older catalogues of songs. I accessed a lot of old sheet music; as I could read music and Slim couldn't, I was able to teach him most of the songs that he didn't already know. One good thing was that he was a quick learner when he wanted to be; he had good ears for a melody and a good memory for the words. Then he got to work to sort out the songs and fit them together. It turned out to be a huge amount of work, but the album and its follow-up were both very big sellers.

By 1962 we had been on the showground for five full years. We were in partnership with Frank in the Slim Dusty Show, Samson the Strong Man and in the Ghost Train. Frank's young cousin, Teddy Trevor, ran the Ghost Train for us. Slim and I had a big and comfortable caravan and we were well settled into this way of life. It was certainly an easier living than night showing, moving five or six days a week. On the showgrounds there was always electricity available for the vans, even if it went off now and then. We could carry a small washing machine and use hoses to run water to the caravan tank and the washing machine. There were the usual frustrations of people taking your hose off the tap and not putting it back on when you were just filling the machine, but that was a minor irritation when you added it all up. There was constant noise and bustle, especially on show days and nights, and a certain camaraderie in the show community. Most of the showies were family people and hard workers, and I still hold a lot of respect for them.

However, we had to look out for the old saying, 'It's the backup that beats you.' In other words, you had to be able to provide the incentive for crowds to keep coming back to see the show. In our case we had been fortunate in being able to move into new territory fairly regularly, but we also moved with the times by incorporating young rock or rock/country artists in capital shows and some big towns.

David was travelling with us all the time, while Anne was often back at school in Sydney, living with Mum and Dad. I was very worried about my mother's health as I knew it was deteriorating. My youngest brother, Stuart, and his wife, Jan, lived with my parents and Anne, and I was able to go back to Sydney occasionally to stay for a week or two.

When my mother died in August 1962, I was distraught. Slim took Anne and David with him to the Adelaide and Melbourne Royal Shows while I looked after all the sad arrangements to be made at home. The quiet little rock of the family was gone, I had no one to talk to and ask advice from, and I felt pressured on every side.

Although Slim and I went on with the shows and spent Christmas on the showgrounds, we seemed to lose heart a lot. We went to Metung to see Mack and Lorna and we bought a small block of ground there. I think that without pinning down the exact explanation of how we were feeling, maybe the answer was that we were beginning to feel stale with our writing and our music. In the enclosed showground life, we were cut off to a great extent from contact with the very people we sang to at every show; we weren't sharing their lives and stories the way we used to do even before we started touring back in 1954. Another thing that was a concern was the way we differed from most of the show community.

The older show families tended to be quite chauvinistic in outlook. Whereas the women were expected to work the joint or the ticket box and such, and then stay out of the way when not working, the men seemed to believe they could do as they liked in every arena. I didn't see why, for instance, the women in our camp had to sit down and write up and roll up the advertising posters while Frank, Slim and the other men went off shooting or fishing. That put me in the black books for a while; not in Slim's, though. He'd been wondering how long it would be before I'd jack up. We were more of a partnership and worked as a team in our planning and aims, after we'd got through the 'growing pains' of our first touring years.

There were few women working the front of line-up shows, I noticed. Frank's sister Frances was a top spruiker and could beat most men at getting a crowd out front, and Shirley Castles used to 'tell the tale' out the front of Tommy's and her magic show. But they were exceptions. There may have been others, but I didn't come across them. Things seem to be different nowadays and women seem to take a much more prominent role in organising and running the joints and big rides on the grounds. But there are no music or variety shows any more.

Slim and I were there towards the end of an era of big variety tent shows, music and magic shows, ghost houses, mirror mazes. It was a fascinating era and I wouldn't have missed it for anything. But I had changed a lot. I had developed from being a singer, musician and part-time radio host to a fledgling businesswoman who wrote and sang songs, played guitar, piano accordion and electric bass onstage, and began to stand up for a bit of equality around the place. No wonder I was a nuisance, and no wonder there was always a pressure to split the partnership Slim and I had. Slim might have thought that perhaps he had bitten off more than he could chew when he married me, but he seemed to be enjoying the taste of it. I believe he encouraged me to stick up for myself and he knew, too, that I was always on his side even when I was disagreeing with him. He was the same with me; he was one of the most loyal people I have ever known.

CHAPTER 11

At the beginning of 1963, we decided that Anne had to go to boarding school if she was to have a good education, which was something we'd both set our hearts on for our children. We came to Sydney for the Royal Easter Show and, as part of the pre-show publicity, Slim appeared on Johnny O'Keefe's *Six O'Clock Rock* TV show, did numerous radio and paper interviews teed up by Frank, and booked performers, while Merle and I got the staff hired and dressed, and arranged the catering. In the previous month or two, Slim and I had got together the material for a new album, *Another Aussie Sing Song*, because the recording company had been so pleased with the success of the first one that they were keen to have a follow-up. Slim recorded this before we headed north with the show again.

While we were all a bit blasé about the routine of showing after six years of showground work, we disagreed strongly with some facets of it, and after one particularly strong disagreement with Frank at Grafton, we decided it was time we got back to our own show and closer ties with our music and background. The showground years had been a remarkable partnership, we had all done well out of it, and it was an experience we would never regret having. Over the years, we have kept in touch with Frank, and it ended up as an amicable break-up along the lines of, 'You take the red truck and I'll have the blue one … and it looks like you should be getting another couple of hundred pounds … that okay with you?'

From Grafton, Slim and I headed to Brisbane, and within three weeks we were on the road with our night show. Barry Thornton and his wife, Pauline, were with us; Teddy Trevor, Frank's young cousin, came as our advance agent; Sid Young brought his ropes and whips but, thanks to a PR stunt that went wrong, he was minus his silverplated Colt revolvers. During the Ekka he had decided to stage a 'holdup' at a big intersection in Brisbane. There he was – long hair, big Stetson, Buffalo Bill outfit – standing in the middle of the intersection with traffic stalled around him as he fired his Colts full of blanks into the air. Police swarmed in from every side and carted off Sid (aka Kid) and his revolvers. They confiscated his Colts, and then gave him a licence to buy new ones. He was so disgusted he didn't bother.

We needed some glamour in the show, so we booked big Julie, the Hungarian juggler. Julie juggled firesticks, but we didn't realise at the time that she'd added a striptease to her juggling act. Once we worked it out, we had to make some alterations to the act. Then we hired a dancer, a lass who was classically trained and who presented a rather high-class act that was a bit over the top for our audiences. Last I heard of her she was in the United States heading a big dance troupe, and shortly after she married a multi-millionaire father of a pop star. True!

We headed out through Kingaroy and other southern Queensland towns; overall, we toured constantly until the end of the year. When we bought our block of Metung land, we thought we could build a sort of en suite cabin that would be useful if we pulled our caravan alongside it for a stay in Metung to see Mack and Lorna and Cora. But in the end we had Mack and Jim, Cora's husband, build us a small house overlooking Chinamans Creek. We spent our first Christmas there at the end of 1963; at Christmas in 2013 my whole family celebrated the fiftieth anniversary of the first home the four of us ever had together.

The following year we resumed our touring life; we planned to tour at least ten months of the year and that meant we had to have a regular touring itinerary with injections of new territory at intervals. Kid Young was still with us and he began telling us to go to Western Australia. We were listening too, especially as television had begun to make inroads upon our regular show towns. Every business felt the pinch with this novelty; theatre owners found audiences smaller, even drycleaners noticed that with people staying home glued to the TV screen there were no longer the usual numbers of good clothes requiring specialist cleaning.

Night showing meant that we moved at least six days of every week, just as we used to do, and with the longer distances in the western areas we had to show some very small places that we called 'petrol stops'. The small houses would possibly cover the cost of the wages for that night plus the petrol for all the vehicles. The larger towns at the weekend would be our profit for the week and the coverage of all the big expenses. Breakdowns were more frequent as vehicles and caravans moved every day over worse roads; travelling hours were longer and harder. But we grew to love the addiction to the road that we developed. We were close to the people who listened to our songs, and they brought us stories and a connection with the land and their lives that we had come close to losing in the heady days of the 'Pub' and the clamour of Sideshow Alley. We wouldn't have missed that showground experience for worlds, but we now found a great satisfaction in building our links with audiences, writers and storytellers all over the country.

Depending on who was with the show at the time, either Slim or I drove a car and caravan, or Slim drove one of the trucks with the big caravan behind. David and I occasionally travelled together, and on one trip across gemstone country I was glad of my five year old's steadiness. The caravan I was towing with the station wagon was loaded to the hilt, and so was the Holden I was driving. The road was rough and stony, and consisted of up hill and down dale, with every 'dale' being a fairly steep gully.

If I didn't want to take off the bottom or back of the caravan – which would happen if I got a run at the steep pull out of the gully, thereby scraping the back of the van on the rocks in the gully – I had to slow down going into the gully and make the wagon do a dead pull out and up the next rise. I had done yet another of these when the wagon just couldn't make it up a particular hill, and it stalled on the steep road. I did not believe that if I got out of the vehicle to chock the wheels the brake would hold the wagon from being pulled backwards, downhill, by the loaded caravan. So as I held the outfit in place with foot and hand brakes, I spoke gently to David and said, 'Would you get out and chock the wheels for me, darling?' He didn't panic for a minute but got out, found rocks from the side of the road and ran straight to the caravan wheels to put the rocks in place, before doing the same behind the rear wheels of the station wagon. He'd seen all of us do it so often that he knew exactly what he should do. Once I was sure we would not slide backwards down the hill, I was able to give the station wagon another go; when we made it to the top, Davy was official offsider, ready and waiting to do it all again.

Moving every day meant, once again, that I had trouble getting correspondence lessons for David, as I had done for Anne. David was a bright young man and sailed through the lessons he did receive, learning to read at an early age. That gave Slim and me a break, as before then I had to read to him in the car, or else Slim had to make up songs and stories to amuse him as we travelled. Once David found he had a knack for making up his own story songs, it kept him busy for a while as he sang them to us. Slim once made himself unpopular with the team by buying David a trumpet that piped up everywhere around the camp. But Slim paid for it the next day as it tooted in his ear hour after hour from one town to the next.

I had a young lass from Brisbane travelling with me to help with housework and looking after David. As I was working every night, Davy needed someone to be with him. But the usual problem cropped up: local lads always liked to check out the new talent in town; lack of young company nearly always led to boredom, and that led to a point where I could no longer take the responsibility I had assumed when hiring the girl. I was out in the Central West of New South Wales when I told Slim that I would have to send her home. It was just another hurdle to get over and it seemed as if there was a long line of those same hurdles coming up all the time.

I am not sure why I said it to Slim, but I fairly wept as I wailed, 'I need someone like my aunty Una!'

Slim, being more practical than me, replied, 'Why don't you ring her, then?'

I think I stopped mid-wail in utter surprise: 'But she can't come out here – she's looking after Grandfather and everyone at home.'

Slim was adamant and just about escorted me to the public phone down at the post office. I was a bit dazed when I told him, 'She said she'd love to come! And when I said we were heading out to Wilcannia, Aunty Una said she's always wanted to see Wilcannia.'

Slim didn't see why Una wanted to go to Wilcannia in particular, and therefore understood that she was having a joke at my expense, but he couldn't wait to get her train ticket booked before she changed her mind.

Aunty Una came to my rescue for a few weeks that turned into eight years. She arrived in Nyngan and joined me in a station wagon pulling a caravan. David travelled with us, and our very first trip was in the rain, out through the black-soil plains towards Wilcannia. She hopped out into the mud and pushed branches under the wheels to give the wagon a chance to get back off the slippery slime, onto more solid ground, every time we slid towards the gutter. *And* she laughed as she did it! I swear she enjoyed every minute of it. It certainly made a change from housework back in town and, after all, Aunty Una was an outdoor lady who loved growing flowers and big tomatoes in her garden, loved keeping chooks, dogs and cats (all strays, of course), and cooking the most fantastic cakes and dinners.

Aunty Una took over supervising David's lessons and pulled him into gear when he preferred to daydream out the caravan window instead of concentrating on his schoolbooks. Then she got Slim under her thumb by cooking him his favourites (coconut apple pie being one), thereby being able to pull him into gear when required. I now had an ally, a helper and confidante who was quite capable of delivering a few straight words in my direction if she believed it necessary. All this was handed out with a good dose of solid affection, and she became Aunty Una to the whole camp.

It was not long before Aunty Una became well known in the outback as Slim and Joy's 'chucker outer' – play up at the show and you were out on your ear, was the message that got around. The rest of the message was that if you were a kid and your parents were down at the pub instead of in the show, you were more than likely to be shepherded into the hall when the lights went out at the beginning. Just sit down where you were put, enjoy yourself with no nonsense and you got a free show, courtesy of Aunty Una. All that part was in the near future, and I couldn't believe my luck. Slim was really in my good books for pushing me into ringing Una.

In the latter part of the year, John Dante joined us for a tour. Dante was the magician who had given Slim and Shorty a job in his show for a while back in their busking days. Slim tracked him down living in retirement in Melbourne, and John was quite happy to get his stage gear together and do a bit of touring again. He stayed in hotels at first, and was quite uppity in his disdain of our 'petrol stops', as he considered the size of these towns somewhat beneath his notice. After he settled in and decided that he was enjoying himself, and he was a great success on stage once more, he had us send a driver to Melbourne to bring his wife, Elizabeth, with their caravan, dog Kim and bird Jo-Jo. I didn't mind Jo-Jo sitting in his cage scattering birdseed as I drove their outfit but I wasn't keen on Kim, a cocker spaniel who turned savage the minute he smelled food of any kind. John doted on him and was not happy with me as I fought Kim over the back seat to save John and Elizabeth's steak from being Kim's dinner instead of theirs.

Elizabeth, previously a professional pianist, was John's assistant onstage and his long-suffering wife offstage. John's white goatee beard would wave in temper as he complained about the length of the drive, the size of the town, the lack of facilities in the park or the back of the hall, and the way all the shady parking spots had been taken before he arrived. He and Slim would have a spat about something – usually John's grizzling – until Slim would feel bad about it and suggest a quiet beer or, in John's case, a half brandy in the saloon bar, while they cooled down and John educated Slim in the finer aspects of stagecraft. John knew his craft backwards, and in his opinion it was a shame the way modern stage performers neglected to study it. He and Elizabeth knew to a fraction of a minute just when their applause would come and how to 'milk it'.

Being such an experienced performer, John knew when his act was going down well or extremely well, and he also knew when he had to work the audience a bit harder to get them onside. Therefore, one night in Rowena, in western New South Wales, he was absolutely astounded when almost half of the audience, scattered throughout the hall, quietly rose to their feet and left through the front door. He came offstage spluttering with confusion and insulted dignity. We were just as flummoxed. Then the pattering on the iron roof of the hall made itself heard; it was beginning to rain. Rowena was right in the middle of a huge black-soil plain and anyone who hadn't left at the first raindrop was fated to spend the night and maybe part of the next day or week stranded in their cars as they headed for home. Next morning there were cars stuck in the mud on every road out of town and the Slim Dusty Show was stuck there too … for nearly a week.

We had our caravans parked behind the hall, and once we finally resigned ourselves to the inevitable we settled in to spending an enforced rest. I don't say 'holiday' because there was nothing holiday-ish about being forced to take one. I think Barry made scones in the hall's supper-room kitchen stove, and the supper room became the team's rumpus room for laundry, bathing and drying clothes. I don't remember if the local hall committee charged us for our stay, but I don't think so. It would have been a bit heartless to do that to us on top of our losing nearly a week's work.

Slim was always recording whenever he could, and as well as his own writing and my songs, he was now collecting and being sent songs or, mostly lyrics, by other writers and poets. This increased as the years went on and it came home to bush people that here was someone who could put their words to music and tell their stories in song to the rest of the country.

Mack Cormack came up with 'How Will I Go With Him, Mate?' that year; Wave Jackson, John Ashe, Stan Coster, Shorty Ranger, Jim Wesley and then Joe Daly and his first wife, Val, were all contributing to the pool of songs by 1965. Another songwriter who became a strong addition to Slim's group of regular songwriters was a bit of a stirrer who was involved in the big Mount Isa strike of that year. Brisbane was even declared a state of emergency during the event, but we did not meet up with this man till a few years later. He was driving a taxi, as his papers at the mine were marked 'never to be employed again by Mount Isa Mines'.

On our showground trip to Darwin, we showed in Longreach in Queensland one night. A visitor to our caravan was Joe Daly, who brought a copy of his poem 'Our Jacky'. Joe, with Val and their young family, lived and worked on the rabbit proof fence in the far west of Queensland, and over the coming years he became a regular writer for Slim, as did Stan Coster. Slim didn't like the title of the poem, though, and changed it to 'Trumby'. It told the story of an Aboriginal ringer, actually a foreman on the station, who died after drinking from a poisoned waterhole because he couldn't read the warning sign. The name 'Trumby' came from a place named Terumbi not too far from Slim's old home valley, Nulla Creek, and we were told that when Slim's recording became hugely popular with Aboriginal people, there was a rise in enrolments in literacy classes throughout the north. One tale we heard, too, was of an old man crying as he listened to Slim's recording, 'That Slim, he should have known poor old Trumby couldn't read or write!'

Stan Coster's wonderful wife, Dot, sent him down to see Slim about a swag of songs Stan had written. Stan didn't have them with him, and Slim asked him to tape them and send them to him. Then, as Stan said, 'Things got going down at the pub – you know how it happens?' And, of course, Slim did know. It took Stan, with Dot's urging, a further two years before he got round to sending a tape of songs down south. We hadn't had much to do with Stan (or Dot) up till then but from there on we managed to meet up somewhere in Queensland wherever Stan and Dot were working; out on the beef road construction camps, for instance. It was a good friendship. 'Return of the Stockman' was the first of Stan's songs that Slim recorded.

We had set our hearts on crossing the Nullarbor, though, and trying out the south and south-west of Western Australia with our night show. So in March 1965, we left the Gippsland and headed for the Golden West.

Our first foray into Western Australia began with the trek across Victoria and South Australia with Teddy Trevor and his wife, Barbara, doing the advance work. We received great news from Teddy to say that Barb had twin girls in Colac in Victoria. We wondered how Barb would manage with twin babies and the long trip ahead, but she managed indeed. We had a new team with us, and had told everyone that we were going over to Western Australia and back again before heading north to catch the Mount Isa Rodeo.

After the previous couple of years touring with a group that was larger than the one on our first two years on the road, we were learning that to travel for months on end with a troupe that included married couples, children and performers who sometimes suffered from professional jealousy was a very different proposition. We became a travelling community; a little world to ourselves. On the showground there had always been lots of other families and performers, many caravans and many other distractions from any irritations that might have sprung up between individuals or families. In our little travelling world, our social life was usually confined to our own group.

On the nights we were not showing, we often had get-togethers in one of the caravans or in the supper room of a hall we camped behind. There were plenty of barbecues, impromptu parties and visiting between our vans. As the years went on we built up a network of friends all over Australia, and this meant meeting up with them whenever we arrived in town. Whoever happened to be touring with us at the time was generally included in whatever social activity was offered.

However, our small travelling community was just that – small – and it was probably inevitable that some personalities would grate on others and minor irritations could become mountainous grievances. It was a huge education in how to keep the peace in the camp while maintaining a certain authority. It was a constant stress. Once we put together a team, we would watch out for the rot to set in at about the three-month mark. Around that time the children would be causing disagreements between their mothers, while the kids had sorted out their differences in no time. Then there were the genuine eccentrics who are a part of any area of show business.

There was a young couple who seemed to spend their time thumping one another or having huge arguments. The husband once landed at our caravan door gasping, 'She's after me with a knife!' As the wife was very young, I was able to stop that with no trouble, playing bossy mother hen; but I wasn't able to operate a stomach pump when she swallowed a box of painkillers, so Aunty Una was deputised to cart her up to the local hospital, where a no-nonsense sister suggested she 'stick her finger down her throat'. As the aspirin swallower muttered, 'Which finger?' it was fairly obvious most of her demonstrations were to get attention, but they were wearing, I assure you.

A male singer and his wife gave us all the biggest surprise when the wife went up to the local hospital with stomach pains. The husband came to our van next morning with a grin a mile wide, declaring, 'I've got a son!' The new mother had been the only one who knew of her condition, and she had been able to fool all of us – husband, women and all. The only one who had mentioned any concerns was Slim; he once remarked that he thought she had the strangest build he'd ever seen. But if we had known, we would not have been happy to have the lady with us. If she had been less than a week later with her confinement, their baby son could have been born in the middle of the Nullarbor Plain. I have done many things, but I am no midwife.

One big problem with running the show every night was that we did not have seat bookings until much later in our career. That is why we nearly always had front rows full of unsupervised children so excited and rowdy; we tried notices out the front of the ticket box – *Children must be seated with parents* – but they were ignored. Eventually, of course, we had to get still more organised and set up bookings. There seemed no end to the jobs Slim and I had to do just to keep the show on the road; anything extra began to stretch us to the limit. But the songs and the stories we came across always made up for the rigorous lifestyle we had chosen. Sometimes I wondered if we really did choose it; maybe the music and the lifestyle just took us over without our really knowing it.

The actual collecting of lyrics, stories and songs began during our time on the long outback tours. Previously, songwriters and lyric writers had approached Slim with their work without any effort on our part. But once I had found a clipping from a country paper of a poem called 'The Wave Hill Track', we both realised that there was an absolute mine of unrecognised writing out there waiting to be found. The clipping was pasted to the wall of the Dunmarra roadhouse in the Northern Territory, not far from the turnoff to the actual Wave Hill Track. It took a while to find the writer, George Crowley, as he used a nom de plume to sign off on his poems.

We soon discovered that there were others the same as George and also Tom Oliver sending their poems to the *North Queensland Register*, a newspaper in the tradition of the old

Bulletin. I used to send our ads with our itineraries to this paper because I discovered that it went to all the outback stations and towns. By listing a two- or three-week itinerary, and altering the listing in each issue, we gave outlying property owners and workers plenty of time to organise a trip to town for the show. And, before long, the charm of finding an unknown poem or story and tracking down its author became quite addictive.

The south-west of Western Australia was beautiful with its tall timbers and many shady caravan parks. The pink salt lake of Esperance fascinated us, and the goldfields town of Kalgoorlie was one of our favourite show towns. The town hall was a real throwback to the days when Kalgoorlie and Coolgardie were roaring goldmining towns; its red velvet seats, tiers of seating and maze of dressing rooms backstage had us enchanted. We even showed in a couple of the small mining towns around the area. When I heard the stories about Paddy Hannan, who discovered Kalgoorlie gold, and the battle to bring water to the goldfields, I wrote 'Ghosts of the Golden Mile'.

I think we were sorry to leave the West as we faced the Nullarbor and its 700 miles of dirt, potholes and bulldust. But we felt we had new territory that would be welcoming to us, and we couldn't help thinking that it would be a great trip to continue north in Western Australia and head through the Pilbara and the Kimberley to reach Darwin during Show Week.

With that in mind, we turned back to the more familiar surroundings of the eastern states and decided to begin planning for the first of the round-Australia journeys of the future.

Slim had been discussing our future with Mack thinking that he should make more concrete plans for the time when we could no longer tour the way we were doing. We now had our house at Metung, and with Mack and Lorna, Cora and Jim, we had a circle of close friends and, indeed, almost a second family. I was agreeable to buying some land and listened with interest to all the information about passionfruit growing that was all the go in the surrounding district. But in the end Slim saw the sense in the argument that he and Mack knew nothing about growing and marketing passionfruit, whereas they both knew cattle. We ended up with about 300 acres in Nungurner, just down the road from Metung, and Mack took over looking after both the land and the herd of cattle we were raising on it.

In order to pay for the land we mortgaged our record royalties for some time to come, and although we were a bit nervous about that, we felt that surely the touring would finance our living and the kids' education. There were moments when we thought we were going to be in debt to the record company a lot longer than we had planned, but we were trying to ensure our future as we saw it. So out on the road we went, with some new members of the troupe, until we turned back to Metung for Christmas with Anne and David, and with my father joining the family there.

The big adventure of the next year was heavy on our minds, but our hearts lifted when we thought of new places, new towns and people, and old friends in now familiar places all over Australia.

CHAPTER 12

January 1966 marked my thirty-sixth birthday and the beginning of the round-Australia tours. There were a lot of other things happening in Australia as well as the news that the Slim Dusty Show was going to attempt its first national road tour, and they were certainly of more national significance than our news. Of course, things such as decimal currency being introduced, and the repeal of the Dog Act – as it was called – carried a lot more weight on the national scene, but to us they were incidental to the big thing we were tackling. It makes me laugh when I think about it now. I didn't give either of those items a thought as I got ready to spend another year out on the roads of the outback, in and out of towns big and small.

We had completed arrangements for the personnel of the tour, sent the poster design to the printers and booked halls and theatres for the first part of the tour. We decided on the format of the show programme and got the scripts of the new comedy skits ready for rehearsal. We traded in two of the beat-up old vehicles for one new one; had checked and repaired anything at all dicey on the two trucks, Thunder and Lightning, and took our big caravan to have the brake system inspected and repaired if necessary. Jack, the garage proprietor, found the van's brake linings burnt to a crisp, he said. Slim went off like a firecracker, informing me that the van was too big and he'd probably be 'cracked up' in it. Jack fixed it, and Slim cooled down for a while.

In the meantime, I worked up a head of steam as school uniforms for Anne and David failed to materialise on time and, when they did, were not always correct in size or whatever. Piles of name tapes all had to be sewn by hand on articles of clothing. The house seemed to exist in a permanent state of chaos with people coming and going. Dad had come to spend Christmas and New Year with us, and to spend the first part of the tour on the road too. Teddy and Barbara arrived with their blonde twin girls crawling everywhere, and set off with their supplies of posters, complimentary tickets and tour itineraries to do the advance work for us. They left about a fortnight ahead of us. Aunty Una was to arrive soon, with car and caravan, from Sydney. And in the back of my mind all the time was the fact that David was going to leave for boarding school for the first time, at the age of seven and a half.

We were to pick up other members of the show in Melbourne and in Terang, our first show town. Setting off on a hot January day from Metung, we got as far as Sale before the new generator in the truck went bung. After trying to move on to Melbourne before attempting repairs, the truck made so much noise that we had to go back to Sale and wait to get a mechanic and parts. The regulator on the generator had been wrongly adjusted and that had caused the breakdown. We were stuck in Sale all day, and knew we would have to travel that night if we were to reach Terang by our date. Then the caravan parking lights refused to work and life became pandemonium again! However, I flatly refused to leave the big van behind. By the time we reached Melbourne and picked up John Dante, who objected to travelling by night but was overruled by cranky us, it had turned cold, and it was freezing and raining at 1.30 a.m. when we reached Terang. Anne and

David were so tired but, as usual, really good and understanding of the situation.

There was a little Morris utility parked with our gear near the truck, and as I walked past a head emerged from one of the other cars. I said, 'Oh, you must be Ray! I'm Joy, Slim's wife.' The head emerged further and informed me he would be glad to get into a proper bed. I sympathised and pointed the way to the bed. After huge rehearsals the next day, we opened the show to a small house of good listeners.

I was driving the new wagon with Dante's caravan on behind, and with Kim the cocker spaniel and Jo-Jo the budgie in the back of the wagon with the luggage. Anne and David took it in turns to travel either with me in the car or in the truck with Slim. Aunty Una reported an early morning conversation to me:

David: 'Anne, can you go in the truck with Dad today?'

Anne: 'No, Davy. You know it's your turn.'

David: 'Yes, I know, but have you seen Dad's face this morning?'

David had a knack of trying hard to be thoughtful but putting his foot in it. Luckily, he has since grown out of that, but one of his efforts was at his father's expense. We carried spare rims and tyres in the truck, and on a trip when Slim was driving the car and caravan with David, Aunty Una and myself as passengers, we got a flat tyre on a rough road on a very hot day. It was the final touch to a most trying morning, and Slim flung out of the car to the side of the road to sit and wait for the truck to roll up.

David, all concern, leaned out the window and said, 'Never mind, Dad, it could have been worse. It could have been two punctures.'

In the resultant uproar from the roadside, Davy turned to Aunty Una and said, 'Gee, I've only made it worse, haven't I!'

'Yes, you have, David. So be quiet!' was Aunty's advice.

By that time, Slim had seen the humour of it and was quite ready to cope with jacks, tyres and waiting to get started.

We had our dog with us; actually, he was David's dog. His name was Hans, which was short for a long pedigree of champion dachshunds. Hans loved the children, and also appointed himself as protector of Anne and me. Slim and David had to fend for themselves, but if any person or animal came too close or too quickly towards either of his ladies, Hans stationed himself out in front of us and bailed up the person – or, as it turned out one day in Boulia, the blue cattle dog who was walking towards us. I thought Hans would be annihilated, but the cattle dog couldn't seem to decide if the animal standing him off was actually a dog or a new species of wildlife, and backed off immediately.

I was glad of Hans's company and protection on dark nights when we parked behind the local hall and I would have to walk to the outside lavatory, or to the toilet block in an ill-lit caravan park. Many a time a late-leaving drunk weaving his way across the hall yard would unknowingly head straight towards me, to be met with a deep, threatening bark out of the darkness, followed with a guttural growl as Hans ran out well in front. In the dark Hans could not be seen for the stocky little dog that he was, and his bark was such that he sounded like an Alsatian.

Hans travelled in the truck or car with me, and with the children when they were with us. Everyone in the camp spoiled him, and Hans's girth expanded as he accepted all the titbits he was offered at dinnertime and at barbecues. I tried putting him on a diet, but it didn't work too well. Everyone thought I was starving poor old Hans and kept slipping him lifesaving goodies. He slept in a basket beneath the dinette table at night, and for six nights a week was quite happy to go to bed when we left for the show and to wake up and greet us on our return. However, he knew when we had a night off because the routine altered. Then, if we didn't take him with us or spend the evening in his sight, we would arrive home to a kitchen rubbish bin tipped upside down, or a bed quilt dragged off our bed and used for Hans's comfort and to make his point that he did not appreciate being left out of the fun on our free night.

As we worked our way west across Victoria and into South Australia, the thought of the looming return to school kept me hemming trousers and skirts, and sewing on name tapes whenever I had a spare moment. Mostly, I sewed as we travelled when either Slim or Aunty Una were driving. My father had come with us for a short trip, and to escort David on the plane from Whyalla in South Australia back to Sydney. He was to start at the Blue Mountains Grammar School as a boarder and I was worried about how the long break from us would affect him. He seemed such a little fellow to be going off to a strange school all on his own, knowing no one else there. When the big day arrived, I dressed him in his white shirt and good trousers, and Slim did his tie and his hair. I think David had as much ice cream as he could eat and I hoped that the plane trip would not result in any ructions with it.

It was very hard to say goodbye; I didn't want to cry and David wouldn't cry. I tried to lighten things a bit by saying, 'Now, Davy, you look after Poppa for me.' He grinned and said, 'Yes, Mum. I'll keep him out of the pub!' We all had to laugh – even Dad, the good sport he was – and I thought, yes, it was just like David to make it easier for us, even at that age.

I was lucky I still had Anne, who was not due to leave for another week. She was singing in the show, and proving extremely popular. Any night she didn't feel like stage work (she was only thirteen, after all) she stayed home in the caravan and very often baked a cake for our supper. I was still sewing on name tapes till I thought I was sewing them in my sleep, but it seemed no time after David left that we had to go into Adelaide and put Anne on the plane too. I was absolutely desolate after she'd gone; I missed them both so badly that I'm afraid I was a real watering pot for weeks off and on. I couldn't wait for the day each week when we could ring them up, and I was never so happy as to hear Davy asking if we could send some more 'tuck' and another Corgi model car, but with doors that opened.

While we were in Adelaide to put Anne on the plane, we recorded an appearance on Reg and Heather's weekly TV show, *Country Homestead*, recorded in Adelaide and viewed through the Channel Nine network. It was my first experience of television work, and although I found it quite strange and interesting, I still noted that I would not like to do it every week. However, there was no chance of that happening anyway – not out where we were heading! Our next show was booked at the Woomera Village near the Woomera Rocket Range, in the centre of desert country where the heatwave weather made everything look reversed as if in a film negative. Arriving at this village of 6000 souls, in the middle of nowhere with Commonwealth security guards at the entrance, was a strange experience. Once inside, we were welcomed and taken to the theatre. We were so thankful to find it was airconditioned, with showers, dressing rooms, a stage and curtains, and every convenience possible. Cool orange juice and sandwiches were supplied, and we had the feeling that the officials couldn't do enough to make us comfortable and welcome. It was a remarkable difference to some of the heaps we'd played in, and the welcome was very warming. They enjoyed the show so much that they asked us to return and show for two nights the following year.

As it turned out, we would go back to Woomera the following year and this time we stayed overnight. It was a village that had the atmosphere of having been placed in the middle of the desert without any sense of growing or developing. There were blocks of flats and houses available for government employees, but other workers, such as drivers, found accommodation more difficult to obtain. Everything was very official, but everyone was very friendly to us.

On this second visit, we were fortunate enough to have an acquaintance who was in charge of the Optical Tracking station based about 28 miles further out in the desert. After the show, he took us out there to see the huge 3000-pound camera in operation. There were three of these stations, keeping a 24-hour watch on satellites. We heard the American commander speaking to the men on shift and telling them what he wanted done with the camera; we were shown photographs of the moon taken from a satellite. It was rather inspiring but overwhelming to be told we were the first outsiders to have been allowed in the control room while such an operation was taking place.

After that first visit to Woomera, it was back to earth and swapping opinions on this new decimal currency that made its debut in February 1966. At first it felt a bit like we were playing 'shops' with the money, and it was considered that the one and two cent pieces looked cheap and would wear out in no time.

We had the usual minor calamities over the initial stages of using dollars and cents. Aunty Una was most upset when she changed a ten-dollar note as a ten-pound note; I did the wages for the first time in the new currency and managed to do everyone's correctly except for one of our performers. I made his wages up in sterling instead of decimal currency and consequently short changed him by ten dollars. Oh dear!

The Nullarbor crossing was soon upon us and the usual hammering of the vehicles and caravans on the hard, dusty, potholed road began in earnest. We pulled into Koonalda station for petrol, and picked up a parcel to post for the Koonalda station owners when we reached Norseman. Old Eucla was partly or almost covered by sand dunes by this time, with only two old ruins poking up from the dazzling white sands that were creeping up and around them. With the white sand below and the clear blue sky above, and the relentless dunes unstoppable in their slow creeping forwards to cover all the stories of the stone ruins, Eucla was an eerie spot.

We headed down the escarpment towards Madura roadhouse and passed a big semitrailer with a load of new cars and an attractive young woman at the wheel. We stopped at Madura for quite some time for fuel and food – and just to see other people. When Peter, our truck driver, ventured into the bar, he emerged later on to announce that it was full of Irishmen and Scots drivers arguing over who the lass from the truck was going to travel with on the next leg of the trip. We left them to it and headed for Cocklebiddy.

Cocklebiddy roadhouse was run by the McDonald family, who also owned a station north of the road. The original Mr and Mrs McDonald had camped by the road waiting for spare parts to reach them and had found themselves helping out other travellers with tea and food to such an extent they ended up charging for their supplies. That led to setting up the small roadhouse, which grew to a larger petrol stop and cafe and, finally, to the big commercial roadhouse of today. The McDonald twins, Jill and Joy, worked the showgrounds for many years, as did their brother, Billy, though Bill ended up concentrating mainly on the family property.

We had a motley crew with us, when I come to think about it. John and Joyce, singer and dancer respectively, had Lorie, their little boy; Barry and Pauline had Meryl and Brian; John and

Elizabeth Dante were elderly professional stagers; Pete drove the truck and helped out on the door and general work; Ray (Delando) was a variety act with a bit of juggling, ventriloquism, miming and balancing. Delando was never satisfied with his equipment, or his costumes, or even his finished act. He spent the days driving across the Nullarbor stitching sequins by the hundred onto a new cloak, and then managed to cause Dante to explode in fury when he began incorporating small magic tricks into his act, as he came onstage flourishing his satin cape and executing a few dance steps to his taped music.

By the time we had shown most of the south-western towns in Western Australia, the jealousy and dislike between Dante and Delando had passed simmering point and reached the explosion mark. It didn't help that we had to carefully explain to Ray how the stockmen up north would react to his sexy wobbles and footwork, plus the sequinned satin cape flourishes. It broke his heart to drop them from the act, but he did see the need for it.

John Dante's eighty-first birthday was duly celebrated in the camp, and everyone pitched in for a birthday present – that is, everyone except Delando. 'That horrible old man,' he declared, 'is not getting anything from me.' It took only a few more weeks of the more or less silent warfare for Delando to decide that he was not appreciated and would go home, where he was considered in a more fitting manner. That left Dante victor in the battle, yet the wily old character stroked his white goatee and continued to grizzle and grumble about where we played, how long the distance was, the size of the town and the lack of shade for his caravan. He was, nevertheless, held in great affection by most of the camp and respected for his knowledge of stagecraft and magic showmanship.

We always set out for Western Australia in January or February each year in order to reach the towns in the south-west before either seeding or harvest times, which was when people were too busy on their properties to come into town. It made for horrifically hot travelling, though. There was no airconditioning in cars then, and by afternoon on the Nullarbor, for instance, we were driving directly into the lowering sun. When I travelled in the big truck with Slim I kept a bucket of water on the floor in front of me, nestled between my feet. I dipped small towels into the water; laid one across his knees and draped another around his neck, wetting them again as they dried out. I did the same for myself, and with the little quarter-windows angled onto the wet towels, that did cool us a bit.

When we reached Esperance, we all wanted to see the Pink Lake. That desire made us get out of bed early, because the huge salt lake always looked its most beautiful just near and just after sunrise. The further you walked out on the salt crust, the deeper the pink colouring.

Then Slim and I were waiting to ring Anne and David, who were spending the weekend out of school, staying at Heather's. We fairly danced with impatience when we couldn't ring till after 6 p.m. because the telephone lines were being tested. Finally we got through and the children were still up, waiting to hear from us and full of chat. They were both well and happy, though, as Anne said, 'Oh, Mum, David's picked up some *awful* sayings from the boys at school!' I hoped they were not too terrible. David, we were told, had arrived for the weekend without any of his own clothes and was sleeping in a pair of Reg's shortie pyjamas; a sight I think would have been worth seeing.

Laws prohibiting Aboriginal people free access to alcohol were repealed in the years 1966 to 1967, leading to changes in what used to be called the Dog Act. Previously, Aboriginal people as a majority were denied the right to drink alcohol; this sanction was relaxed in the case of proven responsible members of the Aboriginal community who were allowed the right. As in the case of the painter Albert Namatjira, it was almost impossible to ignore or refuse to honour the traditional custom of sharing everything with other members of the tribe or community when asked, even if this included alcohol. In his sad case, he was gaoled for a short time for his transgression.

The prohibition was an unpopular law in everyone's mind, not just in the view of the Aboriginal population, but I have to write what I saw and experienced when the law was revoked. At the time alcohol was prohibited we had played to Aboriginal people who were clean and well dressed and a pleasure to deal with. After alcohol was freely available, we had scores of small children sitting on the hall steps while their parents were in the pub. Aunty Una couldn't bear to see them cold, so she always took them into the show when the lights went down.

We had never-ending trouble with drunks in the hall, and some were violent – drunks, white or black, were a worry all the time. I've been grabbed and dragged by a woman who was roaring drunk; I've had a heavy door slammed at me in an effort to break my arm in it. I've been abused by the best in the nation in places where the lone policeman has been absent on a job in a neighbouring town, which meant he didn't have to deal with the trouble he knew was likely to erupt down at the hall during the show.

In one town the hall had big double doors that opened directly onto the back of the stage. Some big young men started to force the doors open, just as Teddy – the advance agent who was back with the show for a break – came around the side of the hall from the front. He raced over and pulled the two away, giving them a good whack as he did it. Two other men came at him from behind and king-hit him in the face. They picked up sticks and came for him again, but just at that moment Slim poked his head out of the back door. The assailants all ran for their lives, leaving Teddy with a broken nose and requiring hospital attention more than once.

Later that same evening, just to top off an eventful night, Pete collapsed with what looked like an epileptic fit. He ended up in hospital in Perth, having all sorts of tests done. We did not know that he had been in a bad accident two years previously, and doctors thought the fit may have been caused by the effects of the accident.

We were sorry too, to be told that the Aboriginal shearing teams who were regarded as the best in the district were now unreliable. Word was that they only worked long enough to earn a cheque then would down tools, demand their cheques and go to town to drink them. Then, if replaced by white shearing teams, it was the boss's fault, of course. We could see a lot of ill feeling where previously there had been little or none. It was very disheartening. New ways are always problematic to begin with, no doubt, but this one in particular upset me very much when I saw it happening at that time. I was grateful to move north away from this area; but, of course, I saw a lot more happenings in the future.

CHAPTER 13

There were to be many round-Australia tours for the Slim Dusty Show, and we saw changes as we went, but the first thing we discovered as we left towns we hadn't visited before, such as Geraldton and Carnarvon, was that we had miscalculated the time required to cover the distances between towns. Sometimes the roads were just so bad that we had to travel slower than before. The distance between towns was longer too.

Cyclone Shirley hit the coast and near interior in April that first year, and we spent a couple of days on the Mardie Plain waiting it out, and then a week marooned in Roebourne. Shirley had well and truly moved on by the time we arrived there, but the roads needed only a short unseasonal fall of rain to make them impassable. On the Mardie Plain we had company in the shape of a couple of truckies who knew they just had to sit it out. They were more patient than we were.

When we arrived at the caravan park in Roebourne as the rain teemed down and the wind blew, an elderly man asked for our assistance with battening down his large tent. Ted and Emmy were an amazing couple in their eighties, camping out on their annual fishing trip. But their tent home was threatening to collapse in this downpour, so our men agreed to get out in the wet and help stabilise it. This was one time I was happy to take a back seat and just put the kettle on for cups of tea, while Emmy waited with me out of the rain for the tent to be sorted out. We certainly admired that pair of fishing enthusiasts; Emmy was as keen, if not more so, than Ted.

I think ours were the first vehicles out of town when the shire opened the roads. Just the same, to get further north we had to go in a detour circle that took us through the asbestos town of Wittenoom on our way to Port Hedland. The mining boom was just starting and Port Hedland was crammed with people living wherever they could. We had a look at the caravan parks and discovered that dysentery was rife, so we settled ourselves behind the council hall we had booked for the show. The council staff did their best to remove us, but with three small children amongst us they had no hope at all. We stayed put till after the show and got out of the town as fast as possible. By the following year, the council would pass a bylaw prohibiting any camping behind the hall.

Meanwhile I was collecting stories and impressions as I travelled, and some of them provided material for a song I called 'Big Frogs in Little Puddles'. An amusing title, but the stories were not so amusing – just true.

We had over 600 kilometres to travel to Broome, and it was a very wearying trip. We were warned about the Pardoo Sands – an area of white sand on the highway where years of grading to make it passable had resulted in the roadway becoming a bit like a tunnel between walls of solid white sand. It was close to being a one way road in places, with pull-offs to allow vehicles to creep past each other if they were able to back up to the wider spot. Of course, we heard the horror stories of the two truck drivers who tried to squeeze past each other but locked tops and spent a week trying to get out of the mess while all other traffic (what there was of it) banked up at each end of the blockage. So you can imagine the panic when Barry, driving ahead in his car and caravan, came tearing back to warn us to hurry ahead to a bypass because 'there's a dirty big semi on its way!' We all made it safely and actually reached Broome in time to clean up and shout ourselves dinner at a local Chinese cafe.

For this trip we had bought a small generator to run the caravan lighting and refrigerators, and it had even run the show for us at times of blackouts or DC power in a small town. There were no powered sites left in the Broome caravan park, so we went to the very end of the park and set up our generator. We staved off possible complaints from neighbours by offering them lighting powered by the generator. Once settled, we drove around town, looking for the cafe. We finally realised it was the corrugated iron house with the garden out the front. We celebrated with everyone who could come out, and Slim distinguished himself by mistaking the bottle of red sauce for tomato. It was chilli, and obviously made from the bushes of chillis growing in the front garden. You could see the steam coming out of his ears.

To get supplies the next day, I headed to the big Burns Philp store. It was also made of corrugated iron – a big, sprawling building. The whole town was centred around that store, where I remember we bought a beautiful lamp made from a carved seashell. At different stops on trips like this, we also bought carved emu eggs. The dark green of the outside shell was scraped away to make a sculpture or drawing in a pale green or cream against the darker green.

Our next stop was the town of Derby, where we met up with another country performer who forgot to give us a message from the shire president in Halls Creek. We were planning to show there on a Sunday night, and the message was to contact a person in Perth to get special permission. In those times, staging a commercial concert on a Sunday night was not allowed except under exceptional circumstances such as ours. The conditions and distances we travelled to get there allowed us to make application to be exempted from the rule. Without that permit, we would have to turn away people who had come long distances themselves for the show.

We showed in Fitzroy Crossing before we reached Halls Creek. The road from Derby was shocking. My caravan was being towed by Thunder, the Inter truck, and when one of the four tyres on the van blew Slim didn't even feel any difference. By the time we reached Fitzroy Crossing, I had to give him the news that the rim was just about wrapped around the hub. I think there was a very good reason for his explosion that time … There was no hall, so we erected canvas sidewalls in a paddock across the road from the general store. We had a low wooden stage and temporary side curtains, and all our folding chairs set out; the store gave us some power from their generator and that, plus our little generator puffing away, lit up our show and ran the PA system. Local kids spent the afternoon working out which trees gave the best view into the show for free.

Next morning, before tackling the next leg to Halls Creek, Slim and I went out to Go Go Station for him to sing some songs for the children and other people there who had not been able to fit on the trucks to get to the show. I think Slim was wearing the overalls he always wore when driving the truck, but they didn't mind. At least he was there, and singing the songs they wanted to hear.

When we finally reached Halls Creek, the shire president got on the phone to Perth and dragged a judge friend off the golf course to sign the permission for us. That was our first meeting with Ernie Bridge. Descendant of one of the early Kimberley pioneers, Ernie was shire president and town butcher; he owned the airline agency and managed the family cattle station. His brother Ben ran the bakery and probably something else as well. Ernie later became the first Aboriginal politician to hold a ministerial position in the Western Australian government, and I do believe he held four portfolios at once for a while. I wouldn't have put it past him as he was a most able man, as well as being a very good country singer. Sometimes I think Ernie would have been as happy just touring Australia with a country music show as running all the businesses he did.

All the time we drove these long distances, I was gasping at the grandeur of the King Leopold and Hamersley Ranges. In places the spinifex was green with the flame of Sturt's desert pea blazing nearby. The earth changed colour from red to ochre and the ranges changed colour with the position of the sun and time of day.

Driving from Halls Creek to Wyndham, I stared at battlements of stone stretching away to the distance; spear grass waving in the light breeze; carbines and river gums standing on the creek beds. And then we reached Wyndham.

Our first time in Wyndham, the coastal town housing the big abattoirs where so many shipments and drives of cattle ended up, we showed in the meatworks hall. It was about the filthiest old dump ever. Food scraps from the last event lay everywhere, the canvas seats were heaped outside and other mounds of debris were to be found in corners of the dressing rooms. It was a full afternoon's work to clean it and set up the seating. The only thing I like to remember about it is the fact that two men staged a fight outside the hall after the show. It was the funniest sight as the two fighters stood yards apart shouting insults at each other, and the barrackers for either side stood behind their man yelling encouragement: 'Get inter 'm, mate! Don't stand for that sort of ★★★★!' The drunks waved fists in each other's direction, weaving back and forth; I got tired of waiting for any real action and went back to stacking seats. I went to pay the rent next morning and told them what I thought of them and their filthy hall.

We moved onwards to Kununurra and the open air theatre. There were the usual friendly folk and the usual quota of inebriated patrons, including one elderly Aboriginal gentleman who draped his arm around my neck and leaned heavily on it as I escorted him to a seat. There was no bridge across the Victoria River in 1966 but we all crossed without trouble and were on our way to Katherine and Darwin in time for the Darwin show.

On our first foray into the Territory back in 1962 with the showground team, I had met up with Auntie Billie Pitcheneder, a big lady with a big heart to match. She ran a catering company as one career and had a second as the best fundraiser in Darwin. Auntie Billie stationed herself on Woolies' corner and brought in the funds for her various charities. In Katherine in 1962, she had been on a committee investigating improvements for the Darwin showground or something when she spotted me battling with a portable clothesline in the wind while four-year-old David caused mayhem around my feet. Auntie Billie had come through the fence in a moment and scooped up Davy, who hadn't known what had happened to him; it must have felt like a mountain of warmth and cuddles from this strange lady.

Early in World War II Auntie Billie used to drive transports up and down the track between Darwin and Alice Springs, and she objected strenuously to being evacuated to Perth after the Japanese bombed Darwin. She was one of the first people back to the city when allowed. It was really *her* town, or so she considered, and old Darwin seemed to think the same.

We rolled into Darwin from our trek through the Pilbara and the Kimberley, late one afternoon, dirty, dusty and weary. We knew the Howard Springs caravan park, some miles south of Darwin, was a haven of cool water and space for all our vans and vehicles, and we were sure of a welcome there. Every year after that we would arrive as expected and would no sooner be settled with power on, and the vans opened and dusted out, before Auntie Billie would arrive with containers of iced water and heaps of cooked dinners and salads – enough to feed the whole team.

We showed in the little Cavanagh Theatre, run by an enthusiastic band of volunteers. We paid rent for the theatre, but the volunteers – who became friends over the years – always turned up to help with ushering and even with walk-on parts in our comedy skits. There was someone to operate the lights; Auntie Billie with cold water, juice and sandwiches for backstage; and willing hands everywhere for any job that needed doing.

The round-Australia tours gave us many memories indeed. Before we tackled the second one, we made the hard decision that we would not be able to take families of small children on the road with us any more. The heat and the long distances in some of the remote places we toured made for tired small children and even more tired mothers, and it all made for much more tension in the camp than we needed. We were such a small community that every little thing made a difference to the happy or unhappy atmosphere within it.

However, this decision cost us the great contribution of Teddy Trevor as our advance man. So what were we going to do about our advance publicity, hall bookings and putting up posters, and organising newspaper and radio advertisements? Mack and Lorna decided that they would take on the rolling up and mailing of our posters, getting them out to the towns in time to advertise the show. Slim and I planned the tours and then I sent out enquiry forms to the halls. As I got the dates in order, I phoned or telegrammed to confirm the bookings and paid the deposits. We already knew which newspapers to advertise in, and what radio stations to advertise on. There was no community radio network in those days, but radio announcers were usually able to arrange their own programmes and that meant that we could get live appearances and extra ads without too much trouble.

The newspaper ads required photo blocks being sent to the papers in plenty of time; radio ads required scripts for reading or a recorded advertisement on a small disc sent ahead. To get the posters into the towns surrounding the town we were showing in, I obtained the telephone directories of all the relevant districts. Then I typed labels for every store listed that I thought might display a poster in return for a complimentary ticket to the show. Mack used these to write, roll up and mail out posters with a printed form to shopkeepers asking for assistance in displaying them. It was labour intensive but relatively successful, especially as later on I had the young singer Margaret Mile – who by then was part of the troupe – to help me with typing the address labels when on tour.

Having said that, it backfired on us at times such as when we booked a fairly new theatre at Mildura and everyone who had a complimentary ticket not only turned up but brought others with them, and we were packed out with some comp ticket holders being most annoyed with us when they weren't fitted in. We tried seating some on the stairs, but officials naturally put a stop to that. The other trap was when mean-spirited shop owners didn't put up the poster but used the complimentary ticket anyway. In one small town I noticed next to no posters up, so I went around and initialled every complimentary ticket where the poster was displayed. That night, we turned back the non-initialled ones.

Barry decided that he would stay with us, settling Pauline and the children near Metung while he was on tour. We trimmed the show, the following year booking Rocky Page, the Cowboy Hypnotist, and Paulino, the balancer and juggler. We had Margaret, and Aunty Una was still with us out front. In most of the photos from this tour you could see Paul balancing on his hands in every scene around Australia.

It was also on this tour that, while heading north for Darwin, Rock had to make an unscheduled trip back home for a family emergency, leaving us with a huge gap in our programme. Rocky used to do a singing spot, then the hypnosis and a memory act in the second half.

We were able to expand the singing spot by Slim doing extra, and Margaret and me doing the same. At this time I was playing a small electric keyboard instead of the piano accordion. But we still needed something in the second half. So Rocky taught me how to do the memory act and I filled in the time. I was a very nervous performer for the first couple of nights, but gained confidence after that. Nevertheless, I was most relieved when Rocky returned to the show and I could return to my normal jobs.

The annual Darwin Show coincided with the Darwin Eisteddfod and the city was crammed for a fortnight with country people from stations and Aboriginal groups from outstations and every corner of the Territory. Many came for all the entertainment, for the fun at the showground, and for the Slim Dusty Show. There was a bit of heartache amongst those who were unable to get to Darwin and join in. But one lass decided to do something about it when she and her friends missed out on the trip.

Miriam Rose Unganmerr was fourteen years old and living at the Francis Xavier Catholic mission at Daly River. She was already a promising artist, a Moyle River girl and a good scholar. Miriam organised a letter to be delivered to Slim Dusty in Darwin. In it, she told him that she and other children at the school had saved up five dollars and would pay him to bring the show to the Daly when he left Darwin and headed south.

Slim and I looked at this letter very carefully indeed. It was so sincere and naïve that we studied our itinerary, and yes, there was one night we could spare on our journey south to Alice Springs. We pulled the caravans in beside the Adelaide River on the road to the Daly River settlement, and drove in with vehicles only.

What a welcome we got! The children were out in force, adults beaming in the background. We couldn't help seeing that the mission was running on short funds but heaps of enthusiasm and dedication. We heard tales of everything that was happening at the mission and at the missions on Bathurst Island and Port Keats as well.

We had a great time that evening as we performed on a stage in the open, to crowds of people not only from the mission, but from all around the settlement. After the finale, Miriam came to see us and handed us the five dollars we had earned. Sister Francisco had earlier warned us that we must accept the money as it had been a matter of pride that the children had saved it up to get Slim to come. Slim accepted it with thanks and with a feeling of great humility. He then proposed that in future, we would bring the show each time we came to Darwin on tour, but instead of being paid he would like to have the children perform for us after we had performed for them. In the years that followed, that was the deal.

The outcome of our relationship with the Daly River mission was that we also used to visit Bathurst Island and Port Keats missions and perform for the people there. These were not paid jobs, they were part of the friendship we were offered in the north and that we wanted to repay somehow. Transport, a stage and some amplification were provided for us. On Bathurst Island, for instance, there were 800 people, with more across the strait on Melville Island who came across for the concert.

CHAPTER 14

When we went to the Northern Territory with our showground team in 1962, we did the Darwin Show and then moved down to Alice Springs. We settled our large group in a council park while Frank approached the council about erecting our big tent and putting on a night show in the Alice. Apparently the council was not too happy about this until one councillor, Reg Harris, carted two or three of the doubters down to the park to inspect our outfits and see that we weren't a heap of thieving no hopers. Having been satisfied about that, and with Reg's support, up went the big tent and the smaller ones around it, with banners and boards livening up the park and arousing a lot of interest amongst the townspeople.

We invited all the residents of the Old Timers Home to be our guests for the evening, and volunteers drove them to and from the performance. That was our introduction to the Alice, and Slim and I would become very good friends with Reg and Marge Harris throughout all our touring days and after. They were old-timers themselves given the length of time they had lived and worked in the Alice, and Reg was a fount of stories about the early pioneers and characters there.

So when we began our round-Australia night show tours, we looked forward to seeing Reg and Marge in the Alice, and hearing all the latest news of the Red Centre. I also looked forward to seeing my cousin Joan, who had moved to the Alice as a nursing sister and ended up marrying and settling down there.

It was on one of our first big tours that we showed at some of the Aboriginal settlements closer to Alice Springs. We cut across country past Aileron Station to Yuendumu settlement, on the road to the Tanami Desert. It was quite a big settlement with a large community dining room and a kitchen run by an exasperated European cook. We were to use the dining room to put on our show.

Another settlement we showed at was Areyonga. It was set near a creek or river bed that nearly bogged our caravans for the duration; we needed planks and big branches to get across that one. It was there that we met Rubina Namatjira, Albert's widow. She was a thin, tall lady with white hair. Her sons took after her husband with their painting ability, and I later bought paintings by Ewald and Enos, plus one by Herbert Raberaba. Enos used to say that he never tried to paint what he saw during the day because the harsh sun washed out all the colours of the rocks and sand and trees. He said, 'I wait till very late, when I see the real colours.'

We first used to aim to show in Darwin for a week, and in later years for a fortnight, during Show and Eisteddfod Week in mid-July. Then we headed for the Mount Isa Rodeo in August, showing everywhere we could on our way. Over the years we showed all the small towns and settlements along the track between Darwin and Alice Springs. We generally called at Dunmarra roadhouse to say hello to Noel and Mrs Healy. Noel didn't go out to the bowser when a tourist pulled up for fuel but, rather, sat and waited inside at the bar. When the visitor grew tired of waiting and entered, Noel would usually greet him or her with, 'What'll you have?' as he waved a bottle or stubbie, and if the tourist wasn't careful he or she would still be there some hours later, yarning and drinking.

There were old goldmining towns like Pine Creek and bigger ones like Tennant Creek, which was a rough and tough town. In most of the towns where there were Aboriginal children Hans, our dog, caused untold amazement, as dachshunds were practically unseen there. 'Limuty Dog' (Slim Dusty's dog) had a group of watchers following him around all the time, pointing and giggling.

Once we left the Three Ways above Tennant Creek and headed east for Mount Isa, we'd face a very empty horizon for over 450 kilometres, with only two roadhouses and a police station between Three Ways and Camooweal over the Queensland border.

We always checked if the 'Booze and Beds' sign was still up at Frewena roadhouse, and in early years were careful not to get tangled up with an impromptu party at Barry Caves roadhouse. At one stage there was a happy pianist there and a very jovial host, and we'd known of other showies who stopped for petrol and were still there a couple of days later. Barry Caves was cut off by floodwaters one year and, despite pleas, had not received any air-dropped supplies. As food was running short, the owner did the only thing he could – he sent an outrageous report to the media: 'Running out of food. Having to kill and eat our pet dogs.' There was such a furore that supplies were dropped in abundance and the media had a great time. Such was the publicity that the new bumper stickers for Barry Caves roadhouse bore an illustration of a steaming labrador dog being served up on a platter.

We camped by the police station at Soudan, and it was my first taste of yellowbelly. The fish were caught in the Ranken River nearby and grilled on the station barbecue plate. In later times, camping by a waterhole, I cooked Slim's catches wrapped in mud and placed in the campfire ashes, or ditto but in the old camp oven. Yellowbelly always seemed a very oily fish to me and tasted best grilled on a wire grid over the coals, but it was a famous treat of the outback.

We rolled into Camooweal one year to see a new Post Office Hotel, fondly designated by some as 'the biggest woolshed in the West'. After parking ourselves behind the hall, Slim and Barry went off 'emu bobbing' (looking for semiprecious stones and jasper or agate). It became a favourite pastime of nearly everyone in the team, as it could be indulged just about anywhere and served as a talking point for everyone. That year Slim came back with some good jasper and ribbon stone, plus two Aboriginal stone knives of grey stone.

The hall was packed that night, and Slim had to sing 'New Australian Bushman' twice in the programme. At that show a policeman sat in the audience with a prisoner on either side of him. The story was that two station hands, or ringers, had collected their cheques and come to Camooweal a couple of days early to stay at the pub and then see the show when we arrived. It turned out that things got going in the pub, as they do, and the lively pair found themselves in the lock-up on the day of the show. That was more than they bargained for, as the show was the whole point of coming to town. They pleaded and promised the earth to the policeman, who was a bit put out by the fact that if they were still in the cell that night he wouldn't see the show either. So history was made in the hall as officialdom carted the two miscreants down to the hall and sat them one each side of their gaoler. The three of them had a good time – no malice felt by anyone.

The town of Mount Isa was doing well, with copper at a good price, and the whole place was revving up for rodeo week. Stores were dressing their windows for the best window competition, and I think we were to judge the winners that year. The crew at 4LM radio station gave us a great welcome, as did the staff at Menzies Chemists, who organised the bookings for us. (We finally gave in and started bookings in self-defence against all those feral youngsters in the front rows!) We were to show in St Joseph's hall; as the pharmacist had vouched for us, the dean allowed us to park all our vehicles and caravans outside the hall. I wonder if he saw Baz and Rocky remove the St Joseph's archway sign to allow the big truck and van inside? They were very quick in putting it back, so no one was any the wiser, I guess.

I rang the children that night, and they were both at home in Metung for the weekend. By this time Anne was a boarder at St Anne's in Sale, and David now a boarder at Gippsland Grammar School, also in Sale. Mack and Lorna had brought them back to Homewood, our house in Metung, and moved in with them for the weekend. The kids were looking forward to coming to Cairns for the school holidays, and I was able to tell them that I had just booked their plane tickets. They'd both brought friends home for the weekend and sounded happy and full of news. It always made the day for us when they sounded like that. I hated it when, in cases such as the marooning at Roebourne after Cyclone Shirley, there was no mail going out or coming in; Anne, in particular, was terribly upset when she didn't receive her usual weekly letter. We were sometimes very isolated on the outback trips.

By the time we reached the Isa that particular year, things were only middling in the camp. Slim had been digging postholes on the fenceline down at the farm over the Christmas break, and had apparently torn or strained some muscles around the heart. Then at one of the camps the week before Mount Isa, he'd carried a really big branch over to the campfire and seemed to have done a bit more damage. A doctor prescribed tablets to help him get it settled, plus some type of daily treatment, but he was told not to drive the truck or do anything heavy till he felt right again. Of course, he wanted to drive the truck with the big caravan on, because the current driver liked throwing the wheel around with a great flourish as he evaded, or tried to evade, every pothole or corrugation on the road, thus making the caravan's interior an unholy mess of open and emptied cupboards and broken domestic items. When asked to ease off a bit, the driver's alternative was to travel at fifteen miles per hour and make us wait hours for the van to arrive.

We were also all very tired of the whines and grizzles and snide remarks of a family of three adults travelling with us. If there were some way to insinuate that they'd had their sleep interrupted by our arrival home from an outing after the show, they'd find it. The wife, and mother of the teenage girl, had been a nurse's aide for a while and considered herself a medical expert. So everyone was treated to her moaning about her 'heart condition', and loud advice to her daughter whenever there was anything physical to be done, to 'mind your kidneys, now!' She eavesdropped at every opportunity and when she heard no good about herself, came to attack me about what was 'going on' and what everyone had done to her and what I was supposed to do about it.

It was very difficult to put up with this sort of thing, day in and day out. But the particular day she chose to land at my door accusing two other members of the troupe of 'saying things' about her daughter's behaviour, and how they were 'carrying on together', was not a good one. I had been washing the floor, down on my knees, when the surprise of her arrival caused me to lose my balance and throw my whole weight onto my bad knee. Bone crunching into bone was how it felt, and I saw stars. I was already worried about Slim, who was having chest pains, and then this lady started in on me about her colleagues. I lost my temper completely and by the time I had finished my tirade, she was backpedalling as fast as she could. She had never heard me go off like that before and I think she went back to hubby for sympathy. At least I had peace and quiet for the rest of the Mount Isa stay while she worked out her next strategic move. In the meantime, I had guiltily thought, Whatever would Mum say if she'd heard me?

The trio lasted another couple of months, before they pushed their luck too far; in this case it was Slim's as well as my patience that gave way. Slim was unhooking our caravan when the family arrived at the park. The husband stormed up to Slim and demanded, 'What do you have to do around here to get the sack?' then stormed off again. Slim was a bit taken aback and asked me what on earth was going on and what should we do about it. I suggested that perhaps it was time we gave him what he wanted … Slim thought that a great idea and proceeded to give it. Apparently this family had had a feud going with one of the others, who they accused of leaving them on the road with a flat tyre without helping, so as usual they took it out on Slim and me. As we were out in the middle of nowhere, you might say, they thought they were pretty safe in putting us on the spot, but they had forgotten the good relations we had with nearly every one of our previous performers. We rang up young Margaret and then Paulino, who both came up on the very next available transport, and we had peace and harmony and fun for the rest of the year. We cheerfully arranged the exodus of the trio to parts unknown, where they could cause trouble for someone else.

A week later in the Isa, however, we were all rested and happy after days of rodeo fever and being made welcome by all and sundry. On the main rodeo night we'd always do a free half-hour show in the arena, as our contribution to the rodeo week and a thank you for all the welcome we received from everyone there. The crowds were so enthusiastic that it was hard to get away; they used to come to our show on the other nights as well. There was always a Mardi Gras procession through town one night of the week; we delayed opening our doors until it was over and some of the crowd came along to us.

Mount Isa was a roaring mining town, and after its annual rodeo week – with a carnival set up down near the dry river bank and a boxing tent doing loud business there as well; with ringers in town on the tear and the pubs open day and night with entertainment going nonstop; with an air of uncontained festivity and excitement even in the supermarkets – going back to our normal run through Cloncurry and then Julia Creek was a bit of a letdown in a way.

Sometimes we toured the Gulf Country of far north Queensland through to the Atherton Tablelands and down to Cairns. On one tour, Slim and Davy were in Thunder on the way to Burketown. The road was not what you'd call a road, actually, as one part of it was over flat rocks across a creek bed. However, they were almost there when David asked for a drink. Not wanting to stop on that 'road', Slim hauled out a can of warm beer from under the truck seat and they shared it. I think Davy was about five, so I was not amused when I found out.

The Gulf towns were old goldmining towns, and Normanton was once a port on the river for Gulf trade and for export of ore from Cloncurry. I looked around at Croydon (about 150 kilometres from Normanton) the first time I went there, and tried to imagine how it might have been in the days when it supported thirteen hotels. Mullock heaps still lay around outside town; the one remaining pub looked rather tattered and torn, and the hall had an old gas lamp still standing outside it. Just the same, people on the stations used to turn up for the show, and we felt that we were doing something worthwhile when we all had a good time and they had a chance to catch up with friends on the night. In Georgetown, the butcher opened up for us to get some meat for the next night's barbecue on the road to Mareeba. I think it was in Croydon that the butcher's premises consisted of a flywire and wood-battened rectangular building about the size of a bathroom, out in the middle of a paddock. It was big enough to hold the butcher, the chopping block, a carcass or two and one customer. I was fascinated.

We hit the new beef road out of Georgetown and had a good trip through to Mareeba in the Tablelands, where we began cleaning up the caravan for the arrival of Anne and David in Cairns. We planned a stopover there of ten days, in order to give everyone a holiday and ourselves a chance to enjoy the children's company. We washed everything. The terylene curtains turned white again instead of red; the windows, blinds and walls were caked with red dust and we spent ages getting them even partly respectable. Once Anne and David arrived Hans was hysterical with delight, jumping all over them one after the other, and then back to the first one again. It was always lovely to have the children on tour with us and we always tried to have our advertising work done before they arrived so that we could spend every available minute with them.

By this time we'd been doing the outback and round Australia tours for a full six years and we were tired. We were always missing mail, phone calls and telegrams, and to call the children at a certain time from some remote town was difficult. We would line up at the public phone box outside the post office and hope that the talkative person in there would finish chatting before our specified time ran out. There were problems with the phone lines and the line testings, and I would sometimes grow so impatient knowing that Anne and David might be waiting at the other end of the line for a call, and that they could miss their turn as another child's call from home came in.

I'd also been having a lot of pain off and on over the previous two years due to inflammation in my bad hip, and the only way it could be stopped was by getting an injection from a specialist – and try finding that in the Pilbara or Kimberley!

Slim was also showing the effects of constant singing and keeping the show rolling. Even when we closed down the tour over Christmas and New Year, Slim and I had to work to get the next year's show on the road, along with the advertising and bookings. We never seemed to stop thinking, planning and working.

While there was always work to do, we were looking forward to having some time off early the next year, 1969.

I remember how I enjoyed the quiet time at Metung. Barry and Pauline had bought the store at Johnsonville and enjoyed some settled time as well. Slim and Mack made regular visits to the Metung pub; Slim went fishing and cooked bream for breakfast; we were able to visit the kids at school regularly and have them home for occasional weekends when allowed. All in all it was a lovely time.

We went to Sydney late in March for Slim to record material for two albums, and in May 1969 boarded the plane for New Zealand.

We were going there to do a tour for a theatre chain, Kerridge Odeon. We had not expected them to accept our quote but they had seemed quite happy about it. As we thought we should take something different in the way of instrumentation, we invited Alan Swanson from Rockhampton to join us. He had been on tour with us a few years before, and was a fine old-style fiddle player and singer of old-time country. Barry was with us still, I was playing bass, and with Alan on board we thought we would be a neat group and quite versatile for the tour.

CHAPTER 15

After we landed in Auckland and were met at the airport and taken to our hotel, we were keen to look around and find out more about the programme and who the support act for the Slim Dusty Show would be. It didn't mean much when we were told that the act was the Hamilton County Bluegrass Band (the HCBB), as we had never heard of them over in our part of the world. I did think their stage name was a bit of a mouthful, and it took me time to get used to saying it.

I was the first to meet them – or, rather, to see them and try to introduce myself when they arrived at the hotel. It wasn't a successful attempt as they swept past me as if I was the hotel maid doing the rooms. The band had become famous in New Zealand after appearing regularly in a TV show called *The Country Touch*, hosted by Tex Morton, who was back from twelve years in the USA and Canada, where he travelled as the Great Morton, hypnotist. Tex was a multi-talented man, and a huge record seller in Australia before he went overseas; he had called in to his home country on his way back to Australia and ended up hosting the TV show.

The HCBB was a smooth, competent, top-quality bluegrass band the likes of which we had never heard in live action before. They sang traditional bluegrass songs in harmony, backed up with fiddle, banjo, mandolin, guitar, slap bass and dobro, and every musician was far more than competent: he or she was really good.

It was a pity that the band members must have heard some weird stories about big stars from Australia expecting to walk all over the local artists or something. One of them in particular was downright rude every chance he got. I searched a bookshop for a copy of *How to Win Friends and Influence People* to put in his instrument case with my signature on it, but had no luck. Alan's fiddle playing was not the novelty we had thought it would be, because the fiddle player in the HCBB was the classically trained Colleen Bain, who was the star of the band whether she liked it or not. Colleen was a modest person, and one of the first to relax and get to know us when it became apparent to the sensible and nice members of the band that the big bad Aussies couldn't care less who had the best lighting plan or the most rehearsal area or time. We were there to play music and make friends.

By eventually refusing to endorse the efforts of their self-appointed leader to insult one of us whenever possible, the other members of the HCBB began to enjoy themselves immensely. Colleen and Alan played fiddle duets, the bluegrass and the old-time styles blending happily. When Barry starred in one of the comedy sketches, the band members roared with laughter in the wings and wanted walk-on parts; they were more disgusted than we were when a paper review referred to the comedy as 'raucous and tasteless' despite the audience loving it.

Another referred to me as being 'rather static on stage'; I smiled when the HCBB shook their heads in despair at the reviewer's ignorance about electric bass guitar playing. It didn't worry me any, though, because as I stood onstage the reviewer could not see that I am physically unable to dance around while playing bass. People have held vigorous arguments about whether or not I had anything wrong with my leg or foot the last time I appeared in their theatre, and I've always had people enquiring what I had done to hurt myself since my last appearance on their stage. Aunty Una used to just give up trying to convince a concerned person that I'd had that 'bad leg' since childhood!

Once the HCBB and the Slim Dusty Show weathered the bad start, we got on so well. The band members insisted that we had to visit the Waitomo Glowworm Caves; we had to try their favourite NZ wines; family members gave us a warm welcome, and we just loved hearing that band swing into action each night. Here was the country band missing from the scene in Australia, and we all talked a lot about how good it would be if they were able to visit and tour back home. Still, that was pie in the sky it seemed, as a five-piece band was a costly item to transfer from New Zealand to Australia; we were sorry to leave them behind when we left to go home.

Over the years we'd found it very difficult to get studio musicians to play country music with 'feel'. They just didn't know how, even though they were professionals and did the best job they could in an unknown style. In particular, getting a violin player to play double-stopping fiddle was downright impossible. I even took a couple of my records to lend to a very good violinist and asked him to study the style. He brought back my records to explain to me that one player could not possibly sound like that – I would have to have *two* fiddles playing at once to get the effect. How I wished he could have seen and heard Colleen's fiddle flying into it. Australia had Alan Swanson and Peter Mollison and Eileen McCoy (Ada Beard), who all played the old-style fiddle and played it well, but the fast, double-stopping style didn't seem to be there.

The club scene in Sydney began its boom in the 1960s, and with the American servicemen on R&R leave in town, the

Texas Tavern in Kings Cross boasted a country band and singer presenting American-style country. Kevin King and friends had a regular gig at the Crystal Palace near Central Station; the popular country of Merle Haggard and Buck Owens, plus all the Nashville country of George Jones and Tammy Wynette and so on were the styles usually featured. These artists were the top American performers at the time, and we enjoyed their songs very much. Indeed, when Buck Owens brought his band to Australia, the record company invited us to see the show when we were in town.

A very interesting statistic of country record sales at the time is that Australian country artists outsold Americans by seven to one, but it was not Australian country that was usually performed and played (in Sydney, at any rate). That is, until Slim and I began working back in the city again, and we took the same show to a Sydney club that we took to a country one. Later on we took it to the Sydney Opera House too, but that was a long way ahead. It might have been a huge encouragement if we had been able to see into the future, because we were still a minority, although it appears that Slim was a unique minority of one who broke through every now and then with something different.

When we came home after the New Zealand tour, we had to get back to work. We'd had a break before the NZ tour, but we organised our Queensland winter tour during that break and it wasn't long before we were on the road again, up through western Queensland to the Isa and over to the Queensland coast to follow the winter sun. We spent every winter for seventeen years somewhere in Queensland and the north, and, my word, didn't it hurt when we had to stay in Sydney or Metung for the first time over winter!

When we left for western Queensland and the Territory, we engaged a country singer from the Tamworth area, Michael Cooke. The variety act was a dog trainer and his performing kelpies, an outstanding animal act. To top off the singing part of the show, we asked Gordon Parsons (that writer of 'A Pub with No Beer') to come along for the trip and liven up the company. As we were not going to do the round-Australia journey this time, I was looking for any different way of going up through Queensland and over to Halls Creek and Kununurra then round back to Katherine and up to Darwin, and my eye lit on the track from Elliott in the Territory that took a loop through Top Springs and up to Halls Creek. That looked ideal for my purpose, so I wrote to the manager of what I assumed was Top Springs station and received a very cordial reply from one R.C. Hawke. We were welcome to use the verandah as a stage, if we wished, and there was generator power to augment our own lighting plant, so it all sounded like a good stopover to get us across to the main leg of our tour.

Barry Thornton was still with us, of course. Baz was like a young brother or grown-up son to us. He and Slim had a close relationship in music as Barry understood immediately what guitar sound Slim wanted for a particular song and could provide it for him. Baz was a self-taught guitarist who developed what became known as 'bush ballad guitar', and when Slim introduced him to EMI as an instrumentalist they ended up producing two EPs (extended play 45 rpm records) of his guitar solo instrumentals. As well as playing guitar with us onstage, Barry worked about three or four comedy sketches in his other personality of Mulga Dan, the Pest of the West. He used to tear from one side to the other backstage, from his plugged-in guitar to his prop case, where his greasepaint and baggy clothes were handy to grab for a quick change. Woe betide anyone who was careless enough to shift any of the props or the case, because it would cause a total disaster to the programme, and it would not be only Baz on the warpath but Slim and Joy as well.

So we were travelling through the Territory when we all rolled in from a hideous dirt road to discover that Top Springs was not a cattle station at all but a grog shanty. The building and bar sat in the middle of a large yard that boasted 44-gallon fuel drums, full or empty, scattered around the yard, with empty stubbies and cans littered about for a bit of colour. One look and I knew it was another of my new chum disasters. The R.C. Hawke with the strong, heavy signature was a lady, the sister of a well-known strongman, Don Athaldo.

One more look was all it took to convince us that we could not show on the verandah of the bar, which was already in full swing, but the local stock and station agent of the area arrived to offer us the use of his home paddock, far enough from the pub to be a reasonable alternative. We absolutely grabbed at the offer, moved down to his paddock and began setting up the canvas sidewalls again.

We pulled out all the seats we had, erected the small portable stage and wings, and filled the lighting plant with fuel for the night. It was heartening to see the utilities and cars and trucks rolling up, and a good crowd filing in past the ticket box where Aunty Una held sway. The dog act was an extremely good one, and country people all appreciated seeing working dogs show off their skills, so we knew that they would be upstaging the rest of us that night. Laddie and Sunny, in particular, would be showing off as they loved to do; the other three would be offsiders to the two stars of the act, but every kelpie always worked like the stars they reckoned they were.

We opened the show with Michael Cooke, a good country singer and compere, and we were horrified when he was hit with a *full* beer can on his chest mid-chorus. Michael recovered from his shock and went on with his song, but Slim could see that there was more to come, so he roared out onto the stage and grabbed the microphone. I have to forgive his language, but it was along the lines of, 'If you so-and-so such-and-suches want to see the show, shut up and sit down and behave. Any more rubbish like that and I'll close the show and you can get out and go home!' I was waiting behind to help him duck whatever came his way, but there was not a sound out front, and certainly not another beer can. Michael, to his credit, completed his set and introduced the next act.

We had no more bother; Arthur and the kelpies brought the house down; I had the women on my side; Mulga Dan had kids and adults rolling in the aisles, and then Gordon Parsons and Slim had the audience happy as Larry asking for this song and that. We were all relaxed at long last, and closed the show with our finale feeling that we had weathered a very touchy situation.

As we stepped off the stage, the welter began. A huge Islander and a tall, rangy ringer leaped out of their seats and began to belt the life out of each other. It was the signal for every other male in the place to join the brawl. Women and kids cleared out under the sidewalls and the door exits as fast as they could go, and the inside area became a huge arena for the biggest brawl we had ever seen. Slim and I were facing the fact that this could be the end of all our precious equipment; lights, sidewalls, amplifiers, seats, stage, instruments – perhaps our arms and legs as well. Then it sank into our terrified minds that we, and our equipment, were being totally ignored as the battle raged in and around the seats and walls out the front.

Aunty Una and I decided that if they wanted to have a playground brawl, they could have it, so long as they didn't break our wooden seats and did not interfere with our packing them up. So we just began folding and stacking the seats and getting them out of the fighters' way, while Slim and the men began dismantling and packing the stage gear. Every so often a dusty and bloody warrior would appear out of the fog of dirt and dust to assure us that he was protecting good old Slim's belongings and reputation – 'Can't have that sort of thing going on, missus. Teach 'em a lesson; gotta do it' – and so on and so on. If two struggling figures lurched too close in their fisticuffs and wrestling, we poked them hard with the legs of the chair we held so that they lurched the other way and we kept folding and stacking.

As more bodies piled up around the sidewalls and under the seats at the back, someone would haul them outside and drag them into the back of a ute or truck. We were busy suggesting that the dog owner put away his shotgun before some other idiot used it on him or one of us instead.

Gordon was hugely entertained. He had 'been around a bit', as they say, but he swore it was the best donnybrook he'd seen in his entire career – and he had seen some beauties. It made his night when he discovered someone's 'plant' of a carton of coldies underneath old Thunder; as no one claimed it, Gordon reckoned he and the others were entitled to a bit of a party. I just wanted a cup of tea with Aunty Una.

We found out the next day that this brawl had been a catastrophe waiting to happen. How on earth could we have known that there was bad blood between the ringers on Victoria River Downs station and the road workers on the new beef road being constructed? There'd been a few outbreaks, and the ringers resented the fact that the road workers had imported two Thursday Island professional brawlers to boost up their strength. So when the opportunity arose, in the shape of the Slim Dusty Show, for everyone to get together and settle the matter of honour, they could hardly wait to get started. After all, this way they got their entertainment twice; music and fists. What more could a red-blooded bloke want?

It was a relief to reach Halls Creek, driving through Old Halls Creek and the mullock heaps of the early goldfields. By the time we reached Darwin and camped at Howard Springs we were ready to enjoy the company of Auntie Billie, the park caretakers Ken and Dot Kerr, and the little theatre crowd and their wonderful friendships. Each night after showing in the theatre, we would drive back to Howard Springs and our caravans. It was always cooler there than in the city. We were camped in an informal area of the grounds, near the fence that divided the recreation area from the national park. We were able to have a campfire if we liked, and a swim at any hour in the big natural swimming hole fed by a small watercourse.

Gordon was a keen fisherman and often brought me nice fish to cook that he assured me he had caught in the creek on the camp side of the fence – definitely not in the national park area. Far be it from me to doubt, or to look a gift fish in the mouth, but I couldn't help wondering how no one else seemed able to hook one in the creek.

Gordon was very popular in the show, and he got on well with everyone in the camp, so we sailed along very happily after Darwin, down the track and across to Mount Isa for rodeo week. We showed there for the week but it was not long before Gordon fell to temptation.

The caravan was behind the hall, and we always had a quick cuppa during interval as a way of making sure we still had our complete troupe on hand to open the second half. Years of coping with the odd, or not so odd, performer who liked too much to drink – whether onstage or not – had made us issue the rule that there was no drinking of alcohol backstage, and everyone had to be sober to perform in the show. Anyone was welcome to drink him- or herself silly after the show and on nights off, but we had found that if we relaxed the rule to say, 'Just one won't hurt', there was always the person who could not stop at one, or even two, and we'd have a real problem on our hands.

On this particular night I came out and made the tea, put out the snacks and called Slim and Gordon. No Gordon anywhere, and we got the old sinking feeling in our stomachs. Sure enough, it was three days before he showed up again, with a monster-sized hangover. In the meantime we had worked hard to fill in the time his act was supposed to have been onstage;

we knew that once he'd started on the tear, there'd be no way he would stop. The town was full of rodeo riders and GP admirers and Gordon could not resist the camaraderie of the bar at every Isa pub. He trotted out the usual regrets: 'A man shouldn't do this sort of thing'; 'Well, I suppose a man should get out of the way after this'; 'It's a bad thing to do', etc., etc. I informed him rather tartly that I reckoned he enjoyed every minute of it. Gordon thought we should pay him the cash for the plane flight home and he'd 'get out of the road'; I thought I should just buy the ticket and, in person, see that he actually got on the plane home, where he would be safer than let loose in roaring Mount Isa Rodeo week.

Just the same, we missed him very much – and not just because his leaving made work that much harder for us. We missed his happy personality around the camp and his cheery outlook on life, so we shook our heads and told each other, 'Well, that's just old Ned (as Slim called him) and he'll never change!' Neither did our affection for him, let it be said.

The club scene was flourishing, and next thing we knew we had agents wanting to book us. The most interesting request came from Papua New Guinea. We thought Ted Whittaker and Raphael Boivan were entrepreneurs from Port Moresby who approached us for a short tour. Actually, they were an ex-patrol officer and his offsider who'd had a win in the Queensland Golden Casket lottery. They'd decided to invest in a tour with Slim Dusty because he was the best-known singer in the Pacific area. Apparently radio announcers in PNG liked to call him 'King of the Jungle Airwaves' – not that Slim or I knew this. We had no idea of his huge popularity right throughout the Pacific and even in Asian areas such as Hong Kong and Singapore. We were so isolated on our outback tours that such news never reached us. When we were once told how a fan had bought Slim's records or cassettes in Abu Dhabi or Dubai, we weren't too sure our legs weren't being pulled … hard. However, the other thing we did not know about all those sales was that they were pirated records and cassettes. We didn't make a penny or cent from them, and nor did our record company.

Anyway, we couldn't resist the offer from Ted and Raphael, as we'd never been to PNG and it was a very good offer of a tour in May 1970. We accepted it, and then planned the rest of our year's touring around it. We put together the new programme for a Western Australia tour early in the year, before the PNG trip, and then booked the artists for the Queensland and Territory tour in the second half of 1970.

CHAPTER 16

In late 1969, the Poseidon mining company had announced a big nickel strike just outside Kalgoorlie in Western Australia, and we landed there with the show the following January. We always looked forward to showing in Kalgoorlie with its old-time atmosphere and sense of the romance of the goldfields. Its twin city, Boulder, had the mines still roaring away, but Kalgoorlie itself was the opposite with the old town hall and its red velvet–covered seats; the rabbit warren of tiny backstage dressing rooms up and down steep stairs; and the statue of Paddy Hannan, who first struck gold at Kalgoorlie, outside the town hall till vandals made it necessary to move his monument inside the town hall foyer.

Kalgoorlie kept up a couple of traditions from the roaring goldfields days, one being the two-up school. When it was proposed that it should be officially closed down because it was obviously illegal, there were screams of protest everywhere. Not only did the players object but so did the tourist operators. 'What would Kalgoorlie be without the two-up and cockatoos on alert and all the attraction of being able to go to a known illegal entertainment?' they cried.

The other tradition, of course, was the street of lights – red lights, mainly, but some establishments went to town on their decorations. I had seen the 'houses of ill repute' the first time we went to Kalgoorlie, when we had accidentally driven along the street looking for the right way to our caravan park. These were small houses with corrugated iron fences on either side, closing each off from its neighbour. That way, no visitor at one house could be seen by occupants of the next. I wasn't driving that time, so I was intrigued by all these bright houses where scantily dressed ladies sat or stood under the doorway lights. Slim had tried to shut me up as I'd exclaimed in wonder, 'What on earth is going on there?' and I finally discovered that from then on my husband made sure he knew a better route to the caravan park. I never did get to see them again.

When we hit town in January 1970, Kalgoorlie was full of mining types in every hotel, bar, mining office, stockbroker's rooms and on the streets. The town was raging the way I'd always imagined it used to back in the goldstrike days. Everyone was crazy about buying mining shares, not just Poseidon's, which had gone through the roof in price while the bubble lasted. The excitement in the air was thick enough to be felt and we were a part of it.

I remembered, though, showing at two nearby old gold towns, Menzies and Leonora. Menzies had a bitumen road to it and that was a welcome treat, but the air of desolation was disheartening when we reached the town after passing old mine workings and old houses, made of a lovely pink-coloured stone, that were tumbling down everywhere. There was one petrol bowser and one hotel still operating, while the town hall boasted an imposing brick façade disguising a corrugated iron building behind. We left there and headed across the desert to Leonora, having been assured that we would have a good crowd for the show. The town had one long street with closed shops and hotels, and faded signs such as the one on a deserted building: *Meals and beds 2/6.*

The Federal Hall in Leonora had antiquated picture theatre projectors lying around, and even an old magic lantern sort of thing that had us intrigued. Even with its seats and our own, we still didn't have enough seating for the crowd that turned up that night. Looking out of town to the desert had not made us think that there was anyone close enough to come to the show, but the old hall was filled to capacity. There were station people and fossickers, miners and families. Some had come many miles from out in the desert. During the afternoon a trip to Gwalia, a ghost town about two miles away, was a real eyeopener. Out in the middle of the desert, the Sons of Gwalia mine was discovered in the early 1900s, operational about 1933 and still going in the 1950s. You could wander in and out of old mining buildings and look at old log sheets that dated as far back as 1911.

Most of the houses were made of corrugated iron and had doors flapping open in the wind, or they were remains of houses gutted by fire. Old shops were shuttered, with their faded signwriting a pathetic reminder of a once-thriving community. A fine old brick hotel, the most solid building in the town, had iron over the windows; the deserted mine had huge machinery lying idle, and wheelbarrows were left where they were last used. I was not sorry to leave what was left of the town; my imagination was working overtime.

When we crossed the Nullarbor that January we had the performing dog act with us, along with Michael Cooke, Margaret Mile and the Vilsteys. Bill and Vera Vilstey were old friends from the Frank Foster showground days, when they worked with us. Originally from Hungary and Germany, they had migrated to Australia after the war and worked in circuses with their dental trapeze act. They actually worked their act on the high trapeze in the circus ring, but when they performed on the grounds and in clubs they adapted their trapeze very cleverly. They had the scaffolding built so that the putting up and pulling down of the trapeze became part of the entertainment. Bill had also perfected a small magic act specifically to appeal to the children in the hall, so that particular year's programme had a lot of variety in it.

Crossing the Nullarbor that year was fraught with menace. We needed to stick together when camping because there had been two murders on the crossing. Two hitchhikers were camped with their host at Ivy Tanks. The next morning, another traveller noted a figure under a blanket in the car and enquired if he was sick. He was told, 'No. He's just sleeping.' As the traveller had seen three people in the car the previous day, he thought it a bit strange. Later, towards Norseman, he saw the car again but he couldn't see the third person, so he reported it to the police station. They found the car in a back street with the owner's body in it, and the two hikers trying to hitch a ride out of Norseman. Around the same time, another man travelling alone camped not far out from Ivy Tanks. His naked body was found thrown into the bushes nearby. Understandably, we were all nervous, and for once we had no trouble keeping the troops all together on that crossing.

Our camp problems began in the west when the dog trainer's wife could not seem to get on with any of the other women in the troupe, except Aunty Una, who wouldn't stand any of her nonsense anyway. The woman's drinking, which went on unseen day and night, turned her nasty and people began avoiding her to save unpleasantness. At times she could not assist in the act as she should, and by interval each night she was getting bleary eyed and ready to start an argument with anyone handy. She antagonised everyone in the show, men and women both, one after the other. When Aunty and I were the only other women around she was not too difficult to put up with, but she hated Vera and barely tolerated young Marg. As it turned out, the dog trainers were from Perth originally and it was convenient for them to leave us there. It was awkward for us, though, as we had provided them with a caravan which we then had to freight back to the East. But the peace and quiet for the rest of the tour, and back home, was worth it.

We noticed smaller crowds at some of our shows and realised that television had only started in the west in November. So it was doing to us in the west what it had already done to us and everyone else back home in the eastern states. In the meantime, a cyclone was wreaking damage north and east, and heating up the whole southern area as well – but it didn't cause as much damage in our little travelling community as our dog lady had done. We were glad to get to Geraldton and did not complain about the constantly blowing wind. The first time I saw the trees along the coast to Geraldton, I was fascinated by the way they were bent over parallel to the earth. The wind is so strong and so ceaseless that they grow that way.

The heat was stifling in our caravan homes, as many parks had little shade. Working every night meant that we needed a rest in the afternoon so our energy did not flag as we reached the second half of the show. But the relentless furnace that was the West Australian summer when a cyclone was near would usually wreck any sleep we tried to get. Still, it was amazing and cheering to see how we all livened up the minute the lights went out in the hall and footlights went up on the stage.

I found a spot under a high tank stand with a leaky tank, and Hans and I made the most of it one afternoon. The best way to cool off was to pour water over yourself while fully dressed, then turn on the fan and stand in front of it. It was 110 degrees Fahrenheit (43 degrees Celsius) that day, and 94 degrees (34 degrees Celsius) that night. By then we were concentrating on survival only, not comfort.

The Eastern Highway was three feet under water in one place towards Kalgoorlie, and the Eastern Railway was cut at Southern Cross. In Cue houses had been unroofed by the cyclone. School was being held in the hall because the school building no longer had a roof. Cyclones were a fact of life over in the north-west, but fortunately we were never to experience the full force of one.

We had turned our heads for home after Cue and showed our way along the Eastern Highway that, thankfully, was dry again. In Merredin I looked in the front row for the two old people I'd seen in the audience before. Sure enough, there they were. I had made enquiries about them after they caught my attention the first time I saw them. They were music teachers in the town; he played piano accordion and his wife played piano and organ. They always sat in the front row, and they dressed up for the occasion. He usually wore a black velvet jacket and stiff white shirt, while she wore a long velvet skirt with a formal blouse. They were outstanding in their dress and in their reception of the music in the show. They applauded generously, and gave especially warm applause for any musical solo or song that they particularly enjoyed. People were not aware that from the stage I could see many of them very clearly, and it was a pleasure to witness pure enjoyment on someone's face down there in the audience.

As we toured many towns nearly every year, I used to look for familiar faces. We got to know some people like the old music teachers, and another family over in Queensland, from the fact that they always sat in the front row. In Charleville, Fred and Edith Warner brought their family and friends in from Boatman station, 130 kilometres out of town. They were always there, even if one year the boggy roads stopped them from arriving till nearly finale time. It was the old music teachers at Merredin and Fred Warner at Charleville who gave me the inspiration for my song 'The Front Row'.

The May tour to Papua New Guinea was upon us before we knew it, and we left Sydney for Port Moresby with the old team of Slim, Barry and me, plus Michael Cooke and another country singer, Kevin King. Anne and David also joined us. Anne had recorded a few songs with Slim over the years, so she was singing in the show on holidays, and David came along to do any odd jobs that turned up.

Ted and Raphael and about a thousand locals met us at the airport. Ted was an Australian and Raphael was a Sepik River man. They had done a great job with the publicity, to the point that there were people sitting up in the trees around the motel where we stayed, hoping to catch a glimpse of any one of us whenever we ventured out the door. If we tried to take a walk down the street, within a hundred yards we had a following entourage of admirers. We visited the markets and were mobbed there as well, and we were glad to get to the Port Moresby football arena for the first show of the tour.

We took a look out at the crowd and thought that if public interest during the day was anything to judge by, the crowd should have been bigger. Still, we lowered the lights, lit up the stage and went into the opening number. Well, talk about tidal waves ... that was what it was like at every point in the high fence around the arena. People swarmed over the top of the fence and filled the arena to capacity; those who missed out climbed the surrounding trees and watched from there.

Ted and Raphael couldn't believe their eyes, but their takings at the ticket office when compared with the size of the crowd certainly made them understand what they were seeing. I felt very sympathetic towards them. It was a harsh lesson in crowd control for two very genuine men who were, nevertheless, amateurs in the tough world of entertainment promotion. When we showed Lae in the hall made of Besser bricks, built in accordance with the demands of the local climate, it allowed half the population to stand outside and look through the generous gaps in the walls.

We flew between shows in DC3 planes; old but reliable, we were assured. And as we sometimes flew in mountainous country such as Mount Hagen, any nervous passengers relied on such assurance. We discovered that the local people were amazed that Slim was not an old, old man. He had been singing for so long that they were convinced he must have been on his last legs and were pleased to find out that he was not. In one town Slim was a bit surprised by a comparatively lukewarm reception as he walked onstage. He couldn't find his hat at the last moment as he was announced, and he went out to the microphone leaving Michael and Kevin madly searching for his Akubra. Kevin found it and raced out onto the stage, slamming the hat onto Slim's head as he was singing his opening number. The audience erupted into cheers and laughter, and Slim could do no wrong from there on. Without his hat, they hadn't been too sure if he was really Slim Dusty or not.

Ted took Slim and Barry over to Honiara in the Solomon Islands to make a couple of appearances, as they couldn't afford the full show. I travelled back to Australia with the rest of the team and our equipment. Slim and Barry told us all about the amazing reception they had received in the Solomons, and how they performed at an open air show down at the docks, the only place to hold all the crowd.

There were so many people around the hotel where they stayed that the hotel manager asked Slim to come outside and make an appearance before the people trampled what was left of his gardens. By the time I heard all this, I thought a bit of 'down to earthing' was in store for my husband before he expected some sort of special treatment back here on his home turf.

I needn't have been concerned, as there were plenty of jobs waiting for him when he arrived. First of all, there had to be a very big discussion about our future. We had booked our

Queensland and Territory itinerary, and the artists for it, before we left for PNG, but there were more personal matters to be decided upon, and fairly quickly too.

We had always tried to make a living out of touring, while saving the royalty cheques so far as possible. That was, until we mortgaged them to buy the small farm near Metung. But the most recent cheques were bigger than ever before and the record company was asking for more and more material, plus a lot more business contact with us. Anne was in her last year at school down at St Anne's. She was aiming to do well in her final year and get a Commonwealth scholarship to university, preferably in Melbourne. She and David had both recently topped their classes, and we were thrilled that they were doing so well at school. Our problem with Anne's uni plans was that we knew not a soul in Melbourne and could not face having Anne move there on her own. She would have some of her school friends, but no older person as a backstop. To move her to Sydney, where we had relations and friends, was the most sensible and the safest thing to do. From every angle it was the right decision, but it meant moving our home base from Metung, away from Mack and Lorna and all the second-family friends we had there.

That was a really hard choice to make, but it was made and we bought a comfortable home at Carlingford, not too far from Macquarie University nor from Kate and Gerry Ormsby in North Parramatta; we were still in touch with Gerry, the instigator of the *Melody Trail* programme. Slim and I did not plan to move in to the house until after our Queensland and Territory tour, so we headed off with a different team once again.

We were showing Tennant Creek on our way back from Darwin and heading over to Mount Isa for rodeo week in August when Slim received a telegram from his older half-brother, Victor. It said, *Ring me at 5 p.m. Urgent. Victor.* We knew it could only be about Slim's mother, Granny Kirk. Sure enough, when

Slim got on the phone, Victor told him that their mother had died half an hour earlier. She had not been ill but had been living in the geriatric wing of Kempsey hospital, and at 80 years of age she was just tired and weary of life. Slim's old friend Shorty had written to Slim at Camooweal but Slim had not yet received the letter that said his mother was failing. He hadn't received her last letter either. Our isolation hit home bitterly.

Slim did the show that night. People had come from near and far and they'd never have known anything was wrong. I spent hours both that night and in the morning trying to get transport from Tennant Creek in the Territory to Kempsey on the mid north coast of New South Wales. Finally we went via Adelaide, Melbourne and Sydney, and in a hire car reached her funeral in Kempsey with half an hour to spare. We hadn't even told her that Slim was to be presented with an MBE in October; he'd wanted to surprise her. We'd had a phone call earlier down at Metung to ask if Slim would accept the award, and he had not hesitated to say yes. To us, this was more than an award to Slim – it meant acceptance of what he was doing, and what we and other country artists were doing: keeping alive Australian music and Australian stories. If the award drew attention to the fact that bush ballads and country music in Australia were worthy of recognition, it was an exciting thing indeed. Maybe it was a signal for all those people who had hidden their country records to pull them out again.

In October, Sir Rohan Delacombe presented Slim with his MBE; Mack and I were there with him. We couldn't take Anne and David, as only two people were allowed to accompany Slim, and Slim felt that I should be one of the two. We could not take only one of the children, so Mack took the part of our other family member. Later in October there was a Melbourne Gold Record presentation for Slim as well. Bob Hawke, then the head of the Australian Council of Trade Unions, did the honours on that occasion.

The last show of the tour was generally held at Bairnsdale in Victoria and as usual the proceeds were donated to the local Noweyung Centre for the Intellectually Disabled. Lorna, Cora and Mack were foundation members of the small group that established this centre. Lorna and Mack's daughter Allison had been born with a dead thyroid gland, and brain damage was done before the deficiency was found a year later. Like so many other parents, the main worry for Lorna and Mack was, 'What will happen to Allison when we die?' That's why the parents of such children, like those Gippsland parents, work so hard for the establishment of halfway houses and homes and carers for these children who become adults and orphans. Every dollar we raised with our annual concerts was designated towards the building and maintenance of one of these houses. (After Slim's death, Anne and I would attend the opening of Noweyung's newest home, Slim Dusty House. We were very proud that day.)

At the time of the last show of this tour there was an aura of change in the air, in more ways than one. With Granny Kirk's death our isolation had been brought home to us in a very sad way, and we felt we could not remain so far away from the children all the time. We were worried about Barry too: he was having attacks of some sort of faintness where he would turn chalk white and have to lean up against a support so that he didn't fall over. He refused to see a doctor until we got home to Metung, and when an appointment with a specialist in Melbourne was not available for three months, I called everyone I knew in Sydney until we got one there in January. We all packed up – Slim, Anne, David and me, plus Barry, Pauline, Meryl and Brian – and moved to Sydney to get Barry to the specialist.

The diagnosis was not very satisfactory. There was some early concern about a brain tumour but, thank goodness, that concern was eliminated. After hospital tests we were given a rather vague diagnosis involving blood vessels in the brain as well as an imbalance in the middle ear. However, we were able to relax and stop worrying about him all the time. And Baz seemed the least worried out of all of us.

Change was everywhere in our lives. Anne finished school and prepared for university. David was still in high school in Sale, and, given the choice, he had opted to stay at Gippsland Grammar for the time being rather than come to a Sydney school. Slim and I had discussed our future in touring and recording, and we faced the fact that with Anne out of school and David now in high school, we needed to be around a lot more than we had been. Further, as there was much more recording to be done, we needed to be closer to the studios and to the musicians.

We also realised that we could work in clubs now if we wished, and we could do shorter tours. As Slim had to do a fair bit of recording, and as I generally helped with the selecting and finding of songs in those days – plus sometimes writing one and keeping our bookings under control – we were both flat out. I went to every recording session and had always done so from the first time I went to sing harmony for him on 'Losin' My Blues Tonight' in 1953. It was a support for him, and I was on hand to sing harmony or back him up if we had any problems on the day.

When we first began recording, the control room was out of bounds for the artists. The engineers wore white coats and a lofty expression most of the time. We would have three hours to complete six songs; halfway through the session the tea lady would bring a trolley of tea and biscuits to the studio. It took some years before artists penetrated this wall of 'Go away, you're only the singer.' Having two of us pushing for the same things helped us to gradually wear down the wall. Recording sessions have gone to the opposite extreme now, perhaps.

CHAPTER 17

It was a strange beginning to the new year of 1971. No Mack leaning on the doorjamb reciting his latest effort with Lorna interjecting 'Speak up, Mack' as the verses softened into an embarrassed mumble; no Christmas stockings hanging on the fireplace mantelpiece; and no fresh fish for breakfast. Instead of looking out the kitchen window over the trees and along Chinamans Creek, I overlooked a swimming pool and small backyard and over the fence to a paddock with some horses grazing there. That paddock was a big selling point to the house for people like us.

When we had discussed this change the previous year, Slim had thought it was the best thing to do and had looked forward to being close to the recording studios, and to being able to do shorter tours and bigger one-off concerts and promotions instead of the nonstop eleven months of the year we had spent outback touring. When the real thing began, though, he was not so impressed; in plain words, he became an absolute pain in the neck. He grizzled about being in the one place all the time; he didn't want to do anything around the big front yard or even the back. As for the swimming pool, which he enjoyed using, it was a cleaning and maintenance duty that he didn't want to know about, and when he did do it he complained loudly and constantly.

There was a bus strike in Sydney when the university term started, and between us we had to drive Anne to Macquarie University and back again each day. That didn't suit either, although Slim didn't begrudge Anne the assistance. It was all *my* fault, somehow. Anyone would have thought I had put handcuffs and leg ropes on him and physically dragged him to big bad Sydney against his will. This time it was me who was about ready to divorce my husband, not the other way around.

There was a heap of recording to be done, though, and that kept Slim very busy for quite a time. Luckily, he loved recording. Moreover, we had friends and relations in Sydney; Gordon Parsons was a regular caller who was on the phone with yarns and news every couple of days, Barry was around the corner more or less, and the songs were being collected and written and rehearsed. About this time, the flow of material from all over Australia began to gather momentum. This was a great encouragement to us because it demonstrated the reach of Slim's music, but, as could be imagined, many of the poems or songs we received were not suitable for Slim's use. We checked every one, though, believe it or not. There were some gems amongst them, and sometimes we'd find a lyric that was not quite good enough but we could see that the writer had the ability to come up with what Slim wanted if he or she was encouraged to keep trying. In quite a few cases, that's what we did; if Slim didn't ring, I would write. It was remarkable to see what had been lying around in old exercise books or writing pads in drawers until the bush people realised that here, at last, was a voice for them.

All the time we were on tour, we heard stories and experienced things that affected the people and the country around us. One thing that stood out in the late 1960s and early 1970s was the number of strikes that occurred all over the nation, seemingly all the time. Freighter ships didn't like having to unload in Darwin because the wharfies were likely to throw a strike on at a moment's notice; there were electricity strikes, rail strikes, petrol strikes, bus strikes, strikes at the Mount Isa mines – you name it and there would have been a strike about it. I got fed up with it at one point – the same as the rest of the population – and wrote a song I called 'Ned Kelly was a Gentleman'. It let me blow off steam, and Slim was going to record it in his next session.

When we arrived home after a tour, there was a pile of parcel mail waiting, including a new album from John Ashe in Townsville. I looked at it and was appalled to see a song listed, by the same name as mine – 'Ned Kelly was a Gentleman'. It was a completely different song but the whole idea was the same and I was horrified. What if John, a good friend and a lovely man, thought I had seen and heard his record *before* I wrote my song? I couldn't wait to get in touch, and John said, 'Well, I would have wondered what was going on!' It was one of those coincidences that could have caused the end of a friendship if not straightened out in the very beginning. Just the same, I have kept the little notebook with all my original scribblings, words and rewritings.

Songwriters are a funny bunch; that includes yours truly. Too much attention given to one of the bush ballad writers and the others would get offended. If the printer made an error on the record cover – say, a name was left off or written incorrectly – you could bet the injured party would be convinced that it was done deliberately by Slim or by me for our own reasons, whatever they thought they were. Over the years we tried to be diplomatic, as every writer was a friend, really, even if some had very short fuses. One took offence over something, and to this day I don't know what it was, and he sent a fiery letter withdrawing all his material and berating us for whatever he thought we had done. We let him cool off for a couple of years, then he woke up to himself and we ended up great mates despite it all. In the end, after 30 or 40 years of being nice about the shenanigans, I did lose patience with some and said my piece. They say there has to be a dragon in every team.

We were in at the EMI studios one day in March that year when who should turn up but Colleen Bain – except she was no longer Colleen Bain but Mrs Paul Trenwith. She and Paul materialised, to Slim's amazement, and he gave them a rather laidback reception, saying, 'What on earth are you doing here?' Having left the Hamilton County Bluegrass Band in New Zealand lamenting the fact that we were all on two different sides of the ocean, it was a happy shock to see them. We were even happier to find that the HCBB had taken the big step of getting themselves to Australia to do some work with Tex Morton. They were, of course, looking for all the work they could get and Slim lost no time in asking Colleen to put down a couple of tracks on the album.

The HCBB now consisted of three originals – Colleen, Paul and Alan Rhodes – and two new members, Graham Lovejoy and Miles Reay. They were a very compatible and cheerful group, and while we did a lot of good work together in the recording studio, we all looked forward to the day we could tour together as well. However, they were committed to the promise of work with Tex, so we just worked together when we could. The band members were great company and were often over at Carlingford for rehearsals and barbecues, but the promised work for the HCBB was not forthcoming.

With all these young people around all the time, we found ourselves exposed to a lot more styles of country and bluegrass music. Anne had joined the Bluegrass Club at university and unleashed a completely different voice as she sang songs by Paul

Siebel and other new singer songwriters, plus all the country and bluegrass tunes she learned. Slim and I knew many of them as well but hadn't sung them for years.

Meanwhile, in Melbourne, an EMI retailer who ran bookshops and record stores happened to glance through the record catalogue and see the Slim Dusty listing of releases. 'This man's got more releases than the Beatles!' was Greg Young's reaction. As he and a colleague did quite a bit of concert promotion, he immediately made contact through EMI and booked Slim and the team for three Melbourne concerts. Two were in the Melbourne Town Hall and the other at Monash University. We took Barry and the HCBB with us, plus Anne and guitarist Colin Watson, whom she'd met at university.

The two Town Hall concerts were fine, but when we set out for the university Slim was definitely touchy about it. Having suffered jibes for years about country music, and especially the bush ballad, he was expecting more of the same from a hall full of uni students and he was prepared to give as good as he expected to get. He was pumped up as he strode out onto the stage, and was flabbergasted when those university students rose to their feet and gave him a standing ovation before he so much as uttered a sound. 'Why, didn't you know you have a cult following in the university crowd?' Greg explained. Well, no, Slim didn't and neither did I, of course. But it was a huge relief to find out in such a nice way.

We had a short Queensland tour booked to begin in June that year and, after the mammoth recording stint, got ready to leave for the north. Anne would have a young married couple living in the house with her while we were away, and David was boarding at Gippsland Grammar. Still, I was not happy when we left for Queensland. Anne was fine, but I worried about Davy. I was concerned because, although we had discussed the changes in our life with David, and given him the right to think about and make the final decision of what he wanted to do, he had opted to stay at Sale with his friends and with Mack and Lorna at Homewood on long weekends. Again, this was a sensible decision in theory, but in practice the fact that Anne was no longer in Sale at St Anne's and that we were in Sydney, and then on tour, meant that David felt much more isolated than he thought he would.

Being a decisive sort of boy, he did something about it. He and three others took off on an unauthorised trek from Sale to Sydney. David was the leader, and his teachers later remarked admiringly on his leadership and compassionate qualities in the way he organised the trip and took great care of a friend whose health was not strong. But the boys didn't get too far before the school and authorities caught up with them and, amid a flurry of phone calls and telegrams, managed to get the boys back to school. That was fright number one for us; we felt that if David was so unsettled now that our base was really Sydney, he should move too. But, to begin with, between us we thought he would give it another go at settling down.

In early June 1971 we left Sydney in a convoy of three to meet up with the rest of the show at Warwick, over the border in Queensland, and open the tour at Kingaroy on 7 June. Barry drove Lightning and one caravan; Slim drove Thunder with the big van on behind, and I drove a Holden station wagon towing a loaded caravan.

Winter seemed to come early that year, and it was bitterly cold and raining cats and dogs by the time I passed through Tamworth and headed up into the Moonbi Ranges on the New England Highway. Slim and Barry were well ahead of me, but that didn't worry me too much. It was the lights of the trucks heading down to Sydney for the morning markets that worried me a lot more. They used to come over the crests of the hills towards me and blaze into my eyes before the driver lowered them in return for my lowering my own headlights.

The problem for me was the fact that cars of the day had the dimmer switch for headlights on the floor, not on the steering wheel as they do now. That made three pedals on the floor of an automatic vehicle, and I had only one foot that worked to use those three controls. My left foot, polio affected, was of no use and under normal circumstances my good foot was fine to control the brake and accelerator while the headlights were on normal brilliance. But in the rain and black night on a windy mountain road, I needed the high beam to alert me to the turns. As a truck came over the crest towards me, I had to take my foot off the accelerator and quickly hit the dimmer switch, then get back to the accelerator before the load in the wagon and caravan pulled me back on the hill. It was in those seconds that I felt out of control of my outfit, but I certainly had the foot juggling down to a fine art by the time I left the mountains behind.

As I passed Armidale and headed for Guyra I travelled by the Devils Pinch, a stretch of road with a drop on one side. I was finding the regular sweep of the windscreen wipers a bit hypnotic and had begun singing to myself to make sure I did not go to sleep at the wheel. But as I saw the drop, I couldn't help wondering how long it would take Slim to find me if I lost control when the truck lights blinded me and went over the Devils Pinch. That was when the story of 'Lights on the Hill' began unfolding in my mind and in the song I was singing to myself. The music kept time with the sweep of the wipers, the words were fitting to the music and the story was being told in my head.

When I reached Warwick, Slim was already unhooking Thunder and the big van. It was about nine o'clock, I think.

'I wrote a song while I was coming,' I said as I opened the door of the caravan.

'Well, you'd better put it down before you forget it,' was his reply and, funnily enough, that's what I did.

I hauled out one of the guitars and the little cassette recorder and recorded a rough demo of 'Lights on the Hill'. Then I put it away and more or less forgot about it until the end of the tour and of the year.

As we headed up the Queensland coast to Cairns and Mareeba and out towards Mount Isa with a new team, the show seemed to be going well. Going to Mount Isa before rodeo week was a bit of a gamble, but we promised ourselves that the following year we'd be back at rodeo time. We showed three nights in the Star Theatre, and I remember being excited and very emotional when I walked out onto the stage the first night to be greeted with a standing ovation. The hard miles, and the hard times, were worth every bit to know that I was part of these people's lives, and that they were happy to have me back in the spinifex and granite country. It made me all the more determined to keep going to the outback, to the Territory, and to keep searching for the stories and songs these people had in store for us to find.

We were on the way home down through New South Wales when we received a phone call and then a visit from the Dubbo police. We were showing Mudgee that night, but the phone calls told me that David had run away from school for a second time. He had set out on his own and made it as far as Eden, on the south coast of New South Wales, before a fatherly policeman spotted him and took him home to his wife and family where he got on the phone to us.

We were distraught; we got David on the first plane we could and flew him to meet us at Bathurst. He walked across the tarmac at that country airport, and he seemed to have grown up and out of not only his school uniform but also his little boy era. I felt for him and could only put my arm around his shoulders or I would have fallen in a heap. I grieved for his upset and his obvious need to be closer to us and to Anne.

At twelve years of age, David was too young to live at home and attend a day school without us being there all the time, so we had to find a vacancy for him at a good Sydney boarding school. He was quite agreeable to that, as he knew our situation. I was terribly worried about his future and his happiness: I knew he was a bright boy and I had great hopes for him, but I also faced the fact that we might have a job to get him into a suitable school at short notice and mid term. His teachers in Sale recommended Trinity in the west of Sydney, and his headmaster sent an introductory letter to the principal.

Anne and David were with us when we went out to Innamincka to visit the Moomba Gas Fields. Years earlier, in Alice Springs, we had met a bush pilot and flown in his old Auster plane out to Ayers Rock, as it was still called then. Slim went out to the airport at Alice to have a look at the plane, and came back to me with a bit of a grin on his face.

'You know, this plane has zip fasteners in the wings so you can inspect the inside struts.'

'Sure, sure, and every wing has extra propellers, I suppose.'

Slim: 'No, hang on. Its shell is made of Irish linen.'

I put my husband down as a leg puller, but not a good one. I did a double take when I got to the airport early next morning to fly out to Ayers Rock, because he was telling the truth.

Artie Hearne, the bush pilot, and his family were now camped at Innamincka while he (and a new plane) flew supplies and contacts everywhere from Queensland and Adelaide to the gas fields. We flew via Broken Hill, where Artie picked us up and took us to the camp. It was on this trip that we visited the famous Dig Tree at a waterhole on Cooper Creek near Napper Merrie station, and went out to the gas fields to give an impromptu concert of two people for the workers there. It was a side of outback living that we had not seen before: the small settlement of Innamincka; Artie's camp nearby with the plane on a small, rough tarmac. He was a major part of the supply chain, flying goods to the men on the gas fields.

It was a very different picture from Sydney, where upon our return we went back to working in the big clubs that were booming in the early 1970s. The entertainment in these clubs was amazing, really. We took bookings of four nights in places like Marrickville and St George clubs. The programme usually included a ballet, other acts and singers or variety acts, plus the Slim Dusty Show, which was usually a full hour of Slim and the band. We had promised ourselves a year of change and a break from the eleven-month outback tours, and we certainly got what we promised. We could not get used to the club atmosphere, but we found that audiences were just the same as those we played to out in the bush, and Slim gave them the same performances as he gave everywhere else. We had been away from the city ever since rock 'n' roll took over, and we'd become used to having to defend our country music preference against lofty putdowns by rock, classical or jazz lovers, or even from other musos. But during the 1960s and '70s more and more country people were forced to move to the city for work, and they were making their own wishes heard: they wanted a lot more country music, and especially they wanted to see Slim Dusty, whose records they played at home. Then the concert and clubgoers who had hidden their country records under the nearest rock during the time they were laughed at decided to pull them out and also start asking for live country music. Somewhere along the line, city listeners had started to hear about Slim Dusty too. So we enjoyed the break and made the most of it.

Then, with Paul and Colleen, we went down to Homewood at Metung to stay for a while over the Christmas and New Year break. It was then that I remembered 'that song' I'd written on the long, rainy drive from Sydney to Warwick. I ratted around the box of cassette tapes and found the one on which I'd recorded a rough version of 'Lights on the Hill'. I wanted to play it to Colleen and to hear her play her double-stopping fiddle behind it. Imagine my frustration and, indeed, my indignation when I discovered that Slim had used the tape to rehearse some song or other and wiped out a good half of my song. I was sounding off in good old fishwife style and Slim quite blithely said, 'Oh, you can write it again!' and then went out fishing.

As he took Paul and Colleen with him, I thought I might as well try to resurrect my poor neglected song. I got the vamping bass going on the old piano to help me find the feel of the melody and I started remembering most of the words as I went along, banging away on the stained old ivory keys. I still have the little notebook with my rewriting of 'Lights' and I wasn't too disappointed with the result when I sang it to Colleen that evening. She played fiddle behind it as soon as she heard it, and she and Paul were adamant that it would be a good one for Slim to record.

Slim, however, was not impressed: 'Too many words. You'd have to change it so a man could get enough breath in between the lines.'

'No, you wouldn't! Just do it like this!' and so it went.

'No, it's not my style, give it to someone else,' was the other argument.

This was the first, and only, time that I argued against Slim about one of my songs. Normally, I let him hear anything I wrote and it was up to him whether he wanted to record it or not. But I believed in 'Lights', and with Colleen's support and genuine agreement that it would be a good song for Slim, I didn't want to give way. I was quite certain he'd sing it easily once he got used to the idea.

As it turned out, I let it be for a while, but the band didn't. By the time Slim began recording in February the next year, with the HCBB in the studio with him, they had lined up a Kiwi electric lead guitarist they knew and Slim recorded his first version of 'Lights on the Hill'. He found it difficult because it was a totally different style of song for him, but Slim was a natural singer and once he did get the feel of 'Lights', to my way of thinking he was the only singer who really dug into the rhythm of it.

Slim recorded 'Lights' in early February 1972 on EMI's new sixteen-track recorder; it was released as a single in the following month of March. By mid March we were on tour in Western Australia and we sent to EMI for a supply of the singles to be shipped to us in Busselton. When the discs arrived safely, Slim bought plenty of brown paper, string and light cardboard, and we packed up each disc with a personal letter to a radio announcer we knew who might play it on his programme. Those were the days when announcers had the privilege of playing their own selection of music for special programmes. It was not like today, when everything is programmed in the capital city and farmed out to the country stations; and talkback radio had not taken over country stations either.

Our amateurish effort to promote 'Lights' paid off – it was such a different song for Slim that it was played and played. It became one of his biggest solid sellers after the 'Pub', and for more than twenty years it was his favourite closer for the show.

All the time we were on this tour, I was worrying about David and whether or not he was happy and willing to settle down at his new school. He flew to the West to join us for Easter, and then joined us in the New South Wales Riverina for the May school holidays; after that I thought maybe I could relax and feel that he was going to be alright. David would go on to be a prefect, School House captain, and a member of the basketball and Rugby teams, but I always hated the thought that he had been so unhappy.

This tour marked the first time we had left our caravan at home and stayed in motels, while the rest of the show used caravans as usual. It was difficult at times to be separated, but we badly needed to be available by phone. We could not continue to be quite so isolated for months on end as we had been in the past. Granny Kirk's death, David's unhappiness at school and Anne looking after herself at Carlingford had been enough to ensure that from here on we had to adjust and do things differently.

CHAPTER 18

It was not just our lifestyle that was changing during this period. Country music as a whole was pushing its way to the forefront once again, and a lot of this was picked up and spearheaded by 2TM radio station in Tamworth, New South Wales. For some years John Minson, better known as Mr Hoedown, had presented a Saturday night country music programme and it had become hugely popular – 2TM had wide coverage and the session was picked up almost everywhere. John had a very engaging personality and a genuine interest in his listeners and the people who called in to say 'hello' or sing a song. Very often, on our nights off in the outback, we could pick up John's cheery voice and hear news of what was going on with other artists around the nation.

When I lived on the farm at Doyles Creek so many years ago, 2TM's midday country music session had been a special listening experience, so I suppose I shouldn't have been too surprised to find that it was 2TM that was getting behind the re-emergence of country music. This time, the management and staff at the station were taking a bigger and more enterprising approach. There had long been a small festive weekend in January where the local country music club held talent quests and concerts. Next thing, 2TM began holding country music concerts as well, and Slim and I became involved in some of these from about 1969 onwards. The radio station and these concerts were becoming a focal point for artists and listeners, and when the idea of a system of awards for country music was suggested, 2TM took it up with enthusiasm.

While this movement was taking place in Tamworth, there were quite a few touring shows such as Rick and Thel out on the road. Reg Lindsay and his wife, my sister Heather, did some touring as well as working the big clubs in Sydney and running their TV show. Tex Morton and Buddy Williams had a fairly public rivalry at times, so it was big news when the two stalwarts announced that they were teaming up for a tour, or some shows anyway. (It didn't last all that long, if I remember, but it was very newsworthy while it did.)

Slim and I took ourselves off to Western Australia again, with a new team that included a German family: Dad, who threw knives, cracked whips and spun ropes; Mum, who had to stand up against a board as her husband threw knives all around her body, and young son who came along for the ride. I couldn't help thinking it wouldn't be a pleasant job for Mum if she and Dad had an argument before the show.

I was having a relatively easy time at the beginning of the WA tour as I'd been told by the doctor that I had to give my voice a six-week rest; Slim probably thought that was a great idea too. But as Anne was able to come along for the first three weeks of the tour, she filled in for me, doing my solo spot and all my backup singing. I think she even did some of the skit straight work for me as well.

The south-west of Western Australia is so beautiful and interesting that Slim and I had a tendency to show it off to anyone new in the team as though we were its proud owners. My dad was with us for the trip, and we carted him down to the Old Farm on Strawberry Hill and the old Whaling Station in Albany, to the Pink Lake in Esperance, and through all the 'up' country, as we called it – towns there have names ending in 'up': Jerramungup, Ongerup, Needilup, Gnowangerup ... I was told that 'up' is an Aboriginal term for water or waterhole or place of water.

Crossing the Nullarbor was becoming easier as the bitumen crept slowly but surely across the desert. But we seemed to complain more about the 300-odd kilometres of bad dirt than we did about the original 1100 of bulldust and potholes and corrugations. We were home barely a month before we headed for Queensland and the Territory with the HCBB, Barry, The Barrons and Tich, the Wonder Dog. That was Tich's publicity tag and, frankly, I think he deserved it. He was a beautiful black and white border collie, and at times you could just about see Tich's brain working.

We headed for Queensland via Bourke in the far west of New South Wales and up through Cunnamulla and Charleville. We hadn't shown Bourke for a while, and I thought about Nick and Koola Peters at the Post Office Hotel. It was Regina, Koola's sister, who used to have hot coffee and a hot water bottle ready for me when I came home late from visiting Anne in the hospital after her appendix operation years before.

I lined up at the local bank and spotted George, Nick's brother, in the queue.

'George, how are Regina and Koola? I must call in and see them.'

George looked at me and said baldly, 'They're all dead.'

I nearly collapsed in shock and it took a while to get the story. George had stayed to look after the hotel while Nick, Koola and Regina drove to Sydney for a family wedding. A car came around a tight corner completely on the wrong side of the road and smashed head on into them. The three were killed instantly. Little Peter had remained with George and his wife. Now, whenever I look through the leaves of my old grey recipe book, I remember Regina as I see her recipes for beans in oil, creamed rice, fish in currants, and the Greek pasta and cream sauce recipe with no name.

The HCBB was all set to enjoy every minute of this caravanning trip to some of the real Australian outback. Alan's wife, Julia, and Miles's wife, Catherine, were also in the team and they began learning all the tricks to running the front of the show. It was a bit different out at Camooweal than it was back home in New Zealand, but the girls soon got the idea and waved the long torches with authority.

They loved the nights off when we camped out of the western towns and lit a big fire with the caravans pulled around it. If we were close enough to town, we would drive in to the motel after the barbecue and campfire; otherwise we would beg a bunk in Vera Vilstey's van for me and in the truck caravan with Baz for Slim. The experiments with campfire cooking were a great novelty, and the entertainment varied each week. No one was allowed to do anything involving their usual talent – it had to be something different. Members of the band seemed happiest acting out silly comedy sketches, Slim had to get Tich to do his tricks, and I polished up my memory act. They met all the people we knew along the way, and we even added three West Australian and Kimberley towns so we could show them more of Australia and the outback.

The members of the HCBB were intrigued with Halls Creek, and then we went on to show Wave Hill. The concert there was a triumph of ingenuity and resilience by the whole of our little team, minus two. We had headed out from Halls Creek on the long trek through spinifex and granite, and then cattle country, reaching the settlement mid-afternoon. As time went on we became uneasy about Barry and Graham in old Thunder with all our seating, lighting and PA system, not to mention a band member, our bush ballad guitarist and comedian, as well. Dusk fell and there was still no sign of old Thunder; panic stations were mounted and a war council held.

The settlement provided us with power from their generator to light up the stage with whatever lights could be found; the four remaining HCBB members prepared themselves to do all Slim's and my band backing without Barry – but who was going to impersonate Mulga Dan, the Pest of the West and favourite of all the kids in the Territory? Speculative eyes roved around the possible contenders and Miles, the bass player, was pounced upon. The station store provided the largest size of baggy pants and bright checked shirt, someone donated a hat that had seen better days, and the girls in the show handed over lipstick and eyeliner and pencils for drawing eyebrows and red cheeks on Miles's fair face. But he absolutely jacked up when they wanted to blacken his (real) fair moustache. Mulga always sported a black greasepaint mo, but this new Mulga was going to stick with his light brown one, full stop.

We got through the show and pronounced Miles a pretty good copy of Mulga; like all the others, he knew the scripts off by heart because they had all spent hours watching and laughing at Barry from the wings. But all the time we were worrying and wondering where Barry and Graham and Thunder were.

Well, they were grinding across country over station properties, over grids and through gates with old Thunder's headlights and Barry's nose the only guide over miles of endless cattle stations with no sign of habitation anywhere. They had been yarning and not looking where they were going and ended up at the aptly named Mistake Creek, many, many miles from where they were supposed to be.

Barry looked at a map and got the idea of where they were, and decided that if he cut across country, they might just make it to Wave Hill in time for the show. Old Thunder did her best, but just as they struck the main track towards Wave Hill, her generator gave up the ghost after all the thumping of the paddock tracks and she sat there puffing. Baz swore, Graham wondered if he'd live to see the daylight, and there they stayed till Slim, with Paul and Alan and settlement helpers, drove out with towropes and petrol to find them in the early hours of the next morning. If they hadn't already made it to the main track, it might have been a long time before they were found at all. As it was, they ate everything in sight when they reached Wave Hill and their caravans.

After this episode, Slim and I were glad to shepherd our mob into the safety of Darwin, the Territory track and over to Mount Isa for rodeo week. In Darwin, the first stop, Anne joined us to stay for a couple of weeks and to sing and play onstage to audiences that had last seen her onstage back in 1960, when she was eight. She was with us when we showed at Daly River, and met up with Miriam Rose Unganmerr and the other girls. We were very proud of Anne as EMI had signed her up as a recording artist and she was beginning to work on the material for her first single and her first album.

By the time we reached Sydney and the recording studios, the Kiwis had spent rodeo week in Mount Isa in a whirl of outback hospitality. They'd met ringers from the stations who had come to town, and seen mobs of horses herded into the yards out at Kalkaringi rodeo grounds, where either Spinifex or Blondie, one of the famous outlaw buckjump horses, was kept in a special yard to be studied and admired. They'd spotted the Isa's famous 'lollypop' mine stacks as they headed east from Camooweal – always a sign that the Isa was within reach.

We had taken them from the Northern Territory and the Kimberley, through the far west of Queensland over to the north Queensland coast. They had travelled through dry country in towns including Cloncurry, Julia Creek, Hughenden and Richmond.

I recalled staying at a roadhouse in one of those towns a couple of years earlier. Things were much friendlier this year, but on that occasion I had walked into the shop and enquired which unit we could stay in. A rather tough-looking lady just wrote out a receipt for the cost and held out her hand for the money without comment or information. I was not impressed at that moment, but by the next morning she had thawed. She and her husband had put their savings into the motel and roadhouse but had found themselves in an unfriendly town, a centre for well-off graziers and, as I found also, a council office with officers who were not very friendly to travelling people.

This woman's son had gone to fight in Vietnam, come home on leave – unwelcomed, unnoticed by the town – and then left after a week. Two years before they hadn't been able to sell because of the drought, but now that the drought had broken they hoped they would be able to sell at last. Nearly all of their family had left, or were leaving. Their daughter and her husband were leaving for Victoria that month. After all, what do you do? Husband helps Dad on the pumps, daughter puts on elaborate makeup, jeans and scarlet nailpolish, and talks to everyone just for something to do. And Mum's hands are swollen and scarred, and there's no makeup and her hair is just dragged back; her toes poke through the tatty remains of strappy sandals below dusty black slacks. And then she smiles at you. And it was at that moment I thanked God I was driving through this town. I didn't have to live there twelve months of every year and suffer the dirt and the heat and the flies nonstop.

Before television appeared to lighten the lack of entertainment, women often told me that they looked forward to seeing the show each year and seeing what new dresses I would be wearing onstage. It gave them an excuse to talk to the neighbours and spend the day in town. It was of no use to tell me things weren't still like that in the early 1970s; I know very well they were.

I will always remember the woman from an outstation that was twenty kilometres from the main homestead. In the late 1950s she was awaiting the birth of her fourth child and staying at the hotel in the nearest town that boasted a bush nursing hospital. I had to stay at the same hotel for a couple of days because Slim and Barry had taken our old Egg caravan back to Longreach to have the springs repaired. In their absence, I'd had a chance to make friends with the outstation lady, as well as quite a number of local women down the street and in the shops. I found out that this particular lady came from Victoria, but as the family farm had had to be divided between two brothers, her husband had elected to take out his share to finance a move to Queensland, where he got this job on a cattle station. Their house was near a creek that flooded regularly with the smallest fall of rain and wiped out the vegetable garden she had planted. Bringing vegetables by train from the coast was unprofitable because by the time they were picked up from the railway siding, taken to the station and then the twenty kilometres to her, the contents of the bag were generally mouldy. So she kept on replanting the vegie garden and hoped that something would survive the elements.

She made her own bread and taught the children their school lessons by correspondence. To begin with the family had had only bore water to drink and it had made the children sick; they couldn't seem to adjust to it. Her husband badgered the boss till they got a tank at long last, and then they waited to get enough rain to fill it. They had no regular vehicle and the single telephone line from the outstation to the main homestead worked only sporadically. Naturally enough, I asked her why she stayed.

'Oh, well, my husband loves it up here, so I guess I'll stick it out,' was her matter-of-fact reply. Is it any wonder I have such respect for women of the outback?

The Hamilton County Bluegrass Band wound up their great Australian tour with a Slim Dusty concert at Tamworth in October where we recorded a live album that aired 'Kelly's Offsider' for the first time. Down at Metung over the previous Christmas, I read a story in the newspaper about a woman and her truck-driver husband or partner, and I couldn't get it out of my head. I woke at four in the morning one time, and crept out of bed and into the kitchen and sitting room in our little house at Metung. I had the whole first verse, words and music, in my mind and I was able to get out a guitar and sing it to myself in the quiet of the night. The rest of the song just wrote itself and I offered it to Slim when I had it finished. I don't know of any other song of mine or Slim's that was recorded 'live' as its first recording.

After a mammoth recording session, the HCBB headed home to New Zealand for Christmas, and we planned to visit them after our own Christmas, but in the meantime we made a quick visit to Canberra to the Playhouse Theatre for the Federation of Australian Commercial Broadcasters' annual awards night. Slim and I were surprised to each receive an imposing bronze trophy for Best Country Album, *Lights on the Hill.*

CHAPTER 19

We were in a state of turmoil after our Christmas at Metung in 1972, as Anne and her friend Maureen were setting off overseas on 28 December. Slim reckoned we were both nervous wrecks by the time we saw the girls off at Sydney Airport. Anne's passport wasn't collected until about three hours before takeoff, and even once they were on board we couldn't settle down because the Qantas plane was delayed for 24 hours in Singapore and we were worrying about them. The girls were happy, though; they got extra sightseeing time. Friends met them in London, and after travelling all over Britain they bought a little red Mini to take to the Continent with them. It was promptly stolen in London, but after it was found three days later, off they went to France, Belgium, Holland and Germany, where they stayed with relatives of Vera Vilstey. The Mini conked out in Austria, so it was sold for what they could get and the girls went off to see Italy. I think they spent their last few coins on a quick phone call home as they waited to board the Qantas plane in Rome, bound for Australia. Slim and I didn't breathe easily until we picked them up again in Sydney.

While Anne was away David, Slim and I went to New Zealand for a short holiday. We visited all the members of the Hamilton County Bluegrass Band, and did the tourist bit all over the country. When we arrived back in Sydney a petrol strike was in full swing, and we drove home expecting to have the car splutter to a stop at any minute. Our main concern was that now we would be unable to attend the very first 2TM Country Music Awards night in Tamworth. We tried all the commercial flights but they were fully booked, and it looked as though we were to miss out. But after a few panicked phone calls, 2TM managed to get us on a charter flight. They were the worst conditions we had ever flown in; pouring rain and violent storms all the way. As there was minimum visibility, the pilot flew and landed by instruments only. Slim is not a fan of flying at any time, so he was not feeling very happy during this particular flight.

What a night we had, though! There was a big crowd to watch the presentation of these first awards; officials and official guests had come from everywhere, with many recording company executives attending too. I was thrilled – absolutely delighted – to win the very first Golden Guitar ever presented, for the APRA (Australasian Performing Right Association) Best Composition of the Year; it was for 'Lights on the Hill'. It was my first award ever; it was recognition by my peers of my writing, and it was hard for me to absorb the ramifications of it. I didn't think of all those things at the exact moment; I was just one very happy lady. Slim received a Golden Guitar for singing the song, as well as two other awards.

This Golden Guitar Award was presented for a trucking song that the industry and fans found difficult to believe had been written by a woman. It must be kept in mind that I began writing during an era that expected women songwriters to excel in beautiful songs about love, romance and maybe a bit of cheating to daringly spice things up, but most certainly – in country music anyway – not to intrude on the manly territory of the bush, the outback and the rougher sides of life. So now I may as well write plainly about a fact that Slim and I kept secret for many years.

Recently, I was asked straight out about the truth of a certain rumour, and as the interview was being recorded and filmed live, I decided it was time to put it to rest. In the 1960s and early '70s Slim sang many very strong bush ballads, and we were beginning the lifelong collection of lyrics and songs from bush writers. I was writing too, and Slim wanted to record most of these bush songs as I finished them. However, it was a bit embarrassing, apparently, for a woman to be writing songs for men to sing, and because of the general outlook of ballad listeners we decided that it might be a good idea to put Slim's name as well as mine on my songs. That should have made them acceptable to the more macho of his listeners and followers.

There was one such change in 1958, but we did it more regularly from 1968 to 1978 with bush ballad style songs. If I wrote a more general style of song, my name alone was listed as composer; and, of course, once 'Lights on the Hill' became the hit that it turned out to be, I was recognised as a writer of stronger style songs and we could put my name alone on everything I wrote from then on if I wished. If this story sounds strange to present day readers, I can only ask you to remember that social and cultural life has changed a great deal in the past very few decades.

After nineteen years on the road with us, Barry Thornton decided that it was time to take a break at home for twelve months. He reckoned he'd be back after that, but as his 'young bloke' needed some pulling into line and was getting too much for Pauline to handle on her own, it was a good time for him to stay at home. Barry was a real part of our family and Slim's right-hand man, and we knew we would miss him and the valuable part he played in our life and our music. But he was settled not far from us, and we looked forward to having him with us again further down the track.

Slim now had to find a suitable lead guitarist, and he began searching for someone who could play bush ballad guitar. Interviewing and auditioning guitarists began, but it was a while before John Minson came up with the right man: Lindsay Butler. Once that position was filled, we set about putting together the touring team for the last six months of the year, getting caravans and vehicles hired, and all the itineraries settled.

Over the preceding few years the administration side of our touring, recording, city performing, songwriting and general 'keeping the show rolling' had become a huge job. I was kept going day and night, and so was Slim, who handled all the PR side with radio and store appearances on tour, plus the many TV appearances offered whenever we were in Sydney, as well as everything else that landed on his plate. I had engaged a part-time secretary, who was in touch all the time we were on tour, sending out the paper advertisements and photo blocks, checking that the radio ads had been received and that the hall bookings were all in place, and so on. Looking at some of my daily road diaries, the listings of jobs on tour and beforehand were endless.

I still kept the books, did the wages, dealt with the accountant and the tax duties such as group certificates and so on. I ordered the record stock, paid the hall rentals, kept in touch with the children and attended to their needs at school, and arranged their travel to us wherever we were. Before each tour, caravan accommodation had to be located, inspected and hired and vehicles sorted out to haul the vans. It would take a page to list all the odd jobs that had to be done and arrangements to be made. That was besides keeping peace in the camp and driving a car and caravan. In the show each night I did my solo singing spot as well as playing bass for Slim and sometimes for other acts, plus doing a bit on the electric keyboard at times. I also enjoyed working in the comedy sketches – that was the fun part! You name it, I was doing it, but I began to pay for it in 1973.

I'd had ongoing hip pain for quite a while but I could manage it most of the time. Neither Slim nor I realised that carrying extremely heavy things like a small electric keyboard or piano accordion put too much strain on that hip. I was physically strong, and managed the lifting quite easily, but I was doing damage. I also found that headaches and never-ending tiredness were pulling me down. My patience and temper became very uncertain, especially as we had some rather irritating personalities on tour that year, but it was not until we were in Queensland again and showing in the Isa that it came to a head.

We were good friends with a very unusual doctor in Mount Isa, Dr Mac. He was a specialist physician who was involved in most things going on in the town and even with the rodeo as a volunteer medico. Slim and Dr Mac were good mates, but Mac was fairly sharp eyed too and he bailed me up with a demand that I get a check-up. He reckoned he would start with basic checks such as taking my blood pressure, which he found to be absolutely sky high. He read the riot act to me and then to Slim, and laid out a litany of what was going to happen to me in the near and far future if I didn't pull my head in and rest up. It was going to be a bit difficult to do that, as we were in the middle of a long tour, but I began to try.

We had bookings solidly from the beginning of August until 23 December that year. The tour took us all through Queensland, down through New South Wales to Victoria and the Gippsland, and back up the South Coast to Sydney. Some club bookings were waiting there, and then we flew to Melbourne for Slim to appear on the Graham Kennedy TV show before fitting in numerous publicity interviews for radio and newspaper ahead of a few Melbourne concerts. They included one at Dallas Brook Hall for Greg Young, who had been instrumental in bringing Slim back to Melbourne a couple of years before. We also went to Tasmania for a week's shows and had a job to get home due to a pilots' strike. Then as soon as we arrived in Sydney, Slim and the show, including Anne, took off for a short tour in New Zealand. The minute he got back to Sydney, Slim packed up Anne and David with some of the band and flew to Brisbane for a series of shows for a promoter up there. They returned home two days before Christmas, and after Christmas and Boxing Day we all headed south to Metung.

It is probably no mystery why I did not go either to New Zealand or back up to Queensland: I was really in need of a break until I could get my health under control. Anne took over my singing spot and my electric bass playing in New Zealand, as well as for the short promoter's tour in southern Queensland. David went along as Slim's drummer. He'd been taking lessons and was also doing a bit of bass playing. So the kids came to my rescue fairly early in the day. The other thing we would try in future was to have a secretary on tour with me, or to arrange for a shorthand typist to do a day's work with me whenever we were in a big enough town.

The 1970s became a whirlwind of requests, publicity, recording, touring, and fielding all the demands that seemed to come from every point of the compass. One thing that made me very happy was that Colleen and Paul Trenwith, together with baby Jeremy, were coming to work with us for a year or two.

We fell into the pattern of spending the first half of the year in Sydney working club shows while Slim and the band recorded songs for a year's worth of releases. As the recording company was asking for more and more material, it was a big part of our work to write and find all the songs, and get them recorded. At one stage Slim undertook to record and release two full albums of new songs each year. That meant there were 24 new songs to be written or found, which is a lot harder than it sounds.

Finding those songs involved checking every bit of mail that arrived. I read any lyrics and passed on to Slim all those that I thought would be suitable for his use; we also listened to the cassettes of songs that turned up. I kept checking everywhere I knew I would find published bush poetry. We were putting together a network of bush writers from all over the country: Stan Coster, Tom Oliver, Tony Brooks, Joe Daly, Keith Dixon, Wave Jackson and, of course, Mack Cormack were some of the earliest in the team, and many came in the years following.

Slim wrote and set to music so many bush poems; I wrote my songs when I could, and when I got the urge. All the stories, all the problems, and all the adventure and people we encountered were fuel for the songs we wrote. I wrote 'The Local Mary Magdalene' during some of this madhouse atmosphere, in the early hours of the morning. I jotted a note saying that even if it was never recorded, I would always be glad I had written it.

Anne graduated from university and proposed that she work in music for a year before considering the future. That year turned into a lifelong career for Anne, beginning with the recording of her first album. She wrote the liner notes in Camooweal, on tour with the Slim Dusty Show. Anne drove her car and caravan and looked after everything to do with her outfit. I went with her one day to give her a lesson in mud driving when you have a van in tow. She's a somewhat nervous passenger and her hair must have been standing on end, but she picked up the tips and didn't get herself bogged when she took over the wheel.

Anne's jobs in the touring show included her solo singing spot plus singing backup at times for Slim and me, and playing bass for either of us when needed. She could play a bit of mandolin behind Paul and Colleen too. We had put together a different kind of show this trip, featuring more music and more varied kinds of country music. Barry Thornton had 'gone bush' out to Innamincka to offside for our bush pilot friend. So once again, we had to change our lead guitarist. His family was with him for quite a while in the camp near the rough airstrip, until conditions became a bit too difficult.

Anne had met a number of musicians in the university Bluegrass Club, and sang a lot with Colin Watson backing her on electric and acoustic guitar. So the Travelling Country Band at this time consisted of Colin on lead guitar; Paul Trenwith on banjo, dobro and acoustic guitar; Colleen on fiddle and mandolin and harmony vocals; and either Anne or me on electric bass and backing vocals.

The Vilsteys came along as our variety act, and Bill developed a comedy clown and magic act for the second half. Bill was like a blowfly around the place; he wanted to catch every fish, shoot anything in sight, and generally keep himself on the hop 24 hours of the day. Vera helped out at the front of house when she wasn't onstage on the trapeze, and her previous experience when Aunty Una had been in charge out there was invaluable. She was able to coach Margaret Pender, whose husband, Don, worked the small sound system and helped with all the general vehicle jobs. We had heeded our doctor friend's orders and hired Carol as secretary and front-of-house assistant.

We missed Aunty Una, though. She stayed home this year, looking after her two brothers (one being my dad) after their elder sister, Vera, passed away. Then she gave me the shock of all time; after having declined at least two proposals of marriage that I knew of during her life, she accepted her schoolteacher friend Tony's and arrived at our home to break the news to me by showing me her engagement ring. They would go on to have about 25 years or more of a tremendously happy marriage before Tony's premature death, but I couldn't help begrudging Tony his monopolising of *my* Aunty Una.

Carol and Anne shared a caravan, with an unwanted (on our part) extra passenger, Pookie. Carol had asked if she could bring her cat, and we had said, 'No'. But when we left town we discovered that Pookie was part of the troupe nonetheless. Before long he had destroyed nearly every flyscreen in the caravan, as he refused to be kept in at night. He fought his way out, and then jumped back in through the same windows onto Anne's or Carol's face or head with all the neighbourhood cats yowling after him. Then the next morning Pookie would not want to move on from his selected township. He would streak under the nearest building and there would be the hilarious sight of everyone in the show trying to find him and coax him out so we could all get to the next town to work. Slim took to the chase with vigour one particular time, because he had found a suitable piece of four-by-two timber just the right size for throwing. When he caught sight of dear Pookie crouched well under the building, defying his pursuers, Slim let fly with accuracy and Pookie screeched out into Carol's loving, waiting arms. Carol glared at Slim and Slim smiled back. I looked the other way.

After showing Wave Hill, along the way back to Darwin we saw a flash new pub where the old Top Springs grog shanty used to be. We hit the Track at Katherine and took all the caravans down to the riverside caravan park. Birds seemed to be everywhere just now; at the crossing, multi-coloured honeyeaters flashed over the water and white cranes flew over. We saw a brolga beside the road from Kununurra, and at Timber Creek there were black cockatoos in flocks. Little finches flitted everywhere, and white corellas massed around the feet of cattle at a bore tank.

Events at the show that night brought me down to earth with a bump. I was onstage with Slim in the second half when there began a yahooing and yelling at top volume from the audience. This kept up till Slim told me to go around the front and fix it. The problem was in the shape of a big, drunk white woman from the largest cattle station in the area. Self-styled Big White Queen of the Territory, she was looking for a fight that I certainly had no plan to join. She'd have made two of me, and I had my stage dress on, too. First Vera and Margaret, and then Carol, had asked her to be quiet so people could hear the show. That only resulted in some fruity refusals and louder disturbances. At this stage she did not even have a ticket, as her husband had gone downtown to cash a cheque to buy some. By the time he came back she had called me everything I won't repeat just now, and I asked him if he could control his wife. He said, quite frankly, 'No, I can't.' So I told him in that case I couldn't sell him a ticket for her, and if he insisted on leaving her in the hall I would have to call the police to evict her. He seemed to think that was an unpleasant fact, and a silly one on my side, but he got the message that we were all fed up with his better half. Next day I was told by locals, 'Just as well you didn't try to mix it with her. She's a gutter brawler from way back.' Their words, not mine.

As we drew closer to Darwin, Slim and I became very worried about his bad throat. At first we blamed it on voice strain complicated by a virus. The voice strain, we believed, was caused by a concert we'd done in a club not long before leaving on tour.

'Does the club have a sound system?' we'd asked.

'Oh yes, of course. All supplied, no worries.'

So we hadn't taken the extra loading of our own system. The worst thing we could have done, as it turned out. The club certainly had their own sound system and it was about the worst we had ever used in our careers. Slim strained and strained all night in his efforts to be heard, and at the end of the night the audience was so much in sympathy with our difficulties that they took up a petition to the club on the spot.

Having someone to blame was no consolation up in the Northern Territory with a full tour booked, people to pay and outback audiences banking on the show being there again that year. It is a tradition that the show must go on, and you might be surprised how deeply that is entrenched in the minds of show people. But Slim was in real trouble. He rested his voice as much as possible but found he was losing volume and range, and he was just about whispering by the end of each show. He persisted, though, and managed by calling on every bit of stagecraft he knew.

We arrived in the Isa for rodeo week and got more bad news. Colin had to fly to Brisbane for some urgent medical attention, and when he was told he was to have an important operation and would remain in hospital for at least a fortnight, and possibly longer, he telegrammed us to get Lindsay Butler to come up. In the meantime, Paul and Colleen had taken over all the backing for Slim, me and Anne. Lindsay was available and came to Townsville to join us, and so did David. Slim was so unwell that I insisted he see a doctor who told us that Slim *still* had the virus he contracted back in April (this was August) and wouldn't get better unless he went to bed for a week. I then set out to cancel some of the next week's shows. I managed to get about ten days' rest for him.

It was a very depressing time: there had been an oil and fuel strike for about two weeks and we were anxious about plane flights being cancelled and preventing David coming to join us. Inflation was running at 14 per cent, with predictions of it being up to 20 per cent by the end of the year, and there were other strikes. Fuel subsidies in the country areas had been removed so that petrol was more costly. Much against my grain, we had to raise our ticket price to $3.50 in a climate of unrest and alarm in the community.

During this enforced break, I was trying to find some specialist treatment for Slim; when we flew to Sydney in September for a charity concert, I was able to book an appointment with an ear, nose and throat specialist known to the stage fraternity. The doctor diagnosed a nodule on the vocal cords and booked Slim in for it to be removed when we would be back in Sydney in October. He informed us that it was a very simple operation, and with two weeks' rest for recovery Slim would be back at work with no problems. A singer friend had endorsed this procedure, saying that she was singing better than ever after her treatment. So we were quite confident when Slim went into theatre and then took it easy through two weeks of silence. I read all his notes scrawled in what I called his 'shorthand,' and we managed to communicate with only a few mix-ups in my interpretations of his scribbles.

I had cancelled all club shows booked for that period and the first four concerts of our forthcoming southern tour in November. But when Slim began singing again, he became more upset than ever. He said, 'I'm not better! It's worse! I'm wobbling all over the place, I can't keep on the note, I've got no control, I can't sing!' He went to the specialist, who seemed to think he was just imagining the problem; Slim even took his guitar along and gave the doctor a demonstration, but he still gave the recommendation that Slim just go home, calm down, take it easy, do all the things he normally did and so on and so on. Anyone would think Slim was having a panic attack or something, over nothing at all. Nothing at all? Just his whole life's work, and almost his reason for being. That was all.

On our insistence that there was something terribly wrong, the specialist put Slim into theatre to have a proper look; he came back to us to say that the vocal cords looked perfectly alright and there was no reason why Slim shouldn't be singing as normal.

So we prepared to fulfil the bookings of the tour. We opened in Ballarat, and Slim had such a terrible time onstage that when he came off he threw his precious guitar onto the floor. He was in despair, and I didn't know what to do now to help him.

His audience decided that he had a dreadful attack of laryngitis and many of them insisted he try their favourite remedy for it – if only it had been just that! We sat down quietly and calmly and Slim made the decision that he would do his best to keep faith with his keen followers by doing the rest of the twelve shows booked. By the end of the tour I was singing in unison with him in the finale, the sound was turned up as high as we could manage without feedback, and Slim was still sounding as though he had laryngitis. The final show of the year was in Tamworth, and a reviewer mentioned the 'gravelly' problem. They were beginning to call him the King of Country Music, but he certainly did not feel like it.

In Sydney, Anne spoke to Slim. She was taking voice production lessons and she said to Slim, 'Dad, why don't you try these? Mr Thew might be able to help you learn how to save your voice or how to help you get over the operation.' Slim was ready to try anything at that point, so off he went to the teacher, who must have wondered what sort of pupil he'd scored this time.

After a few lessons, Mr Thew confronted Slim with the news that another client had told him who this 'Mr Kirkpatrick' was. He then became very concerned, because he knew immediately how desperate Slim must have been to come to him for help. He was frank in saying that if Slim kept singing the way he was, and working his voice as hard as he was, he could expect it to give up on him in a short few years' time. Then he began teaching Slim how to sing all his ballads so that everything sounded exactly the same but didn't strain his vocal cords, as he had been doing for decades.

By working hard on the lessons, Slim's voice began improving, and I began breathing a little easier. He had been very despondent at times, but now he could see that he would be able to beat it – by joining it, I suppose you might say. I wonder what he thought when he heard that the teacher had said to Anne, 'You know, your father could have been an opera singer.'

We went down to Metung for Christmas. We hung our stockings on the old mantelpiece over the open fireplace and had the usual fun sneaking gifts of all kinds, many of them made for laughs, into the red stockings. The tree, a big branch of a native cherry tree, stood in the corner loaded with decorations and presents piled on and under it. On the piano stood a cut-out, almost life-sized, coloured drawing of a black and tan dachshund done by Anne a few years earlier, and inside it was a poem supposedly from a sausage dog … all signed by David and Anne with a pawprint of our own Hans. Friends began calling in as they passed on their way to families for Christmas lunch; Lorna and Mack were coming over to have the meal with us. Then we heard the news.

Cyclone Tracy had devastated Darwin.

CHAPTER 20

We didn't believe it at first. What did they mean, 'devastated'? But the news went on, hour after hour, the details striking home to our hearts as we thought of all our friends in Darwin and around. Margaret Mile, the young singer who travelled so much with us, had gone back to Darwin to settle there and we were frightened for her. She was living in a caravan at one of the caravan parks. What about the Kerrs out at Howard Springs, in a house up on stilts? Should we try to speak to someone and find out what was happening to our friends?

The authorities asked that unless it were absolutely imperative, no one should tie up the telephone lines that were needed for the government to co-ordinate the rescue efforts. So we put down the receiver and began to wait it out while going through the motions of a cheery Christmas Day for the youngsters. But we couldn't stop thinking about it. We wondered how Auntie Billie war faring in amongst all that terror and heartbreak. Doing her best to mend everything all by herself, if we knew anything about her, and if she was alive and safe. That was the thing that kept coming into our minds: we had no way of knowing if everyone was safe, let alone alive. All the team at the little Cavanagh Theatre would have been down there afterwards, trying to protect their precious props, the lighting equipment and such.

It was days before we found out that Margaret was safe in a caravan tied down to pegs; the Kerrs and their daughter, Cheryl, had crouched in the bathroom of their home. Auntie Billie was alive and doing her best to feed the multitude with what resources she had. The folk from the Cavanagh, though, were mourning the loss of their beloved little theatre. It was smashed beyond any redemption.

We were heavy hearted as we headed back to Sydney and then to Tamworth for the January awards, where 'The Biggest Disappointment' won the APRA Award for Song of the Year, and Slim received Male Vocalist of the Year for his recording of it. 'The Biggest Diss', as everyone calls it, has been a consistent favourite in country music; there have been numerous performances and recordings of it. My biased husband proclaimed it the best song I ever wrote. I don't know about that; I always liked 'Marty', though it didn't cause the stir the 'Biggest Diss' has. So no doubt I am wrong, and others are right in their preference.

I have always declined invitations to conduct songwriting workshops or such, because I feel I am not qualified to teach anyone how to write a song. I am not an organised, methodical songwriter by any means. I believe there are books printed that set out methods and frameworks to teach you how to write a hit song, and I am sure they must be a great help. There are professional composers by the number, but I'm not one of them. I seem to be an intuitive writer, if there is such a thing. I have been known to sit down and write a song on a subject suggested to me, but it was usually a subject I had already given thought to, or was familiar with, and was of interest to me.

For what it is worth, I offer the fact that I always try to get words and music roughed out together if possible. That gives me a sense of the rhythm of the lyrics, and hopefully then the song will begin to flow a little. I used always to write as I played my guitar, but in later years I found I could move around more in a musical sense as I vamped on the old piano. I wrote 'Indian Pacific' on the piano in Metung; ditto with 'Cattlemen from the High Plains' and others.

After the success of 'Lights on the Hill' I wrote other truck songs such as 'Riding this Road', 'Worst in the World' and then 'The Angel of Goulburn Hill'. I also wrote 'Grandfather Johnson' about the life of an old Aboriginal gentleman whose story was told to me by Mack and the Gilsenans at Metung. I was beginning to feel that I could write what I wanted, not just what was expected of me.

We went to Darwin in March 1975 on a government-arranged morale building visit, to do a couple of concerts and a lot of visiting and talking to people. Once we got off the plane I didn't quite believe what I was seeing. Everywhere, whole streets were lined with wooden platforms that were once floors left standing on stilts or blocks; what was left of the houses were piles of matchsticks scattered where Tracy had dumped them. The malevolence of the storm, the wind and the rain felt real even months since its occurrence. Cars lay upside down or on their sides like oversized toys; it looked as though a giant child had been playing and forgotten to take home its playthings.

One concert was staged at the Nightcliff high school, housing hundreds in and underneath the buildings. A sense of aimlessness hit me as we arrived. There was no routine or schedule left in the lives of many women and children. Children played in the shade of the casuarina trees; they came to stare when we stood talking with their parents and other adults. The harbour and docks hosted a huge ship acting as a floating hostel; in another time, perhaps, it had been a cruise ship and now it was a halfway house for these hundreds of displaced humans with maybe just the clothes they stood up in. One of the homeless was big Julie, the juggler of a few years earlier.

The little Cavanagh Theatre was gone; we would not show there ever again. Auntie Billie was in the thick of every rescue effort being made; our friends were all safe and well, and we were grateful. Darwin rebuilt and her people began returning, but some never did come back and her character changed from the old Darwin we had loved so well.

Back on the road down south, after a festival concert, Slim and I stayed overnight in a town in an old hotel overlooking the main street, which was also the Hume Highway. Trucks went up and down that highway all night without stopping, and I spent most of the night hours at the window watching the big semis barrelling through the town, their headlights and trailer lights blazing. I wrote a song that night and called it 'I Don't Sleep at Night', and truer word was never spoken. All this time Slim's voice problems kept recurring and he kept getting over them. I always remember that song because when Slim recorded it, I could hear the roughness in his voice compared with its usual sound. His voice was a constant worry for both of us, especially as we knew we had to keep his condition from getting into the media.

We spent a whole eight years with this weight hanging over us. We switched to another very well regarded specialist who operated at least three times, with little success in erasing the problem. Each time Slim had to keep silent for at least three weeks, and we had to dodge music colleagues and friends so that the severity of the problem would not become general knowledge. I became expert in deciphering hasty scrawls and mentally expanding a couple of words I could hardly read into a full request or comment. It was really funny at times, especially if I didn't get it right straight away. Sometimes I could tell what he was going to write before he got it down, and that was a help too. We were very close, and my good guessing made things a bit easier.

However, as soon as Slim began singing again, a watery swelling would come up on his vocal cords and interfere with his pitch and control of the voice. This went on for years, until finally the good surgeon said to us: 'I want you to see a colleague of mine. He operates with the laser, not the scalpel, and I think he might be able to help you better than I can.' I suppose you could say we were desperate, and we had confidence in the goodwill of this excellent surgeon, so we saw his colleague, who operated as soon as was possible. The recovery was so much better this time, and together with the training the voice teacher had given him, Slim was singing better than ever … about seven or eight years after he'd thought it was going to happen.

It was some years later when Slim went for a check-up that he had to see the new surgeon's locum. 'My word, you were lucky weren't you? You know, with Dr — removing that malignancy on your vocal cords and getting you back into form, you know?' Well, we didn't know. If we had been told, the truth had not sunk in, but it certainly hit the pit of my stomach this time.

Except for when we showed the capitals on the showgrounds, our touring had taken us to the country and outback towns of Australia. When the club scene was in full sway and demand in the city for our brand of music came to the fore once again, we worked in suburban clubs whenever we wanted. But we thought it a rather ambitious scheme on the part of the recording company when they envisaged a tour of all the capital cities, finishing at Sydney Opera House. It was with some trepidation that we embarked on this, flying between capitals with the band. We went all the way to Perth and performed in their beautiful Concert Hall, into Adelaide and over to Melbourne.

I felt quite strange standing onstage at the Opera House singing my songs, and then seeing and hearing Slim singing his bush ballads and the truck songs I'd written for him. After those early years of our music being derided by many, it was some satisfaction to be justified in what I think I always knew; music from the heart and from life, simple and direct though it may be, will eventually be recognised and loved for what it is – music of the people and a mirror of who and what they are.

In an eventful year of touring, and constantly trying to keep Slim's voice up to the work, we began to take short engagements where promoters organised the tours for us. We were over in Western Australia on one of these tours, and were waiting to go down to the show room at a venue in Geraldton north of Perth, when we received the phone call we were dreading. It was from Tommy Miles, Mack Cormack's brother-in-law, in Metung. Against Mack's wishes, Tommy had insisted that we should be told the truth about Mack's health: he had lung cancer and there was nothing they could do but keep him comfortable till the end, which could be some weeks away. Slim was terribly upset; Mack had stood in place of his father as well as being a mentor and mate. I thought of Lorna, always patient in her care for Allison and Mack, and my good friend and confidante. We longed for the tour to end so we could get home to Metung to see them.

This phone call from Tommy, though, was to tell us that Mack was suddenly worse and not expected to live more than a few days. Couldn't we come home? If we wanted to say goodbye to Mack, head of our second family, we had to go. It was the only time we ever deliberately missed a show. The hall was filling up; the show was booked out. I was unable to keep my tears under control as I didn't believe we would see Mack again; but the promoter got the plane to Perth held for a short time while Slim, Anne and I threw overnight bags together and headed for Metung from Geraldton. I think I was still wearing my show clothes when we reached the hospital in Bairnsdale, near Metung, about nine or ten the next morning. We'd caught the 'red-eye' flight from Perth to Melbourne, picked up a hire car there and headed for the Gippsland. The promoter had organised everything for us, even though we had wrecked his tour.

Mack was not pleased with us, or so he said. But I noticed how his face brightened when he saw us coming into his room. He was weak and weary, but he seemed to rally quite a lot then. We didn't tell David how ill he was, because David was in the middle of examinations at the end of his final school year. The studio in Sydney was booked for recording but we cancelled everything to be with Mack, who held on till we were able to tell David and bring him down to Homewood. We were all there when Mack gave up the battle just before Christmas.

It was a subdued Christmas that year, after Mack was buried in Bairnsdale. When the funeral cortege moved along the road to the cemetery, a drover had to move his mob of cattle to let it through. It was a fitting moment for Mack's goodbye.

The endless work of recording, writing, collecting songs, and doing business and publicity work took us all of one year in 1976. In the beginning of the year, Anne was off doing her own thing, which included joining a country band that performed in clubs and living in a share house not too far away. Actually, both David and Anne were living at home in January because Anne was between share houses and David, at eighteen, had got a very good mark that earned him a place in Veterinary Science at Sydney University.

At this year's Golden Guitar Awards, I was invited to be one of the presenters, and I was thrilled to present the Golden Guitar Award for Best Female Vocal to my sister Heather McKean for her recording, 'I Can Feel Love'. That was something very special.

We'd arrived home from the Tamworth Awards a few days earlier and were sound asleep when David woke us in the early hours of the morning.

'She's alright, but Anne's had an accident,' David told us. He had answered the call from Ryde Hospital emergency department; we hadn't heard the phone. We raced over to find Anne in a bed, still groggy from anaesthetics and medication. Her face and wrist were stitched, as were her knees. A young doctor had taken a lot of care to see that her face was relatively unmarked by the stitching. She was terribly sore and bruised, but she was lucky to have her two legs, let alone her life. She had done a performance at a club on the other side of Sydney and was driving home when she went to sleep. She'd been rehearsing daily, and inspecting prospective accommodation every day plus working at night, and the lack of sleep had caught up with her on the way home. She'd hit a telephone pole, and because she was sound asleep behind the wheel her legs were pushed up out of the way when the engine was driven partway into the cabin. The chassis of her car had to be chained together to be towed away. She couldn't comprehend how bad it was until I took her to see what was left of her car.

As it turned out, she recuperated at home and I was hoping she would stay for a lot longer. It wasn't long after this that the team from *This is Your Life*, the top-rating television show, contacted me. They wanted to do a segment on Slim, and outlined pages and pages of requests for information and contacts that they needed to produce the programme successfully. Even though having Anne back at home meant that Slim and David knew they'd have to battle it out for bathroom time, I was glad because

I realised there were hundreds of photos to check through, and lists of names and phone numbers to find, and Anne and David would be a great help. They would provide a sort of smokescreen for all the activity going on around the house.

So I put both children to work, much to Slim's amazement. 'What have you got them on to all that stuff for?' he wanted to know.

'Well, it's about time we got some of it organised and sorted out,' was my response, 'so we might as well give them something useful to do besides hang around waiting for uni to start and for Anne to move out again.'

That raised his eyebrows a bit, as it was usually my job to keep the kids out of any strife with their father, not the other way around. It was difficult to stop Slim finding out what we were really up to because we were all working in the same house, and he seemed to always turn up whenever we didn't want him around. He wasn't used to being shunted off from whatever Anne and David were doing, and we were also having trouble making or receiving phone calls about the programme without Slim hearing any conversations. We were at our wits' ends at times, but we survived.

Slim's record company, EMI, collaborated by arranging for Slim to fly to Melbourne on the day of the proposed filming, supposedly for some urgent publicity interviews and photos. They picked him up from Sydney Airport when he returned and brought him up to the recording studios, where he was told it was arranged for him to film a commercial for EMI. Slim was prepared for all that, and didn't even register the odd fact that I was wearing a very dressed-up frock just to welcome him home from an absence of only a few hours.

So he set up with guitar, hat and microphone, and began recording the songs they asked for. The photographer was taking shots as he worked, and someone stood behind the video camera supposedly filming Slim as he sang. I was on tenterhooks after a while; where was Mike Willesee, the presenter of the show? He was supposed to have walked in and surprised Slim in mid song, yet there was no sign of him. Slim finished singing and we asked him to 'Do that one again, please. We missed the beginning, sorry.' This went on a couple of times, and Slim was getting fed up.

'Where's the script?' he asked. 'If I'm doing a commercial, I need a script. I can't just keep singing all night.'

I knew that if Mike didn't turn up soon I would have an explosion on my hands, so I was a bundle of nerves when he suddenly came into the studio. Slim paused with a look of 'Who the hell is butting in *now*?' I held my breath as Mike smiled and said, 'Slim Dusty! This is your life!' Mike's car had had a flat tyre on the way to the studio, and that twenty-minute delay put more than twenty grey hairs on my head.

It was a great night. The TV team had gathered together family and friends, and told our story so well. One of the highlights was the fact that they had found Barry Thornton and flown him from the desert to Sydney. During the show, before Barry appeared, Slim had whispered to me, 'Did they find Barry?' He guessed that they would try, at least, but Barry and the pilot were all over the place from Innamincka to Charleville to Adelaide and all other outback towns and settlements. I whispered in reply, 'I don't know,' which was not exactly true; they told me they had located Baz through the Royal Flying Doctor Service, but whether he would actually be there on the night I was not 100 per cent sure. So when Barry walked onto the set, Slim was so excited and pleased. There were friends and relations and show business colleagues whom we hadn't seen for ages, but I think seeing old Baz turn up was special.

It was special in another way, too. Barry's wife and kids had finally made their way from the desert camp over to family in Canberra; the conditions out there were too isolated for them and his young daughter had been involved in an accident with some of the machinery. All the problems of medical assistance came to the fore then, and though the Royal Flying Doctor Service was superb, Baz's wife, Pauline, wanted to be where she had more resources for the children. We were in contact with them all the time, and after the programme was aired, the two children rang Slim. They asked Uncle Slim if he could 'get Dad to come and see us'. Barry was back at the desert camp having gone bush a couple of years previously, so we asked him if he'd like to record an album we were planning that would feature just Slim and a basic band sound of lead guitar and bass. Baz came over, we organised a trip to Canberra and the family was back together again. They stayed that way.

We seemed to be here, there and everywhere that year. There were awards such as King of Pop, and when we weren't attending industry events and doing one-off concerts, we were in the recording studios. In the past ten years I had recorded some singles, including the song 'Davy, Darling'. I wrote it at Brookton in Western Australia after having to send David to school for the very first time. I'd released several singles and an EP of four songs, and in 1970 I'd released an album called *Country Joy*. But in this particularly busy period, the only recording I did was to sing the occasional solo for one of Slim's albums as well as some duets. I was turning more towards writing, and the management of our career together.

Just the same, I was still very involved in music because I was still finding and vetting suitable songs for Slim as they flooded in by mail. On tour, I sang in my own spot playing acoustic guitar as accompaniment and sometimes playing autoharp for old-time songs. Then, until the HCBB took over, I had played electric bass for Slim onstage and sung harmonies for him. I was even playing bass on a very few of his recordings, such as 'The Man from Snowy River'.

Barry and I got a lecture from Slim before we even started that recording: 'I can't do this over and over; we've got to get it down first or maybe second go, so make sure you don't make any mistakes.' As he had key changes in that arrangement, Baz and I were concentrating as hard as we could, and just about collapsed with relief when we got it down first take after nearly eight minutes of following Slim's voice like a couple of flop-eared bloodhounds. That's how it felt, anyway.

We completed the year by celebrating 30 years of recording with EMI, and 25 years of marriage. Our silver wedding anniversary party was held at home with a house full of friends and family, old and new. Our children were probably relieved that we had made it this far, as there had definitely been times when no one would have believed it possible. Put two strong-willed people working and living together 24 hours a day and twelve months of the year and you are bound to have ructions, but as we usually said, 'The glue was always there.' And it was. Always.

After being off the road for most of a year, we made sure we were back at it as soon as possible the following one. At the Tamworth Awards, we were most interested in a Melbourne band called Saltbush. They had a good album out, and their lead guitarist was writing good material for the group. They won the Best New Talent Award, and we got on well with them. Later on that year, we booked them for the 1978 Queensland tour. They planned to tour in America early in 1978 and were keen to do the tour with us after that.

Anne had been working with her own group, the Anne Kirkpatrick Band, and as we had coaxed her in to touring with us this year, we poached members of her band for touring and recording. They were more country-rock style musicians, but included the familiar Colin Watson on electric guitar, and with the addition of two strong country musicians in Charley Boyter on bush ballad guitar and Mike Tyne on pedal steel, we had a good strong show.

Off we went to the bush, giving the new musos a taste of life on the road. To do them justice, they settled in fairly well. Most of the problem lay in getting them out of bed in the morning. In the 1970s, amidst the days of government handouts to musicians who didn't have full-time work, it became a mindset amongst the city musos (in contemporary country, anyway) that it was beneath their dignity to take a day job; their 'art' was supposed to be recognised by the regular income provided by the government when they didn't have other work. This was an outlook that was completely foreign to us and to most country musicians and artists. We'd all had day jobs to begin with, and built up our professional careers as we supported ourselves.

I remember one Saltbush member commenting very caustically on the subject. 'Let 'em go and get a job and earn their keep like we did.' I have to say that I agreed with him. I couldn't help but notice that the saying 'The harder I work, the luckier I get' applied to most of the successful artists and musicians I knew.

There were times when the laidback attitudes grated on me, mostly when I'd had to almost physically hoist some hungover roadie out of bed. Everyone else would be up and waiting to leave while slugalug snored at ease in his room

I did a fair amount of writing at this time, because Slim was embarking on a concept album about being on the road. I wrote five songs for the album, including the title track, 'On the Move'. There were two that I don't hear so much these days – 'You Know What I Mean' and 'What Am I Doing in This Town?'; the better-known ones are 'Indian Pacific' and 'The Front Row', plus 'On the Move', of course. I'd intended to write 'Indian Pacific' for some time, and when some rather rough efforts landed on my desk, I thought I'd better get a move on. It was really fortunate that the particular concept turned up just at the right time to feature that song.

In the midst of all this, I began to notice that Anne was not mentioning a particular escort of hers. To me, it indicated that the young man was not a casual 'mate' but, in fact, someone more important. I had to wait it out until she wanted to invite him to visit us at Metung over the Christmas break.

CHAPTER 21

It was quite a big thing in our lives to find that our daughter was now engaged to marry one Greg Arneman, who originally thought she must be a physical education teacher or trainer because she looked so fit. He soon discovered that his fiancée's job as an entertainer meant that she worked at odd hours and odd venues, and that she tended to go off around the country on tour.

Planning began for the wedding, which was to take place in late April 1978, so we had time to go up for the Tamworth Awards in January. 'Indian Pacific' was Song of the Year for me and Bestselling Song for Slim.

Anne's wedding was to be a big family event. Friends and family were coming from near and far, and for ages we couldn't find a suitable venue. Finally, we decided that the Wildflower Pavilion in the Ku-ring-gai National Park in Sydney's north would make a lovely setting for a country girl's wedding. At that time Anne had a high profile in the music world, with her albums and awards, so we had to have some security at the entrance to the gardens. I felt that was a bit over the top, but it came in handy mostly because of the media interest. Still, it didn't spoil the day – it was a lovely wedding and Anne was a beautiful bride, wearing a copy of my wedding dress.

With Anne away on honeymoon, it seemed strange to be going out on tour without her, and we missed her around the place, so busying ourselves with arrangements for the Queensland tour helped us get back into work mode.

No one believed we would be able to handle Saltbush, who had already crafted an image as hard-living outlaw-style entertainers, and catastrophe was predicted. But Slim and I had a straight-down-the-line talk with the band and came to a fairly satisfactory arrangement: they had to be sober for every performance, and that meant no drinking during the show. A few other things were agreed upon and we looked forward to a fun tour with a different slant.

It was different, alright. I asked Slim, 'How about giving Chad a go?' and Slim was agreeable to giving Chad Morgan a berth. I thought he would be good for the tour. We included Charley Boyter on acoustic guitar and Mike Tyne on pedal steel as the straight country musicians, and our backing band was the biggest and strongest yet, we reckoned.

Saltbush turned out to be a great hit; they had good songs and a lot of life in their presentation. They had a lot of life in their band meetings too. I didn't tune in to those but I believe the 'discussions' could best be described as 'robust' to the nth degree. Chad, for the most part, got on with everyone and didn't blot his copybook until much further north.

As we headed north from Sydney to start the tour, we did a rather unusual show. In 1973, the third Aquarius Festival was held in Nimbin, a small farming community near Lismore, on the North Coast in the Northern Rivers district of New South Wales. It had attracted students, alternative lifestyle people and those who were usually categorised as 'hippies'. Some of these people stayed in the area, living the ideal of a sustainable lifestyle, growing their own vegetables and fruit, getting into recycling and so on. But they were, rightly or wrongly, classified as pot smoking, drug taking hippies, and the local farming families on the whole avoided them as much as possible.

We had a visit from a very nice young woman with an unusual proposition for us. She and others thought that if Slim would bring the show to Nimbin, they would provide the hall and dinner before the show. Their thinking was that if Slim were to show in Nimbin, the local families would turn up and there would be an opportunity for the alternative people to fraternise with the locals and try to show them they were ordinary family people who wanted to become part of the community, not remain as outsiders.

We thought it over and decided that the show would be an interesting experiment. We rolled up to Nimbin to a dinner of Hunza pie, which was all the go in the 1970s, and a beer or two for the men. The Aquarians didn't seem to want any. We found out later that the publican had given them the beer on credit, seeing as it was for Slim. The Nimbin Aquarians (as I will call them) organised the concert in an informal manner, so that people mingled in the hall before and even during the show. We were happy with the atmosphere, and hoped that the experiment worked for them.

At the Tamworth Country Music Festival back in January we'd met John Lapsley, a journalist with a bent for following up any interesting leads he came across. During the festival he had ended up at a post-awards party in our motel room, along with band members and friends and family. It was a loud and happy gathering, and there were lots of stories being bandied around about things that happened on tour and onstage. John was fascinated. 'Has anyone written down any of this?' he asked. As that had never occurred to us, we simply shook our heads and laughed at the idea.

John came back to us in Sydney and we ended up spending days and weeks telling him about our life together as he began writing it down, and forming it into a book we called *Walk a Country Mile.* It was planned for release in 1979, so EMI thought Slim should make one of his '79 record releases an album by the same name, with songs written to fit in with the story.

I wrote another two or three songs for that album as well as 'Walk a Country Mile'. This was, I suppose, my first formal experience of writing songs to an idea suggested to me. It was a very liberating feeling, as I felt as though I could tell part of our life story in a different way. Once Slim discovered that it was sometimes possible to get me writing on a subject he wanted a song about, he was inclined to get a bit direct about it.

I remember being barely awake one morning years later, after our trip to Carlton Station in the Kimberley, to hear Slim saying, 'It would make a good song.'

'It would, too,' I mumbled. 'What about?'

'The ringers and their jobs, life on the big stations ...' He rambled on for a minute while I pulled up the blankets around my ears.

'That's it! Right ... Call it "Ringer from the Top End"!' I sat bolt upright, looking at him in amazement. He had not only woken me up well and truly but seemed to expect that I would jump out of bed and begin writing a song on his command. I'll say this for him: Slim was never backwards in coming forwards when he wanted something done, and it led to fireworks around the place many a time. Just the same, I wrote it and enjoyed it.

After doing a heap of recording that included the *Walk a Country Mile* album, we took off for a caravan holiday in Queensland and the Northern Territory. We thought we had earned one, and we had a small camping caravan that we could take off road when necessary.

On one of our concert nights at the Daly River Mission, perhaps in 1976 or 1977, Harry Wilson introduced himself and invited us to visit his people at Peppimenarti, out on the Moyle River, west of the Daly River, on the road to Port Keats (Wadeye) on the coast. We hadn't been able to accept the invitation until now but here we were, camped at the Daly waiting for Harry and some of the mob to come back from Darwin and guide us out to Peppi.

When they finally turned up there were six men in the back of the ute and two in the cabin with Harry, all but Harry still wearing ochre paintings from the previous night's corroboree in Darwin. The Daly River was still high after the Wet and flowed into the floor of the caravan, but we were across without any bother.

In the 1970s the outstation movement saw Aboriginal leaders moving groups of their people back to their traditional homelands. In Peppi's case Harry and his wife, Regina, together with two old women and one old man, moved out to Peppimenarti with tents and basic living equipment and so began, or revived, the community there. When we visited in 1979, Peppimenarti was a settlement of A-frame corrugated iron houses with cooking fires out the front; a large building housed the community store and the radio station in the office.

On our way there that day Harry stopped to point out the tree where Nemarluk, the brave Aboriginal leader, was chained after being captured and while he was on the way to prison in Darwin. The road was rough, with boggy patches interspersed with miles of dusty potholes. The billabongs lay quiet with waterlilies floating on their surfaces; we wondered if each one we saw just might be the one to harbour a full-size 'alligator', as Harry called them. During the Wet crocodiles sometimes moved across land from one body of water to another. The Johnson crocodile is a fish eater and harmless to humans, but the 'alligator', like the 'saltie' (saltwater croc), is an enthusiastic flesh eater, be it cattle, kangaroo or human.

At this time the community had a herd of cattle; men and boys were sorted into mustering camps, fencing gangs and settlement workers who kept the settlement in order. When we reached the settlement at about four that afternoon, Harry found a plane on the airstrip with a cattle buyer waiting to inspect the mob of cattle that hadn't been mustered. Panic stations all round, you would think. Harry had to organise the grading of a new road out to where the cattle were, the erection of portable cattle yards and the loading of cattle by the next day. It didn't seem to fluster him at all, though, as he also planned a day's fishing out on the Moyle and a welcome corroboree for the next night. We soon learned that Harry could drive, talk, check fences, look for game and spot tracks all at the same time. So a little thing like an unexpected cattle muster was all in a day's work, apparently.

Peppimenarti was a 'restricted area'. We had to have permits to visit there, and by the people's own decision there was only one area where liquor was allowed: the 'club area', a large grassy patch with a wide hollow in the centre of it. Every man was allowed to buy up to four cans of beer if he wanted, and each woman was allowed up to three ('Women go under more easily,' said Harry in explanation). Harry did not drink alcohol, nor did he smoke. Soft drink was plentiful for children and non-alcohol drinkers. Empty cans were thrown into the hollow to be collected and disposed of by the garbage gangs on the following day. Children played around the family groups, and many adults played cards or traded gossip and jokes as they drank their 'ration' before going home to cook tea.

That year I met Regina for the first time. She was slim, quiet and a truly beautiful young woman with long, glossy black hair. She kept the books and ran the store and radio communication. Her quiet voice and shy manner belied the strength that brought her there to help mould a new community. In the years since Harry's death, Regina has become the matriarch of the community and a leader in setting up a blossoming art movement in Peppi. Even when I first met her, she was one of the best weavers in the Territory and won many prizes at the Darwin Show for her work. Since then she has moved on to painting and has launched textiles featuring her designs. I was fortunate in making a special friend that year; we are still special friends, although distance separates us so that we see each other only very occasionally.

On this visit, in 1979, we were given the use of a house, so we had the luxury of hot water and showers on tap. We pulled our caravan up to the verandah, much to the delight of the children who hadn't seen a van like ours and spent much time in and out of it as I tried to get myself settled and also to move some of the dust outside.

We set up a camping table and stools inside the house, and while Slim spent most of his time fishing or out on the mustering camp, I caught up on baking bread when we ran out, going out with the women and children to find the sweet edible nodules buried at the roots of a certain grass out on the mud plain, and learning how to cook fish without benefit of a frying pan or camp oven on the open fire. My Peppi friends didn't load themselves down with equipment for a day out fishing by the river: a billy, some tea and sugar, plus a couple of pannikins, were all that was needed for a cuppa. When the fish were caught they were thrown on the coals of a fire just as they came from the water. After turning, and when judged sufficiently cooked, they were laid on green leaves from any nearby tree to have the scales and skin removed with a couple of swift pulls. The insides, cooked to a neat bundle, were easily removed and burned in the fire, and the delicious white flesh pulled apart by fingers and eaten the same way. With the river nearby to wash greasy fingers and to supply water for a cup of tea, what else was really needed?

We packed up the van again for a trip to the Wild Life over on the coast, where we were promised a long-necked turtle catch. Driving behind the utility and truck full of camping gear, excited children and relaxed adults became a bit of a worry for me. The children and adults in the vehicles ahead began tossing lighted matches out on either side to burn off the dry undergrowth, so we had to drive through small fires on both sides of the ute and caravan. I do not like fire in the bush, having spent time as a child with a bushfire burning around our home and a paddock where I sat with my sister and baby brothers. We sped up but still I felt very uneasy and I was glad to get to the open area beside the marshes where we camped.

Once again, I was given a lesson in the basics of life – in this case, camping. The truck unloaded mattresses that were placed all over a big square area. Mangrove spears were driven into the ground at intervals around this, to hold up a roof and sides of mosquito netting and complete the communal tent. Cooking fires were set outside, not too far from the tent. Everyone headed for the marshes, wading into the low water, feeling around with bare feet till they came across a turtle which was then grabbed by the neck and unceremoniously hauled out onto land. Later, I saw the turtles turned upside down over the embers of the cooking fires. After they were ready, I was offered some of broth collected in the turtle shell; it was known to be a delicacy usually given to the older members of the tribe, as it was said to be very nourishing.

A group of children came along with some honeybag for me to try; they had followed a native bee in its flight to a tree, then scaled the trunk to rob the hive hidden in a hole. There were some bees embedded in the honey, but the honey itself was strong and dark. The next day some of them caught a wild duck, which was handed from one to the other in turn to pet and to play with. Of course, the inevitable happened and when the smallest boy had his turn, the duck wriggled out of his eager clasp and that was the end of the children's duck dinner.

The launch of *Walk a Country Mile* was accompanied by a national tour that took in the capitals of each state plus several extra West Australian towns. It was the first time our son, David, had taken an official part in a tour – even if it wasn't for the whole trip – and it was a happy time for me to see my whole family together on the road. At that time David was learning and playing drums, guitar and electric bass. I knew all about his drum playing. Once he was practising his kicks at the same time as I was indulging in a long, warm soak in the bath. When my head began bouncing off the rim of the tub, I realised it was time he was given practice pads to use.

David turned 21 in June 1979; he was studying at Sydney University. We had held his twenty-first birthday party at home, with all his friends and band mates, and all our friends and relatives who could make it to the house. It was a great night, but I wrecked things the next day by packing all his gifts into our car, now called Old Purple, and parking it in Castlereagh Street in the city opposite the EMI 301 Studios, where I was to pick up Slim after a mixing session in the studio and take the presents to David's place. I opened the boot and took out some items, which I moved to the body of the car, then I locked up and went to the studio. When we returned, Purple had been burgled and all David's birthday presents were gone. I was so upset; someone must have seen me remove things from the boot and targeted our car. They certainly got a haul, and they certainly spoiled things for a special birthday. But David said, 'It's alright, Mum. The special thing about the birthday was all the people who came so far to be there.' It did comfort me a bit, but I still felt very guilty.

During the 1960s, in one half of the show, I featured many folk songs such as 'Barb'ry Allan', that were popular at the time. For this spot, I wore dresses such as this one instead of my cowgirl dresses.

Camping out by the roadside for our Sunday night barbecue and campfire in the outback. *Left to right*: Margaret Mile, me, Slim, Aunty Una (Hans on her lap), Bernie standing, Vi Skuthorpe, John Brady, Barry Thornton.

Anne, aged six, with my father Silas at Stanwell Park.

Anne with my mother Millie and me on the Moonah Cullah jetty in the late 1950s.

We discovered this roadside model of 'The Pub with No Beer' in central Tasmania in 1961. It was built by a lady from Ranelagh and was maintained by road workers. Anne and David posed for this photo.

Slim, Anne and David with the Gold Record for 'The Answer to the Pub with No Beer'. I think it is my niece Dianne Lindsay hiding in the background.

David, aged three or four, in the outback. He is clutching a treasure, maybe an interesting stone he has found.

Slim, dressed for work, and David with another of his finds, beside the blue show truck.

1966. A rare shot of Anne dressed in one of her stage outfits. This was taken in Kalgoorlie.

David outside the big van. He was about eight years of age and on school holidays with the show.

'Just one more take.' The tension is beginning to show at EMI studios as (unknown to Slim) we await the arrival of Mike Willesee for filming Slim's segment on *This is Your Life*, 1976. (Photograph courtesy of EMI Music Australia)

The first Travelling Country Band. *Back, left to right*: Paul Trenwith and Colin Watson. *Front, left to right*: Colleen Trenwith, Anne, Joy and Slim. By this time, I was playing the Precision Bass instead of the Hofner or the Maton Baroque.

1982. The McKean Sisters, taken during filming of the *Slim Dusty Movie*. Due to technical problems our performance was not used in the film.

Taken at Peppimenarti during the filming of the *Slim Dusty Movie*. *Left to right*: Slim standing, Harry Wilson (obscured), Kent Chadwick (the producer) and me.

Waiting to film Slim singing 'Plains of Peppimenarti' to all the people at Peppi. I was nursing little Anne, Regina and Harry Wilson's youngest daughter. On my latest visit to Peppi, grown-up Anne Wilson was a family woman herself; a reminder of how long I have known everyone at Peppi, and a reminder of what someone there told me, 'This is your second home.'

At Mendi in the Southern Province of the PNG Highlands in about 1990. The women welcomed me and insisted on my joining the dance after they had given me a token splash of red paint on my nose.

Anne and Smoky Dawson unveiled this plaque on the rock outside Slim's old home in Nulla Nulla Creek. The memorial was erected by members of the Heritage Association in Kempsey, headed at the time by Nick Weare. (Photograph courtesy of Joe Dodds)

An informal shot of Slim and me taken in Tamworth one year. (Photograph courtesy of John Elliott)

In 2008, the whole family recorded an album, *The Slim Dusty Family Reunion*, and this is one of a selection of photos taken for possible cover shots. I am standing in front of Old Purple with my family behind. *Left to right*: David, Kate, James, Anne, Daniel and Hannah. (Photograph courtesy of John Elliott)

CHAPTER 22

How strange it seemed to be moving into the 1980s. We had been touring since late 1954 and we'd seen so much change take place since then. The revival of interest in country music and country rock, and in bluegrass music too, meant that musicians were beginning to study how to play true country. This was a blessing for Slim and me because we found it much easier to explain what we wanted onstage and on record. I would not like to get into that old argument about what is country music and what is not – the easiest and most peaceful way to avoid that argument is to say to yourself that if you can feel the country in a song or in the music, then it is country for you. Just putting a pedal steel or fiddle player into the band isn't going to make your music 'country'. I do wonder if nowadays there is quite enough heart in a lot of the music around to qualify it as true country – or is it just pop music dressed up with a country tag? Now settle down, everyone, do!

For us and for our family, the late 1970s and the '80s were a blur of touring, big events, writing and collecting songs, recording, photographic sessions and, for me, looking after the business side of our career. But the old days of caravans and long outback tours on shocking roads were behind us, to some extent. I missed touring in the caravan because it was always more homely and comfortable than living out of a suitcase for weeks on end. In the '60s I had written a song I called 'Hills of Home'; some of the lyrics went, *My road goes over in the mountains/ My road goes down along the shore/ My road goes over all this country/ and will I never see the Hills of Home no more?* That was the way it felt to me at times: I was forever travelling, trying to keep my family together over the distances that separated us, wanting to have some normality in the life I led off the stages of halls, theatres and clubs all over Australia.

When we stayed in motels, I carried a small suitcase with cooking utensils. I know that cooking in motel rooms is supposed to be a no no, but I defy any motel owner to have ever found any trace of my kitchen activities causing risk or damage to either health or property! Salads were easy to do; an electric skillet warmed up a cooked chicken, or grilled a chop or steak. At one stage I was even making my own bread, just for fun. It broke the monotony of motel breakfasts that might or might not have been nicely cooked and presented, but which were usually from the same menu day in and day out, year in and year out, in every motel. There was one outback motel in Blackall whose owners acknowledged this fact and, therefore, made a feature of having something different, such as rissoles and gravy, as a change on the breakfast menu. Everyone leaped onto this item and everyone ordered it, as I recall.

So with Anne and Greg married and planning a trip overseas, and David planning a trip too (a twenty-first birthday present of airfares), I began talking hopefully to Slim about us having the big experience of a trip to Europe and Britain around the same time. 'Think what fun it will be to meet up with the family on the other side of the world,' I cajoled. This and other efforts met with blank silence and a marked lack of enthusiasm.

Then I remembered that Slim's Uncle George was buried in France in one of the war graves holding Australian soldiers from World War I. I checked out the whereabouts of the grave of Sergeant George Kirkpatrick MM. Having just about given up hope that he'd agree to fly overseas, I reminded Slim of George and of the song he'd recently recorded, 'No Man's Land'. But I was obviously not only disappointed but very annoyed with his refusal to take part in the family exodus to parts unknown. Yet as soon as I told him to 'forget it', he turned around and insisted I book the plane tickets and get the whole itinerary planned. What is there about the word 'contrary' that seems to fit the bill at times?

We left home at the end of April, and after visiting friends in Manila in the Philippines and calling in to Bangkok, we arrived in France en route to George's grave in Flanders well north of Paris. The war cemetery was beautiful, if you could call such a solemn and sad place beautiful. The red poppies were in bloom all around; rows of white crosses, with the AIF insignia on each headstone, stood silent and still over the graves of soldiers whose names and numbers were engraved on the surface. At the bottom of George's headstone were the words, *He did what he could*. Slim played his recording of 'No Man's Land' on a little cassette player, and we paid our respects to the uncle he never knew, and whose grave would probably never be visited again by anyone from his family back in Australia.

We met Anne and Greg in Paris on Mother's Day, and with Anne carrying an armful of blue irises; I am sure that the blue iris became my favourite flower from that day onwards, supplanting the frangipani. It was wonderful to sit in a park in Paris, eating a picnic lunch of fresh crusty bread and cheese, talking about Anne and Greg's arrival and their travel plans. They were going to the south of France while we were heading off to Scotland and Ireland before meeting David in London.

Once we were home again we geared up for more recording. This time we were to do a family album with Anne and David. One of the songs Anne recorded was 'The Local Mary Magdalene'. I played my own style rhythm guitar along with hers and sang some harmony. It was a good feeling to hear her record that song about her beloved Nana. David made his debut as a soloist, and altogether we had a good time in the studio. When we had the photo session for the cover shot, Anne held her mandolin well in front of her because she was pregnant with her first child, Kate, although we didn't know then if it was a boy or girl. We were really excited about welcoming our very first grandchild.

Slim was going into the studio regularly to the mixing sessions of this album, and I was back at my rolltop desk going through the piles of mail and the backlog of cassettes and reams of lyrics sent by hopeful composers, when I came across something interesting. Slim was at home from the studio when I interrupted his quiet beer, brandishing a disc sent to him by one Pat Alexander.

'Slim, you need to have a listen to this,' I told him. 'It's really different, and it's a novelty. You wait till you hear it. You could adapt it to suit all different names and it's really catchy!'

That song was Pat's version of 'Duncan'. I could visualise a 45 rpm disc cover with lots of men's names on it and the accompanying rhymes. We were both so taken with the song that Slim did that rare thing, he interrupted his current session to quickly learn 'Duncan' and record it the next day. We had the Saltbush bass player up from Melbourne for that particular recording session, and it is Paul Pyle's voice that calls out 'One more!' at the end.

Well, 'Duncan' went mad and we found ourselves writing all sorts of rhyming lines to fit every conceivable male name. It was in the middle of the 'Duncan' madness that we were about to open a season at the Twin Towns club in Tweed Heads when Greg rang us to announce that we had 'a granddaughter with big smoky grey eyes like her mother'. To say we were delighted was an understatement and we just could not sit still. We caught the very first available flight to Sydney to go and visit Anne and Kate, as she was called, and flew back to the Gold Coast in time to start the show that night.

I'm not the world's best seamstress but I'm a pretty good knitter, if I do say so myself, and with a brand new little baby girl to knit for, I went into overdrive. Kate was the centre of the family attention. However, we were a little taken aback when Anne announced that she was still coming on tour later that year – and she was bringing Kate with her. 'If you can do it, Mum, so can I,' she said. I didn't want to be a wet blanket and I certainly did want to have Anne and Kate with us, but I wasn't too sure what Greg would say or whether Anne would be able to manage.

Manage she did, however, and Kate was a treasured mascot of that tour. Greg was very adaptable and went along with it. However, Kate had the idea that interval time – at 9.25 p.m. most nights – was the time she would wake up and tell the world what she thought of it. She had a good pair of lungs and exercised them to the limit every night. The only way to soothe her was movement; as Anne was onstage straight after interval and I was not, it became my job to look after Kate. I remember driving all around the town of Winton in Queensland with Kate yelling her head off in her basket in the back seat of the car. I drove around for an hour before she went to sleep. In Bundaberg I went up and down the side lane of the theatre in my full stage outfit, wheeling a howling Kate in her pram till she gave it up. The rest of the time she was really good, but at that time of the night she performed regularly.

We had a long tour booked and towards the northern end of it, in Darwin and just before we headed for the Kimberley and onwards, we knew Slim's voice was not going to last. It was the same thing that had been hanging over our heads for years. We began cancelling every second show, and you have no idea of the uproar that caused, especially as some of the shows were in remote towns whose residents took it very personally. The terrible part was that we couldn't come out with the truth and tell the public what a spot we were in.

We managed to get through, and then were told that Slim was not to sing until March the following year. This was October 1981, so we had to cancel the southern tour and the Tamworth Festival concert in January 1982. On top of that, Slim was booked by Jim Sharman Jnr for a concert at the Adelaide Festival. In the end, Anne and I took the band and did a show simply to fill the gap in the programme, but I'm afraid no one appreciated our efforts too much, except Jim, who knew the real story.

I was almost at my wits' end that year. The stress of this recurring problem when we had hired a band on the promise of a year's regular work, with tours and club shows booked and recording commitments to fulfil, almost drove me crazy. Slim was understandably dreadfully upset, and so was I. Singing was his life, and I knew that he wouldn't adapt to anything else. I kept trying to encourage him, and he battled on despite media rumours about cancer of the throat and so on. Fortunately, he kept coming back and putting the rumours to flight.

One thing that kept us interested and motivated was a meeting with Kent Chadwick up in Queensland that resulted in our agreeing to work on the proposal of a movie about Slim's life and our life together on the road.

We'd had people approach us here and there before but with nothing very firm, so we didn't know what to make of Kent for a while. Enquiries turned up the information that he was a well-known and awarded documentary maker who, at the time we met him, was working on a project in Queensland. By the time we said we would do it I found out that the business side of the project involved quite a few visits to Melbourne, plus getting together the necessary information regarding which towns might be suitable for shooting, what the facilities were like and so on. It kept me very busy, but I was glad of that because I'd had very bad news: my father had cancer of the throat.

My sister, Heather, was in the United States, working with the Country Music Association and thereby keeping her husband Reg Lindsay's Green Card open to allow him to work in the USA. He hoped to break into the music industry there while still flying back and forth to do his TV shows in Australia. Their youngest daughter, Joanne, was with Heather but their two older girls had stayed back in Sydney.

Aunty Una and Tony were looking after Dad, and they took me with them to talk to the doctors about my father's situation. The upshot was that although it might not be successful in the long run, Dad could have his vocal cords taken out in an effort to remove the whole cancer. The operation should prolong his life, and possibly keep him healthy for that time.

I agreed that Dad should give it a go if he wanted to, and he decided to do so. The operation took place and then my father could no longer speak to me. I had a call from Heather to say she was on her way home to see Dad. The day she arrived, Reg told her that he was living with another woman and their marriage was over. Heather had had no indication of this, because she had been living in the USA. It had upset his arrangements when Heather suddenly came home to see Dad. I watched my sister go into a state of shock that I could do little to help; it would hold her in its grip for a long while. I found it difficult at the time to forgive the cause. I still do.

CHAPTER 23

My father's health crisis averted for the time being, preparations for filming the movie went ahead, and there were constant meetings, costume fittings and rehearsals for the band. In addition, we were working regularly to keep the band and singers in trim for the filming. In between trips to Melbourne for meetings with Kent and other key people, I kept in constant touch with my father. Slim had the job of telling me that Dad's cancer had returned, and I then began almost daily trips to the hospital to be with him until his death. I sang to him sometimes, and he wrote me notes with little anecdotes of the past or comments on this and that. We buried him on his seventy-eighth birthday, 8 June 1983.

The one bright spot at the beginning of this hard year was that, after more than twenty years, the McKean Sisters appeared on stage again. This was at the Tamworth Awards. After we were asked to perform we had to pull ourselves together and do some solid rehearsal. Our careers had gone in such different directions that we did wonder whether we could blend as well as we used to do. Heather was a strong solo singer, with a Golden Guitar Female Vocal Award to her credit and a lot of television experience; although I was regularly singing onstage and playing bass, and sometimes accordion or keyboard, I had moved more towards writing and industry administration.

As it turned out, we need not have worried. Once we chose the songs and began practising together, the voices and the timing and harmonies just slotted in and we were back into the McKean Sisters act almost as if we'd never been separated. Nevertheless, we were a bit nervous when we faced the crowd in the big factory building that had been transformed into an auditorium for the night. There was never anywhere suitable to hold the awards nights crowd, which had grown too big for the Tamworth Town Hall to accommodate, and this building was another of the stopgap solutions used over the years (until the problem was eventually solved with the building of the TRECC, as it is known – the Tamworth Regional Entertainment and Conference Centre).

We were given a tremendous welcome by a warm-hearted crowd; our girls came on to the stage to fill our arms with flowers of colour and perfume. In a way, the years fell away for us and we revelled in being together again.

After Tamworth I was once more caught up in the juggernaut of the movie. It was planned to begin filming at Mount Isa Rodeo in August, and so a fleet of cars, buses and trucks moved out of Sydney and Melbourne, headed north-west through Queensland. I think there were about 35 vehicles in all; for every facet of the project there was a vehicle, or so it seemed to me. The *Slim Dusty Movie* was a road movie; it told the story in live shots and interaction between segments of re-enacted action. I suppose it was a most unusual way of telling the story but, then again, it was a rather unusual story to begin with anyway.

I don't know that making movies would be my choice of career if I ever had the chance of choosing it as such. There was an awful lot of waiting around and hanging about while camera shots were debated and decided, and makeup and wardrobe worked out. One good thing was that I didn't have to do the washing and ironing for all our clothes each day – they were always dusty and wrinkled after a day at the rodeo arena or hall where we happened to film. But it was a great experience overall.

At Mount Isa the truck trailer was set up in the rodeo ring as it usually was every year when we appeared at the rodeo before starting our own show downtown. This time we drove into the arena in Old Purple to a big announcement on the loudspeakers, and climbed up to the makeshift stage for the filming of several songs for the crowd – and, of course, for the cameras. I remember that the cameras were especially big widescreen ones, to make the most of shooting some of the amazing landscapes we were to travel through. David was with us at the Isa and taking part in all the shooting. Anne was there through the filming, and so was little Kate, who was two and not impressed by cameras, filming, heat and flies.

As I've said before, the Isa is a great town. At rodeo time, in particular, it fills with people from all the Gulf country, from the Territory and just about anywhere you'd care to name. The streets are filled with families from out of town and locals have their homes packed with visiting friends and relatives, 'in town for the rodeo'.

From the Isa the long convoy headed for the coast, filming in the old theatre at Charters Towers on the way. The cameras captured our stage shows and the crowds who came along; outback people queued up to the ticket box to be filmed as they took their seats and listened to the songs. In Bowen we showed, as always, in the Summergarden Theatre, with Lew Williams and his family sitting amongst the crowd in the old canvas seats. Lew was a cattleman who also worked at the abattoirs outside Bowen. We first met him when we were on the showgrounds with Frank Foster and we had kept in touch over the years

I wrote a song for this sequence, called 'Old Feller'. Lew's sons always called him that, and I wrote it as though it was a letter to him with bits of news and opinions on subjects dear to the hearts of people on the land. That was what I tried to do, anyway. We knew at the time that tough old Lew did not have long to live and, in fact, he died three weeks after the filming. But even in his illness, his sons and daughters toed the line when Lew read the riot act; they respected him greatly. He was a storyteller, a cattleman, a bit of a rough diamond, a man who recited bush poetry in the old-fashioned style and an open-handed giver of hospitality. He was a good friend.

We went to Peppimenarti in the Territory to film there. It was amazing to see how the helicopter flew above the car at different heights to get some beautiful shots of the Moyle River, and of Old Purple out on the plains with the black dust rising in its wake. The *Parkinson* team was filming in the Territory at the same time so Michael Parkinson filmed an interview with Slim while they were in reach of one another.

By the time we arrived in Alice Springs we were used to seeing trucks and cameras and lighting crew; we'd made friends with everyone and still stood in awe of the amount of organisation it took to keep this movie on the road and functioning. We were ready to go down to the stage erected in the dry bed of the river, to perform a concert for hundreds of Territorians crammed into the area in front of the stage. To get some of the shots they wanted the technicians hired a 'cherry picker' from the local council. The main cameraman, David Eggby, and his assistant, plus their equipment, were in the bucket of the crane as it lifted them ten metres or so into the air above the stage and the gathering crowd, to position themselves for some good shots.

Suddenly a bolt sheared off from the arm of the crane and the bucket holding Dave and his mate plummeted those ten or so metres to earth, along with the heavy cameras and tripods.

Dave was smashed around to a critical degree and his assistant was also hurt badly. We knew nothing of this until Kent came rushing into the motel where we were waiting to be taken to the venue. It was hard to envisage the seriousness of the accident. The producers had called a halt to filming altogether, although film crew told us later that they would have worked to get the segment on film for us. We appreciated their support, but completely understood the situation – Dave was so badly hurt. However, with hundreds of people sitting patiently in the river bed, some having come miles and miles for it, we were willing to go ahead and perform the concert whether it was filmed or not. So we did, while Dave and his mate were in surgery and arrangements were being made to fly Dave's wife from Melbourne. I think we were all performing on automatic pilot at the time, as the shock of the accident hit home. It was a sober team who packed up the massive amounts of gear and began loading up to get on the train to head down south.

Our concert at the Sydney Opera House was filmed and it highlighted the difference in the places we showed: from the plains of Peppimenarti in the Territory to the Opera House on Sydney Harbour. It was a bit of a contrast, and I could never help smiling to myself whenever I played in some flash venue and mentally compared it with Wadeye or Wave Hill. Wherever we were the show was basically the same, and the effort we put into it was definitely the same.

When the re-creation of our life story began, we were thrilled to see how the set designers built the sideshow alley set. There were the sideshow banners up, with spruikers up on the boards. We even had Frank Foster, our old partner, up on the line-up board telling the tale as he used to do when the Slim Dusty Show was great on the showgrounds. Vi Skuthorpe and John Brady were part of this re-enactment with their ropes and whips; Frank's daughter Tracy wore her mother's Indian headdress and Jon Blake, who took the part of Slim, lined up with gusto. They even had the Sharman boxing tent and all its banners up, with Jimmy Sharman doing the spruiking out front.

The wedding scene was quite eerie in a way. There were Jon and Sandy Paul (playing me) on the steps of a stone church, with Sandy in my wedding dress. It brought floods of memories: the wind catching my veil on the steps of the church; Heather fixing it for me; us posing on the same steps after the ceremony …

The *Slim Dusty Movie* was a huge undertaking; I believe it was the first road movie of its kind in Australia and the organisation alone must have been an enormous job. It was a lot of pressure for me and especially for Slim, and even though we enjoyed doing it and found it exciting, it was nice to get back out on a southern tour. I think the band members felt the same.

Life for the Dustys resumed its even keel for a while, but we began paying the price of the previous few years of hectic work mode and work schedule. I was no longer doing the organisation of the tours as the work had grown too big for me to handle on my own. I was glad to have handed over the job to Kevin Ritchie and Harley Medcalfe, and later to Kevin on his own as Slim's manager for a long while. It must have been while Kevin was doing management for us that he liaised with Arthur Laing from Canberra, a booking agent and entrepreneur who ended up booking club tours as well as theatre tours, and coming on the road with us as tour manager.

I had been unofficial tour manager for many years, but by that stage we needed several other people to do what I had managed to do alone with a bit of help on the side. Now I needed to concentrate on management of the recording and writing side of our work, and on keeping the peace around the sound and road crew, particularly for one era of our touring.

The musicians, the sound crew and the roadies, who we needed to shift all the equipment for bigger venues, could be quite volatile groups in themselves, and when mixed with the others there were sometimes personality clashes to smooth over. Adding Slim to this mix could be the detonator at times, and I admit I was glad of Arthur's knowhow and breezy attitude to keep everyone happy. Over twenty years of working together Arthur and Slim developed a strong friendship.

After the filming and during the preparation for the release, Slim lost 9.5 kilograms in weight as he suffered agonising stomach pain. The same round of specialists searching for a reason came up with no result, so we managed it as best we could. We began a southern tour in Tasmania, but when we landed in Launceston Slim was too ill to meet media at the airport. That night, in Burnie, I had to locate a doctor in the audience because Slim was in so much pain backstage he'd have had difficulty performing in the second half of the show. These attacks of severe pain went on for months without much relief until he took some time off. I think it was the time off that did the trick, although Slim and a mate reckoned the raw garlic he ate regularly and the honey in his tea were the reasons for his gradual recovery.

I was suffering too. I thought I had arthritis all over my body, especially in the shoulders and arms. I tried physiotherapy and swimming, and various diets recommended for arthritis, and I used painkillers regularly. Nothing helped much, but the painkillers and medication managed the pain to a degree and I could keep going. There were spells when I felt better and thought my management efforts were working.

After completing a year of Veterinary Science, our son, David, switched to Medicine. After he graduated he married his fiancée, Jane Bryan, and they spent their honeymoon moving to Perth, where David had a job at Sir Charles Gairdner Hospital. He had the chance of training for an

Emergency Medicine specialty under the head of the College of Emergency Medicine.

Once they were settled, I felt it was a perfect opportunity to travel to Perth on the Indian Pacific to pay them a visit. It was also a chance to have a break away from the relentless touring and recording. It gave Slim and me a chance to see the Nullarbor Plain from the new train instead of from the inside of a car or truck out amongst the potholes and bulldust of the road. It was certainly a very different outlook, and a darn sight more comfortable. Just the same, it didn't seem quite right.

Anne and Greg now had a little son, James, who was a Capricorn like his grandmother (me). I was content in my role as a grandmother and mother-in-law. While Anne and Greg lived in Sydney, David and Jane were on the other side of the continent and so we were happy to know that, after passing his first specialty exams, David was heading home to take up a job at Gosford Hospital on the Central Coast of New South Wales. David and Jane decided to pack up their four-wheel drive and come home by road, the long way round; north from Perth to the Pilbara, Kimberley and Darwin and down through the Territory over to Metung in time for Christmas. Slim and I decided to meet them in the Territory and we had a wonderful reunion in the north.

It was after this trip that my pain caught up with me; it became a constant presence in my life. I could hardly bear to move my arms and shoulders more than a few centimetres in any direction and I was increasingly relying on pain medication to keep functioning. I was getting more and more tired by the day and it was a battle to keep moving at all. I was sitting at the kitchen table one day, feeling beaten at last, with my head in my hands when I heard David's voice: 'Mum! Whatever is the matter?' Within a very short time he had written a referral to a specialist physician and sent me off to the very first appointment available.

It took three weeks to get the results of the numerous tests the specialist required before she settled on a diagnosis, and in those three weeks I began to wonder if I was dying. I couldn't eat properly, I slept in patches of two hours when the painkillers were most effective and sat through hours when they weren't. I was so weak that I just lay about; I couldn't do anything much. Slim was frantic and turned to Heather for help. Anne didn't know how ill I was; she had a baby and a little girl to look after, so I did not tell her the full story. Heather moved in with us, brought a girlfriend to help with the housework while I was still up and about, and cooked lovely meals that I tried to eat but couldn't. My weight plummeted till my clothes were falling off me.

When I was diagnosed with a rheumatic disorder called polymyalgia rheumatica, my treatment began at once and my pain almost disappeared within two or three days of commencing steroid medication. It took well over a year of watching my blood tests and gradually reducing the dosage of medication before it could be said that I was free of the condition. Jane said to me, 'Joy, don't you ever do that to David again. Tell him when you're ill.'

I was never so thankful in my life to feel well again. There was so much to see and do, and I couldn't wait to get started. Besides, I had another grandchild arriving.

CHAPTER 24

David and Jane's son, Daniel, was born in March 1987, and about nineteen months later his sister, Hannah, arrived. I promptly christened her my 'Bicentennial Babe'. It was a great family time in between all the things that were happening.

We tried a few different things in the 1980s. TV personality and theatre entrepreneur Mike Walsh owned the Regent Theatre in Richmond, on the outskirts of Sydney, and we had played there very successfully a few times in the past; Mike had even given us a Gold Record to mark our show as his biggest box office success at the theatre. It was suggested that the theatre would make a good home for country music in Sydney, in the way the old Ryman Theatre provided a base for country shows such as the *Grand Ole Opry* in Nashville, Tennessee. We put a lot of work into it, planning a programme of monthly concerts of Australian artists. Mike's people built sets for the stage, and we thought bus tours from out of town would boost attendance. It was a good idea but ahead of its time. Artists were expensive, whereas (to my knowledge) the Ryman did not pay artists. In the end we had to close down the programme, more's the pity. Still, it was a good learning experience for us.

We were invited to the opening of the new Parliament House in Canberra; we went to the Solomon Islands after the devastation of Cyclone Namu had demoralised the population of the islands. By this time Heather was a permanent member of the team, and the McKean Sisters were regular performers on the show. Our yodelling caused quite a stir amongst the Solomon Island ladies, in particular – they'd never heard women yodelling before.

Heather was also our merchandiser plus fan club co-ordinator. Her whirlwind style out the front of the shows behind the merchandise desk dazzled many a helper. After trying to make himself useful out the front, one hapless recording company colleague informed me that he'd never seen anyone like Heather on the desk. I think she'd moved him out of her way very briskly as she whizzed from one end of the display to the other to serve a customer. I generally kept out of her way myself – it was safer!

On our trip to the Solomons, a film crew from the television programme *Sixty Minutes* accompanied us. Back in Australia they did a lot more filming, including a trip to Birdsville. Now, Birdsville was one place we had never shown. When Slim met Queen Elizabeth II and the Duke of Edinburgh in Brisbane after a concert in which he shocked or amused the establishment by singing a verse of 'Duncan' about Prince Philip, the Duke was quite puzzled by the fact that Slim said he had never been to Birdsville. He even turned back to check that he'd heard correctly, though I don't know why he would have been so sure Slim had been there.

Anyway, they were opening a new ward in the Birdsville bush hospital, I think, and the *Sixty Minutes* crew was going to film it. They took Slim and me along as well. We performed in the small hall, met everyone we could (including Dick and Pip Smith, who had just dropped in on an Antarctic training flight) and then ended up in the bar of the Birdsville pub. There was a man there with camels, and we were more or less coaxed to be good sports and ride one through the bar. That camel was moaning and groaning and grumbling as though it was being beaten to death. Somehow, I don't think I could ever work up too much affection for a camel.

I was sitting behind Slim, hanging on for dear life, as the camel hoisted itself to its feet, still moaning loudly. Next thing, I realised that the ceiling fan was dangerously close to my hair as our steed paced around the bar to enthusiastic applause. So I don't recall too much about that ride except for dodging a whirling and menacing ceiling fan that threatened to scalp me, and grimly sticking to my seat in the process.

When our Richmond theatre venture closed down we bought some of the stage settings, including the little pub set and windmill wings. We knew they would be great additions to the Heritage Tour of 1988. That was a great tour, and our manager and close friend, Kevin Ritchie, was kept busy getting it organised. The road crew had to set up a full stage setting each night and the sound system was much bigger than we usually carried. In addition to travelling to our usual country towns and remote locations, we showed in every capital city, playing two nights each in Hobart, Melbourne, Adelaide and Brisbane, and one in the Sydney Opera House. We had to travel by DC3 on the leg out to Arnhem Land showing Nhulunbuy (Gove), where we met the Crab Man of Gove. He gave us crabs to take with us to Groote Eylandt and I was waiting for them to escape and join us in the cabin of the plane before we could get them to the cook. From the warmth of Arnhem Land we flew direct to Alice Springs, where we showed outdoors and froze, as our devoted audience did too.

At this time, I was taking it easy because Anne was touring with us, and on a couple of the tours – such as our Heritage Tour – her family of Greg, Kate and James came along. Then when we reached Western Australia, David and Jane, with Danny and Hannah, joined us for a while. I didn't mind too much that I wasn't in the show when I had the grandchildren to spend time with, and could see my own two children up on the stage with their dad. It worked well for me, especially as I had a couple of years when I was fighting hip pain daily.

I think it was during this era, on a later southern tour, that I actually had to miss a show because of the pain I was in; Slim insisted that I rest up. That had never happened to me before, and it was quite a blow to my ego: I always prided myself on being able to do just about everything an able-bodied person could do, and that included being on deck for every job I undertook. I used to brag that the only things I couldn't do were run and dance (modern style, that is!). So that brought my pride to its inevitable downfall indeed. I told myself that it served me right, but the lecture from Slim didn't make me feel any better about it.

The year moved on at a rapid pace with so much going on. Back on the mainland, our names were placed on the Roll of Renown in Tamworth, our hands in the Hands of Fame, also in Tamworth, and we were later inducted into the Australian Country Music Broadcasters Hall of Fame.

After our mammoth Heritage Tour we made the decision to go for a trip overseas with Heather. She took some coaxing, but she came to keep an eye on me, I think. We were real novices at travelling overseas, but I had high hopes of finding Rooskey, the little village in County Tyrone, Northern Ireland, where Heather's and my great-grandfather had been born and grown up. After visiting Athens and the Greek Islands, we went to England. Driving ourselves, we headed north to Scotland to do a bit of touring that included trying to find other family history links to our great-grandmother Jessie, who had followed Henry from Scotland to Australia all those years ago.

Heather and Slim were absolutely delighted when, after some false starts, I finally located Rooskey near Gortin in County Tyrone – they could now get on with seeing the rest of Ireland at last. I went to the Gortin church and was excited to find that the local grocer held the original church records in a little journal. He allowed me to sit in his dining room and copy out some family details from the pages. How kind and helpful he was, and how fortunate that the records still existed. That was the beginning of my interest in family history; it's a bit like being a detective, I think, but with nicer results in the end.

We kicked off the 1990s by being flat out with appearances of every kind, in every possible place. We seemed to be everywhere at once, but still I tried to stay home and work while Anne was able to tour with Slim. I was beginning to feel that we were in a sort of revolving door of songwriting and collecting, recording and touring, dashing off from one end of the country to the other to play special shows without really touching down anywhere for any length of time. It was a different kind of pace from the tours we used to have; I missed the close contact I'd always had with people in the small towns and the outback.

In our early years of show business I'd become friends with Vi Skuthorpe, so I was dreadfully upset when, after a six-year battle with illness, she died. A lot of the gloss and glamour of show life went with her; she was the last of the Skuthorpes, famous for their exploits in the rodeo and buckjump shows. Vi had appeared in early Australian films standing in for the riding and daring horseracing segments in place of the leading lady.

By August of 1990 we'd been so frantic with work that I pushed Slim off to Metung to do some fishing and have some quiet time before we got back into the rest of the year's engagements. As usual he was on the phone regularly to Gordon Parsons, and as he'd had some good fishing in the lakes he rang one night to tell old GP about it and rub it in to him that he hadn't come along for the trip.

Back in Sydney, the phone rang by my bedside very early the next morning; and it was Jeanette, Gordon's wife. Gordon had died in the early hours from a heart attack not long after Jeanette had managed to get him to hospital. She knew she had to let Slim know, and I had to ring him down at Homewood. I couldn't soften the blow; I was feeling bad enough myself. Funny, witty, yarn-telling old GP – so charming that he was always forgiven for all his shenanigans, and perhaps Slim's closest and most beloved of mates apart from old Mack Cormack. Slim came home after that and just went back to work. We missed GP's hilarious phone calls and the stories of the most outrageous happenings that were not necessarily accurate but always entertaining.

Not long afterwards I was contacted by the captain of an Australian Army engineering unit stationed in Papua New Guinea. The army engineers were in Mendi, the capital of the Southern Highlands Province, about 130 kilometres from Mount Hagen. Their job there was to help and to teach the local people to build new bridges and roads in their mountainous homeland of ridges and valleys. As the Highlanders were to celebrate the tenth anniversary of their independence as a separate province, they wanted an Australian representative to attend the celebrations that promised to run over several days and be really special. When asked, the tribal leaders said they wanted Slim Dusty to represent Australia at the celebrations of the anniversary. I suppose the request would have come as rather a surprise to the Army but they coped with it in a very cheerful and gracious way.

Once I realised that I was not having my leg pulled, I was enthusiastic about organising the trip. Back in 1969 we'd been to the more accessible areas of PNG, but this trip promised to be something quite different. We were to fly from Port Moresby to Mendi, which is about 1524 metres above sea level and surrounded by sharp, high mountain peaks. The

Premier, various officials and Army personnel, together with schoolchildren, dancers and local tribespeople, gathered at the airport to greet us and were totally disappointed when the clouds came in and our plane was unable to land. We had to return to Mount Hagen, where the Army would send vehicles to drive us to Mendi.

They said they would send a convoy for the three-hour drive from Mount Hagen to Mendi and they arrived in force. There were four Army four-wheel drive vehicles and six police four-wheel drive vehicles loaded with armed police. I was more than a bit surprised to see such a line-up of force just to convey the five or six of us. It was an interesting drive and my head was swivelling back and forth, looking out at the scenery and watching the people walking along the roadside or digging in their gardens, or just standing talking and watching us go by.

At the time I was getting over a chest cold and I gave a sudden short, sharp cough that I couldn't stop in time. The driver braked, swung around and said quickly, 'Joy, are you alright?' Apparently my sharp cough mimicked the sound of someone being hit by a bullet in the chest. To his relief, and my interest, it was nothing so dramatic.

Then, out from the masses of thick long grass by the side of the road, this figure sprang in front of our car, bearded, fierce looking and brandishing a shotgun that he waved threateningly at us. We slowed to a stop while he began shouting demands for money. It was then that I understood our driver's concern about my cough! The amateur highwayman soon stopped shouting when the vehicle ahead of us also came to a halt, and out of the covered back poured about six fully armed Australian soldiers who soon relieved the man of his shotgun and threats. Apparently, there had been a lot of tribal warfare in the district. This had led to raids on villages and destruction of village gardens plus theft of livestock. In turn, this led to hungry villagers taking to the old occupation of highway robbery.

We arrived in Mendi around dark with lights flashing and sirens blaring, making one big show and a lot of noise. I still think some of the convoy had come along for the ride and the fun of it as much as for the security.

We had a wonderful time in Mendi. Some of the people attending the festivities had walked for up to four days to get there, and they all dressed in traditional finery. I was taken over by some of the women in one of their dancing circles; my face was given a couple of daubs of red paint, and I was included in a sort of dancing-on-the-spot effort which consisted mostly of jumping up and down; after a few minutes I was puffing, while all the others looked as if they could keep it up all day and part of the night too.

The Mud Men were there with their terrifying masks; many of the other headdresses featured pheasant feathers, and the face painting was intricate and colourful. We were told that Slim's voice was just about the first European voice heard on radio in the province. They were all curious to see him in person, because they did not expect him to be still alive after hearing him for some years – their life spans under rough conditions were shorter than ours lived under more comfortable ones.

We performed on an open air stage, and the next day Slim took the salute from the Army unit and I tried to get some of my pidgin English across to the women, who seemed quite happy to take me into their circle. I was high up behind the stage where Slim stood as the Army band played and the soldiers paraded, and I looked out over the huge arena surrounded by wave after wave of colourful masks, headdresses and people. The town was enclosed by mountains of thick green jungle, and from this jungle had come these masses of colourful tribesmen and women plus the children. There were literally thousands of people from all over the area; there were hundreds of 'sing-sing' groups and the singing, dancing and chanting went on all day, every day we were there.

We were made to feel so welcome by everyone. One family entertained us at a night gathering where members enacted traditional customs and songs for us. We were showered with gifts, as were the band members. On the last day of the visit we were to be honoured by a feast at night. In the early afternoon, the presentation of a very big pig made me wonder what I was going to do about shipping a very hefty porker back to Australia, not to mention what I was going to do when it got there. As pigs are as good as currency in the area, we knew we were being honoured with the presentation and we appreciated the gesture. However, as it was recognised that we really could not do the accepted thing and take this very important gift all the way back home, it was decided that it would be the centrepiece of the official banquet that night instead. As we left, I knew the villagers would begin their long walks back to their home villages, another three or four days away.

CHAPTER 25

The drought had hit everywhere in the early 1990s, and we could see sheep starving in paddocks out west in New South Wales and Queensland. The rural recession held the farming communities in its iron grip and no mistake. Even country near the Queensland coast was dry and waiting on rain. Apart from that, depressing news filtered into my mind about homelessness, young family battlers and more. Mostly, as singers and songwriters, Slim and I steered clear of politics until either one of us got stirred up beyond control. This was one time I got wound up and I wrote a song I called 'Our Own Backyard'. I was sick of seeing the hopelessness of people, white and black, not only in the country but in the cities; the very fact that in a land like Australia there were men and women, young and old, sleeping on the streets through no fault of their own just got to me this time. Slim recorded it because he was sick at heart too. He released another song, 'Things Are Not the Same on the Land', at the same time.

We were in Bowen, north Queensland, about to be on our way south when Anne rang me from home.

'Mum, you're getting the Order of Australia Medal,' she said.

My reaction was along the lines of, 'What? Dad's being made a member of the Order of Australia?'

'*No, Mum!* You are! You are! And if you accept it, it will be in the June Queen's Birthday list of Honours.'

Anne was quite excited and so pleased for me. But the news took a bit of digesting. Slim had been awarded the MBE back in 1970; it had never occurred to me that I would be eligible for any such honour. I think I actually asked Anne, 'But what for?'

By this time, she must have been getting a bit exasperated. 'It's for your contribution to country music and the music industry,' she said, 'so are you going to accept it? Of course you are, aren't you?' And of course I was, if only to even up the honours in the family.

Anne had recorded several successful albums but she'd recently switched to the ABC label and released an album entitled *Out of the Blue* – it went up on the charts and she was flat out promoting it and performing. She was booked to appear with Rosanne Cash and Mary Chapin Carpenter when they toured Australia later that year, and to top it off, in October she won an ARIA for the album. That was one award she beat Slim to!

We were lucky to be able to get her for the Queensland tour later in the year; I stayed home for the OAM presentation on 12 September 1991 and Anne took my place in the show. I was allowed to take two people with me to Government House, so David and Greg were to escort me. It was just as well Anne and Slim were out of town because, as Anne said, there would have been a tremendous fight between her and David to see who was the one to go with me to the presentation besides Slim.

When the big day arrived, Slim and Anne rang me to give me their love and congratulations and bolster my courage, and David drove me to Greg's office in Crows Nest to collect Greg for the drive to Government House. I waited in the car while David went to call Greg; he came back and said, 'Mum, there are two corsages of flowers for your jacket and Greg says you'd better choose which one you want to wear' (at the time Greg was managing a courier service for florists). So in I went – and nearly fell over the feet of my husband, all dressed up in his best suit and *not* wearing his famous Akubra. I flopped onto his shoulder, shedding happy tears, until my senses came back and I wanted to know, 'What's happening with the show tonight, then?' (And now I come to think of it, I never did get the flowers for my lapel.)

Slim had caused mayhem for the tour manager with flights and car dashes from St George in Queensland down to Sydney, and after the ceremony and a quick lunch he set off back to the show by taxi, plane to Brisbane and charter flight out west. He only just made it to open the show before Anne and the band were set to perform a rather rockier version of his opening number.

By the 1990s, the Tamworth Country Music Festival, held each January, had become a high point in our work year. The Golden Guitars, as the awards night was known, was an important event now, as artists and media realised that the Golden Guitar Award itself had become a coveted symbol of excellence in the music industry, not just in the country music industry. The whole festival had expanded as more and more artists made Tamworth their destination every year, more and more venues hosted live music, and more and more media paid attention to artists either established or emerging. The fact that country music now attracted this kind of attention could be regarded as a reward for those long years of oblivion and hard work and, in a way, a justification of the belief we'd all had in our music.

Be all that as it may, the BAL Marketing team at Radio 2TM who had established the Golden Guitars, and organised them every year, had worked nonstop to build the festival and the integrity of the awards. It was they who branded Tamworth as 'Country Music Capital'. In the beginning, awards night attendance was by invitation only, plus the nominated artists and their families. However, fans were beginning to demand that the awards night be opened to them as well.

With all this enthusiasm building, Slim and I had been involved from the beginning and had attended every festival. We were thrilled to find that each January our friends in the business were not at the other end of the country from us but there in Tamworth; it was stimulating to catch up with everyone and see what was happening with the music, the talent and artists old and new. It was in this atmosphere of expectation just before Christmas in 1991, when everyone's plans for January 1992 were being made, that an incredible announcement came from BAL Marketing. The 1992 Golden Guitars would not be presented at a formal awards night but would be split up and presented at different events and stages throughout the festival.

In fairness to 2TM and BAL, the loss of their sponsor that year helped cause this new structure for the awards. But nothing, absolutely nothing, could have prepared them for the outrage that erupted and fell onto their heads when industry members heard the news. The organisers had had no concept of how much an awards night of our own meant to people like us, who made our living year after year out on the roads of the nation, in small towns and big. For one night of the year, our music was 'top of the heap' for a change. We were in a crowd of our peers who knew the value and quality of the music presented and who came together to support and encourage each other. It made a nice change to be able to dress up and mingle with all our fellow artists, to receive recognition and applause from our peers, and to give that same recognition and encouragement to them in turn.

The row grew louder and louder, and some less restrained people became quite unpleasant. Slim and I were very perturbed and wondered what was going to happen. One day I answered a phone call from Phil Matthews, longtime manager of John Williamson. Phil and John wanted to meet with us to talk about the situation and see if we could control the damage being done. When they came to talk with us we all decided to invite a fifth member of what was eventually dubbed by 2TM as 'the gang of four/five'. This fifth person was Max Ellis, who was one of the original instigators and founders of the awards and the festival. Max had resigned from BAL and headed up his own company, Max Ellis Marketing.

It was this 'gang of five' which decided that we – that is, all members of the country music industry – would have to take steps to rescue our awards night before it was lost to us forever. The rural recession was worse than ever and it was affecting country artists to a huge degree. Loss of the Golden Guitar Awards on top of all this would be another depressing blow we just did not need. Our phone and fax ran hot as we mustered support from other artists and industry figures. In our discussions we identified the need for a country music industry organisation that could speak for us. To establish such an organisation, we had to have funds and support.

I contacted Brett Cottle from APRA, the performance copyright organisation that was a supporter of the awards from the very beginning. I had won the first Golden Guitar presented at the very first awards night, for Song of the Year; that award was sponsored by APRA. Now, APRA granted us seed funding of $10 000. We decided we could raise further funds by asking artists to support us by appearing in a gala concert in January. The response was overwhelming; there were more artists and musicians wanting to help than we could fit on the stage in one night. An experienced producer, John Spence, volunteered to set up the concert for us, and everyone gave their time and talent at no cost. The only venue available and viable was at the Tamworth rodeo grounds. It was rough, at times we could hear announcements and calls made from the racetrack next door, and Max and his team of volunteers had only a short window of time to erect the stage and sound system, plus basic tent dressing rooms offstage.

Crowds rolled up, many bringing their own chairs, and cheerfully paid their way in. The concert was a resounding success, and our fledgling association, the Country Music Association of Australia (CMAA), was established with a large board of artists, musicians and industry figures. None of this could have happened without the goodwill of volunteers from every corner of the town and the nation, really. The volunteers gave more than 100 per cent.

Negotiations began with 2TM and BAL Marketing to allow the CMAA to organise the awards night; to their credit, they eventually, and generously, gave us permission to continue using the Golden Guitar symbol as trophies. Later on, when 2TM was sold by the Higginbotham family, they gave the ownership of the Golden Guitar symbol to Tamworth Council, which still controls it today. I was sorry to part ways with the 2TM people, because we had worked happily with them for so many years, but it was a situation that we could not avoid and I could not have looked at myself in the mirror if I had dodged it.

The radio station and its marketing arm had done so much to establish a festival that became renowned as one of, if not *the* best country music festivals in the world. Yes, they had done it profitably, but it had required a huge amount of work and dedication and innovation. It was now time that the music industry did something about taking over responsibility and ownership of such an important event rather than seeing it dismantled. Fortunately, the town's business community supported our efforts because they did not want to see the awards go somewhere other than Tamworth; they were too important to the festival.

At the awards – presented all over the town that year, for the only time – Anne won Album of the Year and Female Vocalist of the Year. I think she was the first woman to win Album of the Year in her own right as a soloist, and the Female Vocalist Award was the second she had won. Back in 1979 she had won her first Golden Guitar on the same night as Tom Oliver and I won Song of the Year with 'Beat of the Government Stroke' and Slim was honoured on the Roll of Renown. That was quite a family night to celebrate.

For our winter break, we hooked on our little camp trailer and headed for Peppimenarti. After we arrived I drove to Darwin to collect David and five-year-old Daniel to join us for the camping holiday. The other part of our winter break was a trip to Italy and Greece with eleven-year-old Kate, our eldest grandchild. This trip set the precedent we followed with each of our four grandchildren: when they turned eleven, about to enter high school, we took them for about three weeks to a country of their choice. I found that I enjoyed these travels so much more when I saw things through the eyes of the children. I found, too, that it established a bond with them as there were just the three of us and no parents around. If we had any difficulties, the children were involved in solving them as well.

After the trip with Kate, Slim and I went straight back into work, and caused much speculation in the country music world by taking a young Keith Urban on tour with us. He and Peter Drake, his mate and drummer, spent most of their time writing songs and working on the stage presentation. Keith was a bit apprehensive about whether or not Slim's audiences would accept him and wondered if he should change his stage act a bit. After being told to stick to what he was comfortable doing, he did just that and – long hair or no long hair – by the time we got to the finale, when he and Slim sang their version of 'Lights on the Hill' together, Keith was a favourite with the audience. So he should have been, after the blistering guitar work featured in some of his songs.

There were some interesting jobs that came our way at times. The great Northern Territory band Yothu Yindi were to do a tour of some of the towns and settlements of the Territory to spread the message about responsible use of drugs and alcohol. They asked if we'd be part of the Raypirri Tour, as it was called, and of course we were very keen to take part. I got to be on the tour even though I was not performing. Mandawuy Yunupingu was lead singer on all the shows, and the band was a great, vibrant group of singers, musicians and dancers. I liked Mandawuy very much, and I liked the way everyone in the band looked after a blind guitarist who was a band member.

Very often this guitarist would sit down on a turned-up drum or bucket with his guitar and play for the children who'd gathered around. He played left-handed, which is unusual, and I liked hearing his sweet voice there in the open air, sitting out in the dust and heat, just playing and singing. I didn't know then that he was Gurrumul Yunupingu, whose voice and songs in his own language of Elcho Island have taken the music world by storm in recent times. What I did notice all the time was the affection and care shown towards him by all his band mates. Perhaps, too, there may have been a touch of warm respect in their care. They probably knew they had a very special music man amongst them.

When I heard that accommodation for the Raypirri Tour would be tents and swags, I opted for a small motorhome. I reckoned that I would not be very good sleeping on the ground; I'd been out in that country before. The band was offered tents if they wanted to set them up, but with ground as hard as iron and everyone else sleeping under the stars in swags, our Travelling Country Band (or TCB for short) opted for the macho image and swung their swags to the dirt like everyone else (except me and Slim). I must say that the band blokes were quite resigned to whatever turned up, even when we warned them about the accommodation (or lack of it). They were more interested in the trip. They went to some odd but interesting places as Slim Dusty's band and they seemed to thrive on it.

At Uluru the big open air stage was piled with huge speakers and sound system. Behind the stage loomed the bulk of Uluru itself, a massive and impressive keeper of legends. The stars at night were brilliant in the blackness, but Uluru could still be felt and seen in outline against them.

I was back in some of the places we'd been so many years before. Take Yuendumu and Papunya, for instance. I was intrigued by the women's vigilante patrols each night at Yuendumu. Kids out too late without a reason were shoved off home with strict instructions to 'get to bed'. Drunk husbands were given short shrift too, and if they showed fight they got it with the waddies brandished by these matriarchs who were fed up with them. Nice going, I thought, having seen and heard of some violence over the years.

A bit later that year we went to Carlton Hill Station in the Kimberley, where they were to celebrate the one-hundredth anniversary of the station's founding. There was to be a pageant, a concert in aid of the Royal Flying Doctor Service, and other entertainment that was to include the appearance of Dame Edna Everage, who'd had her gladdies flown in for the occasion. A young Troy Cassar-Daley was on the concert that night too, and it was the first time we had met. All these years later Troy is a star, and a good friend.

A highlight for me was meeting Dame Mary Durack. I had a chance to sit and talk with her while others walked up the gorge to visit the huge dam on the Ord River; I'd read her book, *Kings in Grass Castles*, and even had a worn and torn copy of a book written by her sister Elizabeth and herself, of

Aboriginal stories for children, illustrated by Elizabeth. It was in a collection of books belonging to Anne and David, down at Homewood in Metung. We didn't talk books so much, but more about the country her family had pioneered and the developments that have taken place since their first settlement in the area. She invited me to visit when I next went to Perth but, sadly, I didn't go to Perth until after she had passed away.

Another friend staying at Carlton was Ernie Bridge, originally from Halls Creek, where we first met. At Carlton Hill's celebrations he was Ernie Bridge, country music singer, instead of Ernie Bridge, politician and government minister.

At some stage I was invited to sit on a government board, the Music Industry Advisory Committee, which was to enquire into the lack of live music venues in Sydney. It was something I was vitally interested in, because all the town halls in the suburbs were falling into disuse and there were only clubs for people to go to for musical entertainment. The large city theatres, of course, were available for big shows, but there were not enough affordable and suitable venues for families to attend smaller shows. The same thing was happening in country towns where the local hall fell into disrepair while the club flourished. I doubt any of our efforts or conclusions came to anything, but at least we tried.

Around this time Slim went fishing up at Keela Valley, on the coast a few kilometres north of the Queensland town of Bowen, and pulled in a big Spanish mackerel. What he did not know, of course, was that he had a long calcium spur in his left shoulder, and as he pulled in this heavy catch the spur slashed across the 'cuff' tendon of his shoulder.

We got back to Sydney, but the pain was so bad that eventually surgery was the only alternative. That's how, one Tamworth festival, fans were treated to the sight of Slim performing without a guitar, his arm in a sling, and with the TCB and extra guitar accompaniment by Keith Urban onstage at the awards. Slim couldn't play guitar for a long time but he managed to strum on the dobro laid across his knee, and that kept him working on new songs.

My involvement in his recovery was the physiotherapy I had to help him with four times a day, and this went on as part of our daily routine for nearly nine months. Even after he was able to play guitar, the physio had to continue to help him regain the strength in his arm and hand. I became quite expert at some of the exercises, but I think Slim found me a bit clumsy. I sometimes think he recovered well despite my efforts, not because of them.

I was a bit browned off with life at this stage. A little while back, for a nostalgic performance, Barry Thornton and I had revived our days as the Bushlanders playing electric guitar and electric bass behind Slim onstage as we had done for all those years. When Baz and Slim got out old Fred, the Fender guitar amplifier, and turned it up for the act, it reminded me to get myself well and truly out of the way of Fred's high-pitched guitar sounds. Over the years I had not realised the damage being done to my hearing by old Fred. Very often the amplifier had been turned at an angle that allowed Slim to hear it at the front of the stage but the volume of the high-pitched guitar, as Baz played it for Slim's backing, would hit my ears at full bore. On the small stages we had to use, in most of the country halls we played, there wasn't the room to manoeuvre around those soundwaves. I was still playing bass for Slim until the 1970s so I'd had about fifteen years of this constant damage. Gradually my hearing deteriorated; by the 1990s I was wearing hearing aids in both ears and had done for some time.

My only consolation for my hearing loss is the occasional puzzlement on the face of the audiologists who have to check my aids and my hearing. The latest gentleman looked at his charts and looked again at the elderly lady sitting in front of him and said, 'Strange! Your hearing loss is what we expect from heavy industrial noise or from what musicians suffer.' He did not think for a moment that I had been just that; a bass playing, guitar playing, accordion playing musician and singer working in the midst of a noisy stage for many, many years.

From my point of view, the good thing about all these depressing health problems was that Slim couldn't tour with his damaged shoulder. I knew I was in for a difficult few months if he had to stay in one spot all the time, but I was hopeful that it might be a bit of a rest for both of us. Even then, there was a lot of work to be done with the administrative side of our music careers, besides touring and songwriting and collecting, and it went on constantly, no matter where we were or what we were doing. Administration had always been my job and it was often difficult to make my husband understand that it had to be done, and that if I didn't do it, who would?

Therefore I was ready to listen to any ideas regarding a change of scene, or a new area of our career to try out. When photojournalist and friend John Elliott breezed along with his latest enthusiasm, we were both ready to be convinced of almost anything to liven life. John had fronted up to a Sydney publisher and laid out his idea that it was time there was a Slim Dusty 'autobiography' published, and he had a friend who was well qualified to ghost write it for Slim.

When this idea turned up in concrete form via a definite offer from the publisher, I did some hard thinking. Having spent a lot of time providing the research, stories and photos for the previous book, *Walk a Country Mile*, I decided that rather than go through a still longer period of the same for a new book, I would write it myself. I was sure I knew Slim's story, his way of speaking and thinking, and his outlook on life and our life and career together more than well enough to express it in writing. I could only have a go, I thought, and Slim was sure I could do it. So with his blessing and total support, I wrote *Another Day, Another Town* and it was published in 1996.

While I was writing the book I spent a lot of time with my younger brother, Stuart. He was fighting throat cancer, and it was hard to leave him when we headed to the UK for a short tour in 1996. I kept in touch by phone, until the day I felt especially close to him. An hour or so later, the phone call came from Australia to tell me he had died peacefully.

CHAPTER 26

As expected, media and public attention exploded in Tamworth in January 1998 when Slim's honour of Officer of the Order of Australia (AO) was announced. I was prepared for all the activity because for the previous few years I had worked out a schedule to get us through the festival period in one piece. Slim's friend Paul Donkin came with us every year and acted as Slim's 'minder'. Each morning I'd give Paul a typed list of appointments and appearances for the day, then I'd hand Slim over like a bundle of merchandise to be delivered. I knew he'd be well looked after, and I would be too when I was on the media trail with him.

I had to laugh one time when Paul was supposed to get Slim to the top floor of the Tamworth Post Office, where the media centre was established that year. When they arrived at the post office corner, the streets were blocked off each way and there was nowhere to park.

A record executive was in the car with them and, to his horror, was curtly ordered by Paul to 'Hop out and shift those barriers, mate. Quick!'

'But I can't do that, Paul,' the executive said. 'There's no parking, and you can't go through there!'

Paul: 'Mate, if you're not going to do it, I am.' Out of the car, barriers shifted, car parked and Slim was escorted upstairs for the heaps of interviews lined up. Naturally enough, the cruising police spotted the parked car, the obviously shifted barriers, and betook themselves upstairs after the culprit. Paul expansively explained the situation, how he had Slim Dusty there for important interviews, and before Slim knew what was going on he was autographing police caps and thanking the officers for their assistance.

I was proud of Slim's achievement, but we were both pleased with the fact that bush ballads and country music had come of age; that our life of travelling and connecting with people all over Australia, the Pacific and further had made an impression on a wide segment of our nation's people.

EMI presented us with two first-class return tickets to the USA as a celebration of Slim's fiftieth anniversary of recording for the company. I'd been recording with him for about 43 or 44 of those years, so I reckoned I'd earned my seat on the plane, too. Then we received an official invitation from the *Grand Ole Opry* in Nashville for Slim to appear there. Although we both felt that audiences there might need a dictionary to understand some of the Australian idiom, the fact was that many of Slim's recordings had made their way to the United States. We knew of one publisher who collected every album Slim issued. As we were friendly with Tom T. Hall, and had other friends there such as folk singer Bill Clifton, we made the trip the following year. The problem of a band who knew Slim's songs and styles was solved by contacting Keith Urban and his mates, Peter Drake and Jerry Flowers, who were battling to make their name in the huge American market. They were keen to help out, and when Lawrie Minson from Tamworth volunteered himself as harmonica and didgeridoo player, we were set.

When we arrived home, we were informed that Slim had been chosen by public vote as one of Australia's 100 National Living Treasures. I thought I'd have to keep an eye on his hat and, if it showed signs of being too tight, would have to take action to relieve any swelling of the head. But, as usual, he was a bit disbelieving of all the honour, except for saying that he liked the fact the vote was by the public; he was quite happy to say that, yes, he'd be very willing to perform on the night of the big dinner where the honoured folk were to be announced, even though we'd be in the middle of a tour at the time. Sydney Town Hall was the venue for this fundraising dinner in aid of the National Trust of Australia, and there was much pomp and show for the celebration.

I dislike having to walk up many steps or stairs in front of a crowd because I cannot keep pace with anyone else. I have to take one step at a time, not one after the other, because while I'm standing my caliper is not made to bend. On this occasion I was dismayed to find out that I had to walk with Slim up the very front stairway into the foyer of the Town Hall, while he was being announced to the crowd of onlookers. It was not a good start to my evening, but there was no alternative that I knew about. Inside, the interior of the Town Hall was beautifully decorated, and the huge organ pipes covering most of the wall behind the wide stage were lit with changing colours. I couldn't help remembering what it used to look like in the days when Heather and I sang our yodelling songs on that same stage to an audience of country music enthusiasts.

There were tables set up on the floor and the arrangement was that one Living Treasure would be seated at each table as host to the guests. Of course, that meant Slim was on one table, and from his point of view that meant I would be on his table too. All the Living Treasures were asked to go to a back room to wait for their introduction to the guests, and before I knew it Slim had chivvied me along with him. He did not want to be in amongst that group on his own. So I had the chance of listening to Dick Smith telling Hazel Hawke a fantastic story of plans for an Antarctic adventure while hosts of public figures milled around in the small room. I kept seeing faces I'd only seen on television or in newspapers and they were mostly friendly and open. R.M. Williams was there and so was Colleen McCulloch. In particular, Hazel Hawke was lovely, with a genuine warmth about her.

Not knowing what the procedure would be, I was quite innocent of the fact that within the next short while I was going to be lined up in front of the stage with my husband and (supposedly) the other 99 National Living Treasures. No one seemed to care that there was definitely a ring-in on their night of nights; though one man, noted for his acerbic commentaries and learned reviews, leaned into my ear and said with a chuckle, 'I like you … You're a rebel!' I think – I really do think – that he must have mixed me up with someone else.

The other request from the Trust chairman was for Slim and Richard Tognetti, director and lead violinist of the Australian Chamber Orchestra, to perform onstage together. When this came through, I was flummoxed. What on earth would we do? I couldn't for the life of me visualise Slim in his Akubra and Tognetti with his multi-million dollar violin doing a duo act. But it worked out. We collared the Fettler, Mike Kerin, long-time fiddle player with the Travelling Country Band and suggested to Richard that he and Fett should try out the twin fiddle parts of the arrangement of 'Lights on the Hill'. Apparently, they got on well together to such an extent that Tognetti even had Fett playing in a small classical quartet selection before the duo was to begin. (Mike sprang that one on us and nearly gave us heart attacks.) Always interested and always looking to expand his knowledge of violins and players, Tognetti spent quite a lot of time with Mike, who had picked up violin in his early teens, as the son of a fiddle player from County Clare in Ireland.

When the two violins swung into the driving rhythm of the 'Lights' solo, the crowd loved it. Tognetti and the Fettler were enjoying themselves and when Slim started up 'Claypan Boogie' they were competing with each other to play fantastic boogie and jazz solos. The audience ended up with many dancing between the tables ... quite an abandoned performance from such a formal gathering.

We came back to earth next day, catching a plane to Albury to rejoin our southern tour down to Tasmania and back. It wasn't too much longer before it was time for Slim's investiture at Government House. Anne and David came with me to accompany Slim, and it was like Old Home Week when we met up with Gus Williams from Hermannsburg, whose investiture was to be carried out on the same day. Another bonus was meeting the cartoonist Eric Jolliffe, who had been a favourite of ours for years and years. It was a shame that the official photograph taken on the day was faulty, and Slim never did remember to go to the photographic studio to replicate his official photo.

After all this public attention, we both needed a holiday. Slim went off to Metung fishing with a couple of mates; Heather and I went to Norfolk Island for a few days and managed to land ourselves there for a country music festival. We dodged most of the crowds and had a quiet touristy visit. This year, Daniel turned eleven and we were taking him to South America for his trip.

We were prepared for altitude sickness when we travelled in places such as Bolivia. But I found that, whereas Danny and I went along without bother, Slim was getting breathless and pale at times. It was unusual for him and I was relieved when we came down closer to sea level and he recovered from what we put down to altitude sickness. Even at Machu Picchu he was alright while Danny climbed everything in sight, the higher and rougher the better. And five days after our return, we were on tour in Queensland.

Ever since the start of the Golden Guitars, the awards night had been held in differing venues, ranging from the town hall (now too small to hold the crowds) to the Calrossy High School auditorium (ditto) to a circus marquee that threatened to take off in a storm; even a corrugated iron hangar type building at the airport was used. This was as well as the early rodeo arena covered area. As the Tamworth Festival grew and grew, the lack of an entertainment venue for the city became critical. A group of businessmen and stakeholders eventually pledged a large amount of funding over five years and took it to the Council, which then raised the rest of the funds and began building. So it turned out that this year, 1998, saw the opening of the Tamworth Regional Entertainment and Conference Centre, better known as the TRECC. The CMAA celebrated the occasion with the Concert of the Century to open the long-awaited home of country music.

There was also a bit of building – on a much smaller scale – taking place at home. In view of all the years of recording with them, and the fact that they had sold their own 301 Studios, EMI decided to build Slim a studio in the granny flat located on top of our garage. We decided to go a bit further and build a separate office in the back block behind our house and the proposed studio. Our house had only three bedrooms and while one was my office, and another our bedroom, the third had always had to serve as our secretary's office. Slim had his own separate den. We never had anywhere to put up family or visitors. I became very brave and asked for a separate office and we ended up with a small two-storey building that housed the office and archives upstairs, and we planned the downstairs to be an office and meeting room for me. They say the best-laid plans of mice and men will always go awry and this happened to me, too.

My dear Aunty Una and her husband, Tony, lived in Tony's home town of Guyra, New South Wales, where they built a beautiful home. Aunty Una's eyesight had deteriorated to the point where she had not been able to drive for years, but she was quite active and they were very happy in Tony's retirement. When he was diagnosed with cancer of the throat and it became worse, Tony came to me about Aunty Una's future. He helped us change the plans of the downstairs office area into a little self-contained unit for Una, and later on, after his death, she sold out of Guyra and came to live with us.

Shortly after all the building activity we took the band with us to the Solomon Islands again, this time to perform at a couple of concerts marking the opening of the Gold Ridge Mine. The day I returned from the Solomons I heard from Rick Carey that his wife, Thel, had died after her long battle with illness. Thel and I had spent a lot of time together in a shared house in Merrylands when Anne was a toddler. We had kept in touch over the years one way and another when we were both on the road, and we were the sort of friends who might not see each other for a long time but could then pick up where we'd left off, say, last year. I never thought I would be delivering the eulogy at her funeral.

The number of friends and colleagues who had passed away in the recent few years was a sobering thought at times, though I didn't seriously consider for a moment that we should think ourselves in any danger of death. We were both organically healthy; we tried to keep ourselves busy and fit, especially as Slim walked for an hour each day. The effort I expended in keeping up with normal activities actually resulted in keeping me fit; as one specialist had told my parents, 'It takes her twice the effort to do half as much.'

So I was not prepared for any real worry one evening when Slim went to bed early and was still awake at eleven o'clock. I was up and about at that hour because David was staying with us overnight; he was at the kitchen table with his computer, carrying on a conversation with me at the same time. I found Slim sitting propped up in bed looking grizzly and saying he couldn't settle down to sleep. As he usually went to sleep very quickly after his head hit the pillow, I was surprised and commented on it to David.

David closed down his computer and got up. 'I might just go and have a look at him, Mum,' he said. When he came back he asked me to pack an overnight bag for Slim, because he was taking his father to the emergency department of the Sydney Adventist Hospital in Wahroonga, in Sydney's north, for a check and 'just in case' Slim should need to stay overnight. Next morning I went to the hospital to be with Slim because the cardiologist David had contacted was going to do an angiogram to see the condition of Slim's heart. I was sitting beside Slim's bed after he returned from theatre, chatting and joking and asking when he was going to stop being a fraud and get himself moving, when the specialist hurried into the room, still in theatre gear.

The specialist didn't mince his words. 'You have a life-threatening heart condition,' he said, 'with a ninety-five per cent blockage at the junction of two of your main arteries. You are not to get out of that bed and you are not to try to exert yourself in any way while we arrange surgery immediately.'

Seeing that Slim had spent the previous day working in the yard in the summer heat, cleaning out the hen house and doing other fairly strenuous work, it was obvious he'd had a near-miss with a sudden demise. I was shocked and at first I couldn't take it all in; David soon made it only too clear to me. He arranged for a fine surgeon to operate on his father, and had him moved by ambulance to the surgeon's hospital of choice. Slim reckoned that the ambulance airconditioning unit dripped cold water on his head all the way to the other hospital, and that was all he remembered of the trip.

I still did not register the severity of the situation at this stage. Slim was not a tall or big-built man, being rather fine boned, but he was very resilient and wiry, with amazing stamina. His preferred workload caused musicians 25 years younger to complain. (Although I noticed that they all seemed to like working with him, despite the workload on tour and his volatile nature.)

In intensive care after the operation, Slim had the full attention of the specialist in charge, and the telephone operators on the hospital switchboard worked overtime keeping up with enquiries and fielding requests for information from all and sundry. If we didn't know before, we began to realise then how much Joe Blow and his missus thought of Slim.

Slim recovered slowly but well and began working on his recording as usual. I was keeping more of an eye on him because we had to attend lots of awards nights and community functions, such as the launch of a Social Justice paper or a Legacy Charity luncheon. At a CMAA function I received their Achiever's Award for 1999. We postponed touring until June and July that year and began, like the rest of the nation, to look forward to all the celebrations coming up for the arrival of the year 2000. Moreover, EMI was gearing up to release Slim's one-hundredth album. Although these big events were for Slim, they seemed to include me with him and we celebrated or mourned together for whichever way things went.

The year 2000 was going to be huge, I thought, and so I tried to space things, but it was like a steamroller of events and happenings in a year of events and happenings for the whole country, not just for us.

Our main focus was on the content of the one-hundredth album, which was so important to us and to the recording company. Apparently Slim was the only recording artist in the world to have recorded 100 albums all for the one company, and EMI wanted to mark the occasion with bells and whistles. Songwriter Don Walker wrote the songs for Cold Chisel, a top rock band, but he also wrote two or three country songs that Slim recorded. I asked him to write something special for this album and, not having heard from him for a while, apparently I rang and said, 'Don, we're depending on you,' which we were. That put him on the spot, I suppose, but dependable Don wrote the most beautiful song for Slim, 'Looking Forward,

Looking Back'. It has become an anthem of sorts, and it is a special song still – kept only for Slim.

The launch night was very special. Even the invitations were specially created in timber, and friends and colleagues came from everywhere to be with us. For the second time in Slim's career, *This is Your Life* presented the story of the second half of his life – or, I guess, of our life together. No sooner was all this over, than we turned to our trip with Hannah, the youngest and last of our grandchildren. We settled on a trip that took in Spain, Scotland and Ireland.

All Australia was buzzing with excitement and anticipation because the 2000 Olympics were to be held in our country, in Sydney. I was quite keyed up about this because Slim had been invited to appear in the Closing Ceremony on 1 October. John Spence (who produced so many early Golden Guitar Awards nights) was assisting David Atkins, the artistic director of the Opening and Closing Ceremonies. I didn't know what to think when the idea was first mooted, but it was such an exciting offer that it only became a bit daunting when I understood that Slim would actually be performing the very closing song of the ceremony. We went on tour and I tried not to think too much about it. Both of us had confidence in John, and if he said it would work out, we were sure it would.

First up, there was a full-scale rehearsal at a big open ground in an outer Sydney suburban arena and for the first time we saw most of the built sets and 'floats' being readied for the big night. I saw the extent of the long walk Slim would have to make on his way from the dressing rooms under the buildings to across the roadway, then up the long, long staircase to the top of the huge set in the middle of the arena. I thought all the usual things that wives probably think in situations like this one: What if he trips in the dark? What if the children out front don't move to let him through? What if his walkie-talkie mike doesn't work properly, or the guitar sound can't be picked up? But I didn't dare say anything out loud. Slim seemed to be taking it all in his stride. Only now and then did I see some tension, but this was only the rehearsal.

When the big day arrived we spent most of the day in the green room with other artists who were to perform that night – such as Peter Garrett from Midnight Oil, Jimmy Barnes, the Emmanuel Brothers; everyone came and went at intervals during the waiting time. A good half-hour before Slim was due to perform John took him downstairs, where the engineers fitted him and his guitar with microphones and he and John walked around and talked about what was about to take place.

'Just start,' John told Slim, 'and keep walking steadily ahead. The children will part ahead of you to let you through, and then you head straight up the stairway to the top.' John kept going through the instructions; the microphones and transmitters were hidden beneath Slim's three-quarter-length coat.

When Slim stepped out into the glare of the huge lights, he strummed a chord across his guitar strings and started singing 'Waltzing Matilda' as he slowly and steadily crossed the arena roadway towards a mass of children around the bottom of the stairs. Upstairs in the green room, with its long glass windows overlooking his journey, I had my heart in my mouth. When I couldn't stand it any longer, I went out the door and stood amongst the crowd in the tiers of seating. They had their arms in the air; some were shouting, 'Slim! Slim!' and others began singing with him. The whole massive crowd took up the refrain; the electricity from those thousands of people crackled in the night air. I have never, ever felt anything like it in my life. I stood in a daze watching my husband and willing everything to go right for him … and it did.

CHAPTER 27

Each year usually began with our gearing up for the activities of the Tamworth Country Music Festival, but before that this year, 2001, started with Australia Post announcing Slim as their Legend of 2001 with a series of stamps with his image on them. So when we arrived at Tamworth the stamps were everywhere, and we spent three hours autographing first-day covers and souvenirs of the stamp issue before we moved on to the other activities. That year marked the centenary of Federation in Australia, and there was a huge parade through Sydney streets with Slim and artists such as the Wiggles involved. The Golden Guitars brought three more trophies to the collection; the College Graduation concert was applauded as one of the best of the festival; the Walk a Country Mile display (named after my song) opened at the Information Centre; the Australian Bush Balladeers Association held their Star Quest final and all in all, everything went past in a bit of a blur.

I was trying to keep Slim well, and after the heart scare I watched out for him as best I could. But after being off the road for a large part of the previous year, he was touring again for a good six weeks.

In March 2000 we bought back Slim's old family farm at Nulla Nulla Creek. As well as buying the property where

Slim grew up, the purchase included the neighbouring farm that belonged to Billy Kyle in the days when Slim lived in the valley. That was a bonus, actually, as there were many happy memories attached to the Kyle farm and I'd heard so many stories about those days. We had to have a manager look after the farm because we were flat out with our music and touring, but it was great to take the family there to camp beside the creek and walk over the paddocks.

By this time I was sure there was something the matter with Slim. He was nervy and more easily tired than I had ever seen him. Although he insisted on fulfilling his touring commitments, plus his recording, which he loved, I thought he was flagging and blamed it on his workload, which would have been tremendous for any other man of 74 years of age. On more than one occasion I chased him off to his GP for a check-up and he even underwent a special stress test, but as his GP said to me when I rang to say that I was concerned about my husband, 'He's not very forthcoming about his health, is he?' I gathered that Slim seemed to treat his consultations as an opportunity to have a pleasant chat about all and sundry – everything except what was concerning me.

Life was certainly busy but it was so interesting. We went to South Australia to attend the launch of the Year of the Outback, and promised to be in Marree at the conclusion of the Great Cattle Drive in the Year of the Outback the following year of 2002. Next it was off to Alice Springs for the huge Yeperenye Festival, celebrating Federation year. It was held outdoors on a large stage, and to begin proceedings a long, brilliantly lit 'caterpillar' made its way from the hills around the festival grounds, to wind through the crowds on a pathway to the stage. It was a spectacular opening and overall it was an amazing night, sitting around a campfire behind the stage yarning with friends.

After the ARIAs, where Slim presented a special award to Keith Urban – collecting an ARIA for himself in the process and making other appearances – I was beginning to panic. I *knew* there was something wrong but I couldn't seem to get anyone, especially Slim, to do anything about it.

So I rang David, who had no idea what was going on, and as I was getting very upset I realised I was rather abrupt: 'There's something very wrong with Dad, and I just can't get anywhere with finding what it is. *You* have to get on to his GP and *make* him find it or I'm taking him to someone else.'

Once David knew the situation, he moved decisively. Slim was sent, protesting, for a CT scan that showed a tumour on his left kidney. This was on a Wednesday, and by the following Monday he went into theatre to have it removed, together with his spleen.

I was relieved, and yet frightened. Slim made a good recovery, but we celebrated our Golden Wedding anniversary with a quiet family dinner instead of a party.

To begin the New Year and also to allay rumours of Slim's retirement, we held the Family Concert during the Tamworth Festival and he performed at the Golden Guitar Awards. As usual, we began a couple of months of touring after some family doings. We celebrated Heather's seventieth birthday, and Anne even held an early twenty-first birthday party for Kate because Kate was due to leave soon after to spend a year studying in the south of Germany.

Having put Slim's surgery behind us, we sailed into the year. I confidently informed the audience in Tamworth that Slim was up and running again, and that he would have to be dragged kicking and screaming off the stage, if ever the time came. Slim always reckoned he'd prefer to just fall into the footlights. He recorded an album with Anne, who wrote the title track, 'Travellin' Still ... Always Will'. It summed up our lives together, our differences and our similarities, and it told of what she could always see in us; our strength together and our love for each other no matter what else happened. It was always a special song for Slim and me, an understanding of us I had sometimes wondered if anyone would ever see.

We toured all of June and July, one highlight being the concert at Marree in the north of South Australia, the town that marked the end of the Great Cattle Drive in the Year of the Outback. Marree was inundated with visitors, with the arrival of the cattle and drovers (both professional and keen amateurs) under the charge of boss drover Eric Oldfield.

We covered a lot of different country on that tour, the last concert being at Launceston in Tasmania on 20 July. Eight days later Barry Thornton was in Launceston, playing at a record launch, when his fragile arteries gave out, and he died doing what he said he would do: 'I won't sit around waiting for it to happen, mate. I'll go on doing shows just the same.' He was a loss for us; a link to our hard days and good days.

Over the years, I've had far fewer falls than most people would expect. I always said I was padded well enough to survive most of them anyway, if I did have them. But I had one bad fall backstage in Maitland, during the June tour, when my caliper suddenly gave way underneath me. I fell heavily and wrenched my good knee doing it. I thought I must have accidentally bumped the hinge that releases the knee lock and allows the caliper to bend. I got over it in a day or two, but in September I was in the kitchen talking to Slim and Anne when the caliper suddenly gave way again. As my weight was fully on my bad leg, I fell swiftly and heavily, but this time my bad foot caught under the shelf beneath the butcher's block standing just in front of me.

When my shocked family hauled me up from the floor, it was my foot that concerned me. It was speedily X-rayed; I had two broken bones across the foot, and there was no way I would be able to accompany Slim to Perth. I was devastated, because he was going to accept an Honorary Doctorate in Music from Edith Cowan University and I wanted to see the ceremony. Anne went in my place, and I had to make do with photos and press cuttings as I whizzed around the house in a wheelchair, gouging indents in the architraves of all the doors I went through. When my caliper maker inspected the brace, I received a lecture about regular inspections of the elastic that held the hinge in place; and since then it has been Anne who regularly enquires about the strength of the elastic and whether it needs replacing. They say familiarity breeds contempt, and where my loyal old caliper is concerned I plead guilty on all counts.

I noticed the return of Slim's weariness and his lack of resilience and bounce, and despite my efforts to keep him eating well and healthily, his weight began to drop again. After CT scans and bone scans we were told that the kidney cancer had spread, and he would have to begin radiotherapy. Chemotherapy was not an option for this cancer. In the midst of this Slim and Anne were presented with a Gold Record for the sales of *Travellin' Still ... Always Will* and as Anne, Greg and James left for Germany to spend Christmas with Kate, Slim began radiotherapy. He had the last treatment two days before Christmas, and then our battle really began.

January 2003 saw the Family Concert in Tamworth cancelled and the rumours beginning to circulate. Anne accepted Slim's Golden Guitar for Bush Ballad of the Year and kept her head well down during the festival to dodge media enquiries. At the request of one of the venue owners, Anne organised a Joy McKean tribute concert in Tamworth, with lots of different country artists performing one of my songs each. She really wanted me to see this tribute she had worked so hard to mount, so David came down to stay with Slim while I caught an early plane to Tamworth and an afternoon flight straight back. It did seem strange to hear all those voices singing different arrangements of my songs, old and new. Some of the very old ones made me smile a bit, written as they were when I was in my teens and very early twenties. Listening to them all those years later, I thought they could have done with a bit of polishing. But someone must have liked them enough to ferret them out and learn them at this stage, I told myself. Then when one singer commented, as he introduced his version of 'Ringer', 'It is written as though Joy was there herself,' I couldn't help myself and called out, 'But I *was*!' and then subsided in confusion.

We tried to keep life as normal as possible, although the going was rough at times. Slim's treatments made him tired and irritable, and he was frustrated at his inability to do everything he was used to doing. He put on some of the weight he'd lost, and I felt more hopeful. He began working on a new collection of songs for the next album, and before long managed to get upstairs to his studio to record some of the songs with Rod, Mike and the rest of the band.

Aunty Una – now living in her little unit with us – concentrated on being a listening post and support for me, and for Slim too. She cooked his favourite cake and any time I couldn't find him, I'd go straight over to check if he was with Aunty Una having a cup of tea and a slice of cake or a homemade biscuit. But as the year wore on, with the constant juggling of medications, more treatments and a relentless downhill slide, the family rallied and organised themselves into a strong, loving unit of helpers. Kate did the housework; Jane amazed Slim with her ironing speed (as Jane explained to me: 'I hate ironing so I get it done as quickly as possible!'); David took days out of his annual leave to come down from the Central Coast and stay with his father; Anne was there all the time as we coped with mountains of washing and constant administration of medication; Greg and James (and Anne too) became used to having me ring at all hours to say I needed them to help me lift Slim when he fell.

Getting towards August that year, Slim kept working on the album. Mike Kerin often came over to play guitar with him so that he could rehearse the songs, because Slim was not able to play for long. Slim's sister Kathleen, living with her daughter Noeline in Mullumbimby, was failing too. Noeline and I were in touch almost daily for months, encouraging and supporting each other as the times got harder for each of us. My family made sure I had some time off; someone was always there to stand in for me for some hours, a day, a couple of days here and there.

When Slim couldn't make it up to the studio, he lost heart. By this time Jane had organised nurses for morning and night, and hospital equipment so we could move him more easily and therefore keep him at home. He did not want to go back to hospital, and I promised that he wouldn't if it were humanly possible for me to manage it. Nurses said they had never seen a family organise itself and provide the backup they needed in the way that we did. But we are a close family, exceptionally so in times of crisis.

Anne and Jane were with me in mid-September; I did not know that Jane had rung her children, Danny and Hannah, on the Central Coast and told Hannah to pack an overnight bag for David. Then she rang David, who lost no time on the freeway from Gosford to Sydney. We were there when Slim decided it was time to leave. I have always believed, and still do, that when he couldn't sing any more, he didn't want to hang around. So he left us on 19 September 2003, the forty-ninth anniversary of our first touring concert back in 1954.

I remember little of the rest of the day as I sat with Slim. A reporter came to the door; Jane answered the knock and said, 'I don't believe this!' The hapless journalist said, 'I don't want to be here, either.' EMI organised a spokesman, Chris O'Hearn, who had worked closely with us for a long time, and Chris did the interviews and organised press releases.

The state government offered me a state funeral for Slim and I accepted. I was numb and listened dully to arrangements being made and agreed to. The lady who came to our house over the following week to prepare us for the coming ordeal was kind and efficient; she advised Anne and David on how to prepare themselves for speaking at the service.

Slim's funeral took place in St Andrew's Cathedral in Sydney on 29 September 2003. Flags on the Harbour Bridge were at half mast and the mounted police volunteered to accompany his hearse out of the city. People came from all over Australia to stand outside and watch the service on big television screens if they couldn't get inside. Representatives of Aboriginal communities were prominent. Our son David, son-in-law Greg, grandsons James and Daniel, Slim's record producer and friend Rod Coe, and the Fettler, Mike Kerin, carried his coffin. Jane, Kate and Hannah carried some of his awards behind them. Friends and colleagues from different sides of the music industry spoke of Slim; I appreciated every word but could not remember very much of it later on. Both Anne and David spoke lovingly and proudly of their father, and I have kept a written copy of every beautiful word they said.

That morning, David searched high and low for the 'Bible of the Bush', as Slim called it. This was the book of Henry Lawson poetry that was my first birthday gift to Slim back in 1952. The pages are marked here and there with Slim's notes and even with the words of a verse he knew had been omitted by the editors of that edition. David badly wanted to carry the old book to the cathedral. Almost giving up the search, he spoke aloud: 'Dad, you've got to help me.' In a last try, he pulled a couple of books from one of the shelves – and there, in the gap behind, was the old red book. I think he said, 'Thanks, Dad', and while he carried their father's coffin, Anne held the old Bible of the Bush close in her arms.

Everyone from the prime minister and Cabinet ministers attended; fellow recording artists spoke and sang for Slim, and I walked and talked automatically.

My spirit was elsewhere that day.

CHAPTER 28

I was numb with emotional exhaustion and, indeed, physical exhaustion as well. The previous two years of seeing Slim grow weaker took their toll on me at last. I couldn't think straight. At times my mind would clear and I would begin to move onwards to do all that had to be done, then a fog of grief and tiredness would take over and I could do nothing positive. I went to Metung to sit quietly amongst all the mementoes of our outback trips and my memories of the times when the four of us were so happy together in between school terms and tours. At times my grief was a physical pain that hit me in the pit of my stomach, wrenching my insides till I could stand it no longer. I would double up and cry with loneliness.

At last, though, I was empty. I couldn't even cry any more – it was all done – so I returned to Sydney and looked at what lay ahead of me.

A new edition of our book, *Another Day, Another Town*, was set for release in October, and a long line of media interviews had been set up for me. I was given the choice of refusing these, but I said I would do all the publicity that was required. Slim had seen all the additions to the book and was quite happy with them. So even though some people may have thought it odd that I could do all this so soon after Slim's passing, I knew that Slim would have thought it odd if I didn't. We never did shirk the hard yards, and I would not let him down by doing it now.

Our first Christmas without Slim was a hard one but we coped. I was on the board of the Slim Dusty Foundation, working to build the Heritage Centre (as we called it then) in Kempsey. This was a constant pressure, as we found our first choice of site, the historic showground in West Kempsey, was still designated a flood insurance risk should a 100-year flood hit the town. Among other issues, it became necessary for us to search for a new site. This was difficult and took us quite a while; in the meantime we worked on raising funds to design and finally build a fitting museum and community centre structure.

We had bought the Nulla farms in partnership with a close acquaintance who wanted to expand the property by buying an adjoining farm holding two houses. This was sensible, as it gave us an old house to renovate for our own use and a good brick house for a manager, so we invested in this further purchase. Slim's old home – which as a boy he had christened Melody Ranch – was kept in order and a sign erected on the road outside, along with a solar-powered cassette device playing Slim's voice talking about the old farm and singing 'When the Rain Tumbles Down in July'.

I remember one woman asking me what I was going to do with myself now. I laughed out loud then said that I had been left a lot of work to do, and I was 'getting on with it', as was our usual motto, according to Slim. There was the last album recording to finalise, with the usual work to be done for that; there were the mountains of cards, emails and correspondence from all over the world to deal with; there were all the legal matters pending, and on it went. In amongst all this, I had good friends and helpers. My colleagues at EMI were endlessly helpful and thoughtful beyond the call of business, as were nearly all the business and legal people I had to deal with. My family was the rock I leaned on all the while.

My friends in the country music industry came to the fore with the organisation of a huge 'Concert for Slim' in Tamworth the following January, with all the funds from the concert, and the recording and a DVD of the show, to be donated to the Slim Dusty Foundation; these proceeds would later enable us to buy a parcel of freehold land that lay in the middle of some government leasehold land that we identified as eminently suitable for building the Centre. Everyone from artists and musicians to sound and lighting companies and crews, plus backstage crew, gave their time and talent and hard work as a donation to the Foundation. So did the producer, John Spence, and all the volunteers who set up the seats, did the ushering and all the thousand little things that go to make a big event a successful one.

The TRECC was packed on 20 January 2004. Dobe Newton, compere for the night, announced that, 'This is the public wake, this is our chance to celebrate the life and work of the great Slim Dusty.' It was a celebration indeed, a night of terrific performances and a wonderful feeling of warmth and closeness between artists and audience. I felt lifted up by the presence of all these people singing and playing for Slim, with his Travelling Country Band backing them.

On the way home I stopped in Singleton, my birthplace, where I was invited to make the Australia Day address. It was a big compliment to be asked to do this and it marked the beginning of a number of community things I did that year, such as a video supporting a Salvation Army fundraising appeal.

During January I began speaking up for the 'Go Smoke Free' campaign mounted by a coalition of the NSW Cancer Council, the Heart Foundation, the Asthma Foundation and the Australian Medical Association NSW. Renal cancer is one of the many dangerous outcomes of smoking, especially passive smoking. It is not as well known a consequence of smoking as lung cancer is, for instance. But when I discovered that it might have been a cause of my husband's fatal kidney cancer, I was more than willing to stand up for smoke-free work and play places. Slim and I were amongst the first entertainers to refuse to work in smoky auditoriums and, indeed, we had both been told that we should not perform in such venues if we wanted to continue singing. It made us unpopular to begin with, but in the end people began to think that maybe we did have a point.

I recall one club in Canberra where the dressing rooms were on the side of the stage. The smoke was so thick, pouring up from the auditorium onto the stage, that we had a towel pushed under the dressing room door to stop it from coming in and choking us. That was such an extreme example of what we, as entertainers, had to put up with. We took the similarly extreme measure of speaking to the management about the situation and advising that we could not possibly take any further bookings under those conditions. To their credit, management took this on board and invested in a new airconditioning system that lessened the problem. The next step, of course, was to get the auditorium smoke free altogether.

The Cancer Council asked me to address a meeting of government officials and representatives of the Clubs Association and the Australian Hotels Association. Other people there were members of a working party that was to report to state parliament on laws concerning smoking in pubs and clubs. The seats around a very big table were all full. I was told later that many were impressed by the fact that I spoke without notes. I spoke without notes because I was passionate about my subject. I spoke about the passive smoking that was actually more dangerous than active smoking; I emphasised that all my young colleagues were forced to work in these conditions and if they protested they were told to go and work someplace else then. Musicians starting in the business have to work anywhere and everywhere they can, and as for the bar and waiting staff, they were expected to work and breathe carcinogenic smoke day after day.

I told them about an old musician friend, and I named him. He had never smoked in his life but he had lost first his legs and then his life to the effects of passive smoking suffered in the years of playing in an upmarket function room and its like. The only men in that room who could not meet my eyes were the two from the Clubs Association and the Hotels Association. Frankly, I would not have been surprised if they agreed with me but had to do their job, which was to disagree with my arguments on principle.

A matter of days later, I had an unexpected phone call. The government minister who was involved told me, 'Joy, we will do it. It is going to happen.' I could have cried knowing that the will was there. It did happen, not just because of that one meeting but because of the concerted pressure from so many organisations and individuals – and the undeniable evidence all around us. I should add that both Slim and I were smokers for years, and were aware of the difficulties in quitting nicotine. We did it, eventually, but suffered the consequences of delay with my husband's life, and for that I was very angry at us both.

The last studio album was released in March, and although it was unfinished in that it only had seven tracks on it, it had the usual charisma about it. Slim's recording studio was named Columbia Lane after the lane every recording artist had to traverse to access the original EMI (Columbia Graphophone) recording studio in Homebush, a Sydney suburb. I went there with Slim when I first began singing on records with him and always thought the studios were rather an afterthought tacked onto the main brick building. Nevertheless, when the local council began replacing the old wooden street signs with flash new metal ones, 'Columbia Lane' disappeared one night. Years later, after Slim talked about the lane, the sign appeared on our front verandah, courtesy of a music industry mate of Tex Morton. The yellow sign is still fastened above the stairs to Columbia Lane recording studio where Slim and his family have sung so many songs, and *Columbia Lane – The Last Sessions* is what we called his last album.

Aunty Una had settled into her little unit very well, and was happy to be living with a family again. She had been a constant in my life since I was a little girl, and she was a shoulder to cry on and an ear that listened to everything I wanted to tell. Some good advice came my way at times, because she was never afraid to speak her mind no matter the recipient.

Una had been an expert car driver till her eyes let her down, and she had a very modern take on life in many ways. Una and Tony had been keen dancers, and I remember the exclamation marks on an X-ray report that reported a broken bone in her foot: 'Hurt it jitterbugging!' She was in her late eighties at the time.

Una had a couple of good friends, George and Margaret, and often spent a few days staying with them. It was around April, I think, that she went down to spend a week or two with George and Margaret in the Gippsland; they stayed in our house in Metung. I came home from an appointment one day to find Anne waiting for me.

'Mum!' she said. 'Aunty Una is in hospital – she's been in an accident.'

Una's left leg was badly broken and the other one cut and bruised. When I heard the news, just after lunchtime, she was in Bairnsdale Hospital, but while I was getting ready to leave Sydney they moved her to Latrobe Valley Hospital in Sale, which was larger and had more resources. I packed a bag, fuelled the Land Cruiser and set out on the ten-hour drive to Metung. I stayed overnight at Goulburn, left again at 6 a.m.

and when I arrived at Metung had a shower and set off on the next two-hour drive to Sale.

Una was in plaster from her waist to her toes. The damage to her leg both above and below the knee was bad, very bad. They had moved her to Sale to operate on it, but discovered it was impossible to insert a supportive metal rod because she'd had knee reconstructions in both legs. She could not walk, although she tried to move from her bed by hopping a bit. I knew I had to get her back to Sydney as soon as possible. Air ambulance was the best option; once I was able to arrange a bed in a nursing home near my place, Una was flown to Sydney.

She was there for a couple of weeks while debate went on about what to do with her leg, then she developed pneumonia and entered Hornsby Hospital. I spent most days up there with her and just before I left her at about eight o'clock one night more than a week later, she said to me, 'Joy, I think I'm losing my cool.'

'Aunty Una, don't you dare!' I replied, thinking nothing of it.

'You know I love you, dear, don't you?' was her next remark.

'And I love you too, Aunty Una. You've been so good to me.'

I hadn't been home more than half an hour when the hospital rang to tell me that Una had been talking to the nurse as she was readied for the night's rest when she gave a little sigh and just went to sleep, for good. I went back to the hospital and sat a while. I found out then that she had been told that day that nothing could be done for her leg. That meant the rest of her life in a plaster cast, or in bed unable to get out and around. Right or wrong, I am willing to bet that Aunty Una's way of thinking would be that it was better to go to sleep than to live like that. She was a lady of independence and strong will.

I gave the eulogy at her funeral in May 2004. I'd even managed to get a little bunch of violets for her; they were her favourite flower. But when we were about to leave the chapel, I lost all control and wept my heart out. On top of losing my husband, I had lost a dear aunty who loved me all my life and hers.

I'd been handling all the legal affairs arising from Slim's death, and now I also handled all those arising from Aunty Una's. It's amazing how much has to be done and how long it takes to get it done after someone dies, no matter what assistance you have. When we had sorted out Aunty Una's wishes, she left me with enough money to help pay for a small motorhome. We'd always talked about getting a motorhome so it would be safer camping in the outback, and I decided that I'd do just that. You might ask why, and perhaps it was a rather way-out thing to do just off the top of my head. But the idea had been there for many years – it was just that there never seemed time to put it into action. I planned a long holiday and a trip to see the Territory again and visit my friend Regina at Peppimenarti. I could just see Aunty Una egging me on!

Once the idea was planted in the back of my mind I began planning the trip for the following year. For the present, though, I was tied up working on record company business, fielding offers to take over our archives and manuscripts, attending Foundation meetings and conferences, and sharing the care and development of the Nulla farm. At the same time well-known entrepreneur Michael Chugg put forward the suggestion that we mount a touring musical of Slim's life. He brought his team with him and they set out an attractive and practical proposal with scripts and designs; the whole proposal was set out in a practical, experienced manner but in the end, after many meetings and a lot of work it had to be abandoned. With the 2006 Commonwealth Games in Melbourne coming up, competition for sponsorship was fierce and a project of our size needed that support. I knew Chuggie, as most in the industry call him, did not enjoy telling me we could not continue with the project; but having been around for a long time, I understood only too well the way things go in this entertainment game and appreciated the upfront way he explained it to me. He always had a lot more gumption than many people I know.

I also received offers from national institutions to house our archives, manuscripts and photos, but with the prospective Slim Dusty Centre in mind, I had to keep possession of everything that would be needed for the museum. An erstwhile colleague in radio and heritage work was now at the National Film and Sound Archive (ScreenSound today), and he persuaded me to have the originals of our private movies housed there and DVD copies given to me for my use. I appreciated the good advice and acted upon it. These were just some of the things I had to deal with at this time.

As 2005 arrived, Anne accepted Slim's thirty-seventh Golden Guitar at the awards night in Tamworth and held it high in pride. I still have it.

Before long, I began searching for a suitable and affordable motorhome that I could drive and handle. I found a Trakka conversion on a Mercedes-Benz Sprinter chassis that suited my needs, and took delivery of it in May 2005. It has two single beds, a shower/toilet facility, gas stove and oven; with solar panels on the roof, I am able to camp out with hot water and battery-powered water pumps for up to a fortnight if necessary. Anne and I took it on a trial run during one of the rainiest weeks of the year, so it got a good workout on its first trip.

I planned to fly James and Hannah to Darwin during school and university holidays, pick them up there and drive the motorhome to Peppi. I'd carry a small tent and sleeping bag for James, and Hannah could share the van with me. On my way to the Territory I went to Paul Donkin's sixtieth birthday party in Lithgow on 11 June. It was a great night in celebration of Slim's old 'minder', and the next morning, groups of music industry friends waved me off in fine style to start my big drive. I swept out of the motel feeling like some brave adventurer and got as far as Wellington, past Mudgee, when the adventure dropped out of the story along with the gearbox efficiency. The motorhome just didn't want to go any further.

I ended up in the cabin of a very large tow truck driven by a friendly lady who loaded my little home onto her big truck with no worries and took me into Dubbo. As the motorhome and Merc people were aghast at my phone call explaining what had happened, they offered to put me up in a motel until they could get a new gearbox up to me from Melbourne. However, there was not one motel in Dubbo that would take me because I had my little dog, Penny, a miniature long-haired dachshund, with me. So much for hospitality for the benighted traveller in Dubbo! I had the Trakka unloaded onto a spot in the caravan park and settled in for the night. I tell you, the Merc people and the Trakka people had me back on the road in another day and a half, and the motorhome never missed a beat to Darwin, Peppi and back to Sydney. It wouldn't have dared.

I headed for Bourke and on the way there made a phone call to our farm partner and his partner. To my dismay, she told me her cattle dog was dead of strychnine poisoning. I was distressed for her, and quite shocked at such a terrible thing to have happened. A couple of days later, our partner rang to talk about his suspicions regarding the dog's death, but as his comments were about the manager's family, not his work, I made no comment. By the time I reached Winton, my son David rang to say our partner had sacked the manager and given him seven days to get off the property. I had not been consulted, and was most concerned at the speed of this action and the reasons for it.

David spoke to the manager and his wife who said they would rather leave as they felt there was no trust any more between the partner and them, but they were concerned that I knew nothing about the situation. I rang our partner to suggest that it would be fairer all round to give the family at least two weeks to make the necessary arrangements to move and find accommodation. They had no home of their own. This was not received favourably but agreed to. When I changed the subject to whether we should sell the cattle he had recommended we sell, he seemed to become suddenly angry and shouted that when I returned to Sydney, our partnership would be dissolved. I tried to soothe him, knowing how distressed he was over the death of his partner's dog, but my efforts were unsuccessful and he hung up on me.

So there I was in the middle of outback Queensland with absolutely no idea what was going on back in Sydney or up on the farm, and very upset about it. I could not understand why the partner wanted to dissolve the partnership so suddenly. I did not have the funds or the interest in having a huge cattle run to play around on: I only wanted to keep Homewood Farm and its history in my family and it needed to pay its way for me to do that. After Slim's death he had mentioned once that he felt he did not have the interest in Homewood that I did, and as he had bought an adjoining property perhaps I'd be better off not having to share costs on the larger place we had at the time. I recall replying that I would have no house and would need to be able to build another, and he said, 'Let's leave it for twelve months and see how we are then.' That's how I left it.

This rumpus took the shine off my journey for a while, but as there was little I could do about it up at Longreach and Winton, I was forced to leave it for the time being.

CHAPTER 29

When I first announced that I was driving to Darwin on my own, Anne and David were most perturbed. They didn't like the idea of my being alone on the long stretch from Mount Isa to the Three Ways above Tennant Creek in particular. I invested in a satellite phone and told them that I could always be contacted, or nearly always. They didn't really relax until I was able to tell them that Max Ellis from Tamworth, a fellow board member on the Foundation and our longtime colleague and CMAA fellow founder, had heard me talking about my trip and asked if he and his elder grandson, Finn, could visit Peppimenarti with James, Hannah, Penny and me. That was a great idea all round, I thought, and my two worriers settled down at last.

I think it took Max two days to swap his car for a four-wheel drive, throw his camping gear into the back of it and set out to catch up with me at Longreach. The first advice I gave him on arrival was to go back to Barcaldine and visit the Heritage Centre there because there was a very nice display about his grandmother, Constance Ellis. That was a surprise for him. A few days later, we reached Darwin and I was glad to get there.

Once we had Hannah, James and Finn we headed for Peppimenarti, where Regina was waiting for us under the tamarind tree. In a very kind gesture, she had a vacant house for us to use, and day after happy day we appreciated the showers and the cool after being out in the sun. We had a day out at Pandella Falls, everyone either fishing or swimming in the big lagoon at the bottom of the high falls. Hannah had her heart set on some weaving lessons from Regina, and she was given a demonstration of the whole process from the very beginning of finding the right roots for getting colours, and shredding the pandanus leaves, to spreading them in the sun to dry and then dyeing them. After that, Hannah was started on her first weaving effort; a small table mat. Another day, they were taken up to the summit of Peppimenarti Hill where Regina's husband, Harry, is buried. It is a very special place. James and Hannah wrote 'Resting Place' while they were at Peppi, about the special feeling and the special place. I was sorry to leave, as I always am. On our last night, dancers farewelled us and we sang a few songs in return. We left a different world behind us and returned to the more materialistic one ahead.

Originally, my sister Heather was to fly to Darwin to join me and travel back to Sydney with me, but unfortunately she had to undergo urgent surgery. James and Hannah left from Darwin, Max and Finn headed for Borroloola, and I turned the motorhome to the south and home. I didn't stop anywhere much on the way; I just drove, ate, slept and drove again till I reached Sydney and faced all the farm problems. Indeed, I found the next few months fully occupied with the winding up of the farm partnership and finding a suitable manager for Homewood Farm, as we called the merger of Slim's old 'Melody Ranch' and Basin Flat. There was a clearing sale of machinery and engines, cattle sales and purchases and a hundred and one things to be sorted out. By Christmas, everything was settled and I could concentrate on getting the farm into order, and maybe building myself a house there.

My life changed a lot in the past couple of years or so. It was only to be expected. I was no longer involved in touring and songwriting, except on rare occasions. I didn't have the incentive to write songs any more at this time, but Anne kept all the scraps of verse she found, and came to me one day to say she was working on a new album.

'Mum, I found this verse in my drawer and I love it,' she said. 'Can you finish it for me?'

I had a look at the verse that was actually a sort of chorus, and it was about the cradle Regina had made and given to Anne. The cradle meant a lot to Anne, as it was sent to her when she was expecting Kate. Since then, it has held each of my grandchildren as babies. I wonder who will hold it next, before it goes into the museum at the Slim Dusty Centre?

I sat at the old piano and began to write the melody and the rest of the lyrics. It was not an easy task because I had written the original words more as a poem, without thinking of how a melody would fit them. By the time I finished it as a song, I hoped very sincerely that it would do well for her album, because I'd put a lot of hard work and thinking into it.

Anne began work on *Showman's Daughter* in 2005 and released it in 2006. At the 2007 Golden Guitar Awards, she took out the Bush Ballad Award with 'Peppimenarti Cradle'. I was so proud of her and of the fact that she was now writing with a lot more confidence. I have always rated her song 'Showman's Daughter' as a first-class piece of writing. It must have been really daunting to have two songwriting parents around the place and I was glad to see her using her talent more.

When we released the original CD and DVD *Best of Slim Dusty*, I did all the publicity interviews – phoners, face to face, radio and TV. I went to Canberra at the invitation of the National Library to take part in oral history recordings and to see the Rob Willis and Noeline Kyle presentation of music from the Nulla. On one of these visits Heather came with me to do the oral history recordings too. I understood that this type of historical archive was very important to future research and understanding of the development of the Australian song and music, and I also began thinking I should do something along the lines of recording, on film, some interviews with people who were part of our story over the years.

With this in mind, I arranged for the interviewing and filming of Frank Foster and his cousin Teddy Trevor when they were in Sydney at the Royal Easter Show. That footage (amongst others) is valuable material for my grandson James, who is nearing completion of his ambition to make the definitive documentary on the life of his grandfather.

I was wearing a collection of different hats, you might say, as I moved from farm matters to Foundation board meetings and financials, from publicity interviews to archival work. I also began going to plays and concerts; a luxury I could not indulge when out on the road. I even booked myself on a month's cruise in the Mediterranean. It was on a small cruise ship. I visited many of the ancient archaeological sites I'd read about in places such as Egypt, Greece and Turkey. I'd never had a holiday more interesting than that one.

I threw myself into work and activity of any kind I could drum up. Yes, it was there to do, but I was frantic to keep myself busy. I missed Slim with a vicious kind of missing. I wanted to tell him what was happening; that was the hard part. I couldn't ask his opinion on what I was doing; I couldn't talk things over with him and yet his presence in the house and the garden was strong and pervasive. Many times I caught myself beginning to tell him something. His den was full of his presence; I had to close the door before it overwhelmed me.

There was never any time when I didn't miss him. On my special holiday, I had no Slim to talk to and to laugh with about the things I was seeing and people I was meeting. I had no Slim going crook about something that didn't suit him; if I could have heard him 'sounding off' I would have been so grateful. I think I felt cheated of the years we could have still had together. A bit of anger was sometimes the remedy for the hurt. I missed his sturdy support whenever difficulties arose; though I doubt some of my problems would ever have arisen if Slim had been around. But … I just 'got on with it'. There was no alternative, anyway.

In March of 2007 I had to go to our house in Metung, where a neighbour had destroyed some lilli pillies and was starting to lop a tree when he was sighted and reported. As it wasn't the first time this had happened, I had to go down and see what could be done to discourage the behaviour. On the way home I stayed overnight in Cooma; the next morning, as I came into Bredbo and stopped to pick up a coffee, I decided to leave the highway and make a detour to the east and look for old Anembo. This was the site of one of the little half-time schools my father, as a twenty year old, was sent to for his first teaching post. It wasn't the first time I looked longingly at the road heading out there, and on impulse, this time I did it … I headed out to look for Anembo.

The road soon changed to gravel, and my map showed a junction where the road swung north to Anembo, and south to Jerangle and Peak View. Dad used to talk of playing cricket against Jerangle club. I was poking along at about 60 kilometres per hour looking out for any sign to show me where to turn to find Anembo. I came up a rise and into a turn and then the world went haywire. There was a loud noise as the front driver's side tyre blew out and the Land Cruiser hurtled out of control, off the road towards a huge tree. I managed to miss that but scraped another. I was too late to pull up before I hit the fence. The fence would not have been too bad, but on the other side of it was a large log lying alongside the fenceline. I remember seeing dirt and grass all over the windscreen and thinking, So this is how it's going to be, just before I must have blacked out for a few seconds as the Land Cruiser somersaulted.

When I opened my eyes, I was hanging upside down in my seatbelt and the engine was still turning. I immediately tried to reach the ignition and turn it off. Next thing, I tried to reach the seatbelt catch to undo the belt. It took me quite a while and quite a bit of struggling; as I was trying, around the end of the passenger seat, walking on the interior roof came Penny, my little dog. She tried to lick my face and though it didn't help my efforts to get out of the seatbelt, it did reassure me that she was still all in one piece. Out of the belt, I tried the door but it was jammed shut. Penny and I crawled over to the passenger door that was concertinaed forward and we squeezed out into long grass … right on top of a fresh cow pat. I found a dry spot and flopped down to gather my wits about me.

Finally, I got to my feet and had a look at the vehicle. It was upside down on its roof; the cooler had given up its contents so that a dozen eggs and a container of Thai green curry was strewn around the cabin and back of the four-wheel drive. My luggage was covered in everything else that was in the Esky, I hadn't seen another vehicle since I left the highway, and I didn't have a phone that worked. No coverage on mine, anyway. After about half an hour, a motorbike rider went by but then, thank goodness, a utility pulled up. It was a Country Energy serviceman doing some overtime, and he saw me waving from the paddock.

He was very kind and efficient. He wrapped a rug around my shoulders and gave me hot tea from his thermos, and chocolate from his cooler. He sat me down and gave me a chance to tell him what happened. Then he rang the local police constable and proceeded to collect my belongings and take me – plus dog, luggage and briefcase – to Cooma hospital for checking. He even waited till I was cleared to leave and then took me to the only motel in town that would allow me to have Penny with me.

I rang David and told him my sad story, asking him to ring Anne and tell her not to be alarmed as I was unhurt and safe. Penny must have been thrown around as if she was in a washing machine, and all she wanted to do was lie still. I was sore and bruised, but I was all in one piece and that was more than anyone could have expected, including me.

David arrived next morning to pick me up and take me to see the Land Cruiser at the Captains Flat depot. I was desperately glad to see him. The poor old truck looked dreadful and I think David turned a paler shade of pale as he looked. I collected a few things I'd missed, but I've always been sorry I didn't remember to collect the sheepskin seat covers. Soon afterwards, David took me home to Sydney.

Enquiries from fans about new recordings were constant, and one line of enquiry was always about the possibility of the family as a whole being more active in music and recording. It was with this in mind that Anne, David and I began looking at the viability of recording an album. Anne, of course, had her own recording career, and David was a regular member of a Central Coast band, playing guitar and singing. James played guitar, sang and wrote songs, Hannah sang, wrote, and played flute and keyboard; Kate sang lead and harmony, especially bluegrass. And Daniel was a good listener, he reckoned, but when called upon could sing too.

Once we got rolling on the project, everyone began writing and then rehearsing. We had Slim's recording of Don Walker's 'How Good It Is'; Paul Kelly walked up the driveway carrying his guitar and sang 'Pick It Up and Pass It On' into a cassette recorder for us to learn. Pete Denahy sent 'Took His Saddle Home'; we loved Eric Bogle's 'The Dreamer', which fitted our family story, and then the family wrote the rest of the songs, such as David's 'Old Purple', Anne's 'Road Dreamer', and James and Hannah's 'Resting Place'. In a drawer at Metung I found Slim's handwritten verses of 'Family Reunion' which he must have written on a piece of leather and hung on the Christmas tree during one Christmas at Metung, so I set them to music. To top off a family album, we included Slim's recording of 'Sunburnt People', a song for which I'd written the words and some music, and Slim wrote all the rest.

The family album was recorded in Columbia Lane studio, amongst all the mementoes of travel and music. There was a lot of fun and memories mixed up with those recording sessions. I always love the photo of Anne, Kate and Hannah dressed up in three of my early stage costumes, around the microphone in the drum booth, taken the day of the cover photo shoot by John Elliott. The reason I have my hand behind my back in the cover shot is because I'd had surgery on my middle finger; it was bandaged up like a fat white sausage and I wanted it out of sight.

Our family album release was planned for 2008, and I began organising a family tour to promote it and fulfil the constant and numerous requests for family appearances. To use one accurate description, I have to say that this task was a bit like 'herding cats'. Anne had stage bookings; David had rosters at the hospital; and Daniel, James, Kate and Hannah all had university and work schedules to juggle around my requests. In the end, it did happen but I have not been able to even *think* about doing it again, despite complaints from the states and the towns that missed out. I would love to, but my family are hard to get in one place just for Christmas, let alone for a month or more of touring.

CHAPTER 30

During all the recording and family touring, the house on Homewood Farm was built. While I waited for it to be finished I used the motorhome and camped in the paddock near the big shed, behind the shell of an old farmhouse.

Over on what we called Graveyard Hill towards Basin Flat Gully was a cement block with a little metal plaque to mark the grave of a tiny baby who died nearly a hundred years ago. She died on the day before Christmas, probably in the severe heat of that time of year. I couldn't bear to think of little Florence Rebecca being forgotten, so I had a proper little gravestone with the story of her death, and her family and neighbours, placed above her resting place with her birth and death dates inscribed on it. A strong metal fence protects it from cattle intrusion, and I like to think little Florence Rebecca sleeps in peace with the soft hills around.

Although I could now stay up the Nulla in comfort, I had to spend the greater part of my time back in Sydney. The Foundation had raised the funds to hire a reputable firm to design the layout of the museum installation at the Centre, and construction of the Centre building itself began in 2009. This meant that the curator we had engaged, Linda Raymond, began work in my home in mid-February. Her job was to put together the collection of memorabilia, awards, manuscripts, photographs, stage costumes and all the other items intended for the museum display. She had to catalogue everything, check the condition of each item and recommend conservation work or otherwise, and then pack everything safely for storage while awaiting further funding to pay for installing and displaying in the final stage of the Centre.

Linda is small and cheerful, and if she was daunted by the size of the job, she did her best not to show it. She certainly needed an assistant for part of the big effort because it was a very big, and unique, collection. Linda worked in the house and over at the unit beneath our office for nearly two years, and she needed me, and Anne, to be on hand for nearly all that time to identify items and find them for her. Our standard joke used to be that if anyone stood still long enough, Linda would tie a tag on them. Her trusty computer had files upon files of photographs and information fed into it. There were boxes of all shapes and sizes with stage clothes, boots, hats and other textile items in them, and then there were other boxes and special plastic sleeves holding photographs and fragile manuscripts such as scrapbooks and letters.

I'd never realised the full extent of our collection until the packing of items began. It was almost as though we were packing up my life in front of my eyes. There were Slim's scrapbooks, begun on the farm and ending as we began touring; he'd taken an old exercise book of mine to use for the latest mementoes and photos he wanted to keep. There were two of his old hats, the front of the brim on each bearing the traces of where his hands turned it down every time he put it on his head. Old guitars and my piano accordion all reminded me of the stages they had appeared on. The lines of Golden Guitars and the Gold and Platinum Records all had reminders for me of the years they were awarded, and the miles we travelled then. There were paintings, and Aboriginal artefacts given to us in the outback and Northern Territory. Whenever I looked at something, I remembered the person associated with it and the time and happenings around it. Some special things were kept in the house still, but with a tag to remind me of its final destination … the museum.

All these things will be displayed in such a way as to tell the story of our journey, Slim's and mine, and even the story of touring country music shows and of country music here in Australia.

The first part of 2009 was taken up with the curatorial work as Linda got a hold on the extent of the collection, and we had meetings with the design firm to discuss the layout of the display and to be brought up to date with the technical side of multimedia displays that could (at a big price!) be used to tell the story.

I was talking to Alan James (known as AJ), the manager of Yothu Yindi. Mandawuy Yunupingu and AJ set up the Yothu Yindi Foundation, and the Garma Festival – in aid of the foundation – was held in Arnhem Land in August of each year. The foundation aims to help move towards a future where Indigenous people of Australia have the same opportunities for education and advancement as non-Indigenous people and it offers non-Indigenous visitors the chance to see for themselves the lifestyle and culture of the Arnhem Land peoples.

Mandawuy and AJ invited me to attend and Anne, Kate and James decided to come with me. The journey involved flying to Darwin and thence to Nhulunbuy (Gove) in East Arnhem Land. The site was huge, with a tent city scattered through the scrub. The dirt tracks wound through the trees and scrub to the different tent venues, where lectures were given or exhibitions held. There were some buildings for shower and toilet facilities, for the main entrance office and such. Each morning talks were given on the culture, crafts or stories and music of the area. On different days, there were activities and lectures to choose from. I was fascinated to attend a healing camp run by the women of that land. We watched as an arthritis sufferer was placed in a hollow in the earth where fire had warmed the ground; special tree leaves were massed above hot stones, and as water was poured to generate eucalyptus-smelling steam the woman was laid on the leaves, and covered so that the steam would penetrate her aching bones to help relieve the pain.

The last night of the festival concentrated on music, dancing and display. Every community contributed to the spectacle and band after band of dancers and musicians with didgeridoos and singing sticks performed to the crowds lining the arena. The highlight of the evening was a performance by Yothu Yindi. During one of the day visits to the surrounding community settlements and the local school, we met up with Mandawuy, who was very ill with kidney disease. He had dialysis regularly and looked very weary that day. His smile was just the same, though, and when he took to the stage on that last night you would not have thought it was the same man we saw at the school.

He lit up the stage in the same old way, walking up and down and singing with all the power in the world... 'Treaty! Treaty!' and the crowd went with him. 'Treaty! Treaty!' He was the consummate performer, and the will of the audience lifted him to his limits that night. Mandawuy Yunupingu was Mandawuy the singer and leader in front of the dancers and singers painted up for corroboree, and he lived the part as though he'd never had a day's illness in his life. I never saw Mandawuy again.

Back in Darwin, the city's festival was in full swing and I met up with Regina, who was in town for an exhibition of culture, painting and weaving at the Gallery. Peppimenarti was very well represented with paintings and weaving, and with a great variety of T-shirts featuring Regina's designs.

Back in Sydney, I had to find a buyer for Betsy the Second, a beige-coloured Ford humpy-backed car that Slim had bought in memory of his precious black Betsy the First. Betsy the Second wasn't exactly the same but she reminded us of the old original. However, she had been sitting in the garage over at Epping, our first home, for years and was not roadworthy. As I'd been approached to sell the Epping house, I needed to clear out the garage, and I also needed to move the big living caravan that also sat in the backyard for years. The Foundation volunteers in the shape of board member Kevin Farrawell and mates from Kempsey had a look at the van, got it loaded onto a mover and deposited it in Kevin's work shed for renovation. It now sits in the Centre behind Old Purple, our car, and looks much the same as it did when I lived in it for years on the road.

Since 2006 I'd had either Daniel or Hannah living with me as they attended university in Sydney. Danny had been gone for a while, but Hannah was still with me until halfway through the year when she went to the USA to study. David, Jane and Danny would go to America to spend Christmas with her, returning in early January. The rest of us were going to Metung, and we were going to Skype each other during the holiday season, especially on Christmas Day.

Our Christmas tree was a branch of a gumtree that Anne cut and hauled across the road from the gully. By the time it was decorated up with lights turned on it was just like our trees of previous years at Metung. The stockings were hung along the mantelpiece in front of the fireplace, and the aroma of roast pork and crackling made it smell like Christmases of old as well. On Boxing Day we followed the tradition of recognising my Mum and Dad's wedding anniversary. At exactly 11 a.m. we used to serve them a slice of Christmas cake with a small glass of sherry. That would be Mum's ration of alcohol for the whole year. So this year we remembered and set it out.

I wanted to move Mum's piano from Metung to Sydney but I was a bit sad when the removalists came to pick it up to take it to store in Melbourne until the end of January, when they would deliver it to the house in Sydney. The old piano was suffering from extremes of heat and cold in the empty house, and I wanted it at home at long last. But the little room at Metung looked bereft when it moved out.

Anne and Greg went home on the thirtieth and I spent a quiet New Year's Eve on my own, declining invitations to watch the fireworks on the lake from the village. There was a whole new year ahead of me, and I wondered what it would bring. I had plenty to do: there was the Foundation and the Centre to work for, the recording catalogue and the farm to look after, and apart from those responsibilities I wanted all those very normal things like getting my vegie garden in order, using the motorhome and keeping my weight under control!

But what else might happen? Sometimes, life will take you into a channel you didn't expect and sometimes you meet challenges that you didn't want. I was still looking forward to see what was over the next hill, the same as we always did. Whatever happened, it could possibly make a nice change to meet the unexpected.

I turned 80 years of age on 14 January 2010 and celebrated with a party at home amongst friends, neighbours and colleagues. The big day of the party arrived at last, and the marquee on the back lawn looked festive with lanterns lit, table and chairs set out, and the musicians setting up. Anne did a great job of getting it all in place, and Jane had organised a huge sponge cake with eight candles (how would you fit 80 on one cake, after all?), with white chocolate topping and the figure 80 in gold. Friends came from Melbourne; Heather and her family were there, as were most of our band mates, neighbours and friends from all over. There were flowers from everywhere. Everyone had a wonderful time but I think I had the best time of all!

The day after my birthday I drove up to Tamworth. The Australian Country Music Foundation held a concert as a tribute to the Lady Pioneers, and Lily Connors sang her trademark song 'Happy and Free Yodel'. In the early days of our careers, Lily had always made Heather and me green with envy of her beautiful stage outfits, bought in the USA. On stage this day, she looked and sounded great. At the reception afterwards I cut my second birthday cake – a chocolate one this time. Blow the diet, I thought, I'll have at least one piece.

The next day, a Sunday, I attended a press conference and blew out the candles on an orange cake this time, thinking, Forget that diet till I go home! At the conference there were a lot of questions about the direction of country music. This was because Guy Sebastian, a rock/pop act, had been engaged to headline a concert at the TRECC during the festival, and the Council had hired another rock act for the festival as well. The perception out there amongst artists and concertgoers was, for the moment anyway, that the festival would end up being just another rock festival instead of the unique and huge country music event that it is.

There were other disturbing factors arising that year, as Council made a move towards 'owning' the festival. Up to this point the festival had grown because of various people and organisations mounting concerts, and artists appearing in those concerts and putting on special events of their own. Rural Press Events ran the Country Theatre at the TRECC and there was quite a stir when Council decided to take it over themselves and employ someone to do the bookings and organising. There have been different approaches employed in the development of the festival entertainment, and change always takes place. But I left with the feeling that, as always, things would sort themselves out in time.

I attended the Star Maker finals and congratulated the winner, Luke Austen. Next day I presented the trophy to the winner of the Australian Bush Balladeers Star Quest, a young man from Victoria named Dave Baldi. I always kept my eyes and ears open for young artists who showed promise of taking up bush ballads where Slim had left off, but to date I have not found one with sufficient dedication plus talent and charisma. It is not an easy road, this road we ride when we love the heart and soul of our music to the extent that we did.

I also attended the Bush Laureates Awards in Tamworth Town Hall. I knew I was to be introduced to the audience as the patron of the awards, but I was unprepared when I was awarded a Golden Gumleaf trophy, 'in recognition of a lifelong contribution to Australia's Bush Verse Heritage'. I was very, very touched by this and thanked the organisers sincerely. Jim Haynes, the compere, read the words of 'Indian Pacific' as an example of my work. Standing up in front of all those bush poets who annually presented one of the most popular concerts of the festival, keeping alive the old bush tradition of reciting verse aloud, made me feel more than ever that I had been honoured in a very different way.

The Family Concert for my eightieth birthday was a most special night for me. The photo they used to publicise it had been taken in Townsville in 1957. David sang 'Looking Forward … Looking Back' for me and James sang 'Do You Think That I Do Not Know', Slim's musical setting of the Henry Lawson poem. Everyone sang favourites for me, and I sat in the wings of the Capitol Theatre stage listening, applauding and loving every minute of it. I played my little accordion to 'Our Wedding Waltz' and guitar for 'Kelly's Offsider'. Kate, James and Hannah all sang for me and I had a series of photos taken after the show to remember it by.

The day after the birthday concert, at Bicentennial Park it was announced that Anne Kirkpatrick's name was to be added to the Roll of Renown. It was a great honour for Anne, and I was absolutely thrilled to see her plaque unveiled on the Rock of Renown outside the TRECC. Anne had earned her place there, as someone who had opened doors for the women of country. Not as a pioneer of our days but as a herald of new days for female singers. One critic said words to the effect that Anne 'dragged country music kicking and screaming into the new age'. Whether she did or didn't, the fact remains that she was the first female country artist to take out the ARIA for Best Country Album, and I think she did the same thing as a solo female singer for the Golden Guitar Awards too. Whichever way it went, she was deserving of recognition for her trailblazing career, and I was one proud mum on the day.

I came home from the Tamworth Country Music Festival and took stock of myself, of what I had done in the past year and what I would try to do in the year ahead. I was reasonably healthy, despite two setbacks in the past year: a terrible bout of neuritis with furious headaches, and a few months of back pain and wearing a brace to relieve it. Both were under control now, and that was that.

I had friends and family who loved and supported me, and I had a very busy and challenging lifestyle and career. Most 80 year olds were retired and taking it easy, while I was working as hard as ever in my chosen career. Work had rescued me from sinking under the weight of losing my husband, my mate, my fellow music maker. But when I looked back at my life I realised just how much change I had seen over a long period of years, not only in the history of our country but in the history of music in Australia.

I saw the passing of the big tent shows that travelled the roads of Australia, bringing entertainment and glamour to towns that experienced nothing else like it for the rest of the year. I saw the beginning of small hall shows with a few almost amateur acts, travelling from one small town to another, leaving their signatures on the walls backstage of one drab hall after the other: 'Remember the Sloggetts', 'The Slim Dusty

Show, Always a Good Show'; 'Rick and Thel were here', and even 'Dante, the Magician'.

The showgrounds with their noise, sawdust, thrills, magic and mystery, with the thump of the big bass drum outside the boxing tent, and the rodeos with the horses and buckjump riders – all these and more were part of the passing parade of show business on the roads of Australia. I saw most of these, and was a part of some of them. I was part of the new era too, and I had to adapt to the change – from pounding my little portable typewriter on the back seat of the car between towns to the sophisticated touch of the latest computer; from using the very first portable tape recorder to learning how to handle MP3 digital files after preferring to record on a cassette tape. Yes, I changed and am still changing. But I wonder how much longer and how much change I will cope with?

I was riding the roads of Australia in the days when potholes, dirt, mud and bogs were the norm; I revel now in dual highways of tar. I was riding these roads in the cab of an old Inter truck, or in an old car that vapourised the petrol in its lines the minute it got a bit hot; I was riding these roads before we had cars and caravans of comfort and reliable performance. But do we have the romance and challenge of the road any more? I also wrote songs about those roads when I had stories to tell and people who wanted to hear them. I performed – Heather did, Slim did, Anne does too – for the love of it, and because I couldn't live any other way. Do we sing now for the satisfaction and happiness of it or do we sing for the awards and the money we might make from it? I know the answer from where I sit, but I wish I knew the answer from those who are following on.

Maybe it is alright for me to think I have seen the best of it – but maybe, too, the best is yet to come. I've had a great time one way and another.

It's been a very interesting ride ... so far.

INDEX

Praise for *Of Kings, Queens and Colonies* and the *Coronam* series

'A clever and exciting collision of space opera, high adventure, and devious politics. Insightful and highly entertaining!'
Jonathan Maberry, *New York Times* bestselling author of *Relentless* and *V-Wars*

'Political and prophetic, comprising battles and betrayals, bourgeoisie and brutes, and the persistent hum of bees, *Of Kings, Queens & Colonies* is a masterful epic of exploration and exile. A cautionary tale for citizens of the Old Earth. Sure to be on the award lists.'
Lee Murray, Bram Stoker Award winner and author of *Grotesque: Monster Stories*

'Worthen shows himself a master of style and substance.'
Michael R. Collings, 2016 World Horror Convention Grand Master

'The worlds of Coronam, with their mixture of old and new technologies, create a unique setting for an ageless story about humanity.'
Daniel Yocom, Guild Master Gaming

'Johnny Worthen is a bold and imaginative writer; his Coronam work is a fascinating look at our troubling history through the lens of tomorrow.'
Bryan Young, author of *BattleTech: Honor's Gauntlet*